PIZZA IS ONE OF THE WORLD'S GREATEST FOODS but also one of the hardest to perfect in a home oven. If you think you can't make pizzeria-quality pizzas without a professional pizza oven, think again! With award-winning Italian-American chef Marc Vetri as your guide, mind-blowing pizza is within your grasp any night of the week.

The secret? Dough hydration. Vetri offers various hydration levels for Naples dough, Roman dough, pizza al taglio, and more, so that the dough can be customized to absolutely any type of oven for the best possible results. *Mastering Pizza* also dives into other fundamentals—pizza stones, baking steels, flour types—to help you find the best tools for getting your ultimate crust, be it airy or crispy.

To top your dough, Vetri offers recipes for popular standards like Margherita and Pepperoni, as well as innovative combinations like Fresh Pears and Guanciale, Sicilian Tuna with Shaved Vidalia Onion, Butternut Squash with Crispy Sage and Taleggio, and Wood Oven Crème Brulee Pizza. You can pick your dough, oven type, and toppings, and then mix and match pizzas to your heart's content. With step-by-step photos for making and shaping dough, and clear, encouraging instruction, *Mastering Pizza* is an inspiring book that will help you craft the pizza of your dreams.

MASTERING PIZZA

THE ART AND PRACTICE OF
HANDMADE PIZZA,
FOCACCIA, AND CALZONE

———

MASTERING PIZZA

———

MARC VETRI

and David Joachim

Photography by Ed Anderson

TEN SPEED PRESS
California | New York

TO EVERYONE WHO HAS WALKED THROUGH THOSE VETRI CUCINA
DOORS OVER THE LAST 20 YEARS.

WE HAVE CREATED, WE HAVE INSPIRED, AND WE HAVE
SPREAD THE WORD OF ITALIAN SENSIBILITY AND HOSPITALITY.

THIS BOOK IS DEDICATED TO YOU!

CONTENTS

RECIPE LIST

EVERYBODY LOVES PIZZA

IN MY PHILADELPHIA NEIGHBORHOOD, everyone ended up at Rizzo's. They had the best pizza. It was your typical round American pie, and everybody in Abington loved it. Even the big, plain cheese pizza matched the restaurant's family atmosphere perfectly. On weekend nights, all the families went to Rizzo's for pizza. After Little League games, all the kids gathered at Rizzo's. Sometimes, after pizza, my mom would even take me to 7-Eleven for a Slurpee! Those were the days!

I've always loved pizza. After cooking pizzas for more than thirty years, I've also learned that people get very passionate about their own love for pizza. Everyone has a particular favorite, from thin crust or thick crust to Naples style, Roman style, New York style, and Sicilian style. Some people want only the classic margherita pizza of crushed tomatoes with mozzarella and basil, while meat lovers prefer sauce, mozzarella, sausage, pepperoni, and ham. Well, this book is for *everyone* who loves pizza. I give you a variety of different dough recipes so you can make a variety of different pizzas with a variety of different toppings. I show you how to make better pizza in whatever oven you're working with—from home ovens to wood ovens

to grills. The recipes start with the pizza doughs and then move on to all the different pizzas you can make with them, including dozens of toppings. The doughs, shapes, and toppings are all interchangeable so you can choose any pizza style and any pizza topping to go with it. Experiment with different combinations to find your favorites.

Even though I fell in love with pizza in Philadelphia, I started baking them in California. In my twenties, I moved to Los Angeles, and sometime around 1991, I started working for Wolfgang Puck at Granita. That's where I first learned to make pizza. A guy named Danny Farr showed me how to mix up dough, shape it, and work the wood oven. Danny got me totally hooked on making pizza. I fell in love with the whole process. L.A. celebrities would come into the restaurant and just stare at us making pizzas by hand. That's where I learned how to handle the dough, and I got pretty good—so good that I once made a guitar-shaped pizza for Neil Young. But somehow Danny's dough always came out better. We made the exact same recipe and mixed it the exact same way every time, but his dough looked nicer, rose better, and stretched easier. It took me a while to figure out why.

I eventually went to Italy for a few years to become a better chef, and that's when I really dug my hands into Italian cooking. I made bread, pasta, desserts . . . you name it. And I tried all kinds of pizza. Those were some of the most formative years of my life, and I still return to Italy every chance I get. When I got back to the States after that first trip, I started working at Bella Blu in New York City. They had a big wood oven in the middle of the restaurant just like at Granita. New Yorkers would come in and watch us stoke the fire and make pizza for them. Being New Yorkers, they pretended not to care, but I knew they did. They kept staring at us, at the oven, at the dough, and at the bubbling pizzas. The pizza chef, Matteo Pupillo, was from Puglia, and he taught me that you must have a relationship with your pizza dough. He said, "The dough is the star of the show." Matteo helped me understand that the person behind the dough is as important as the dough itself. It's the relationship between you and your dough that really matters. That's what was missing from my dough compared to Danny Farr's dough. You have to get a feel for your dough. Anyone can follow a recipe, but observing the dough and sensing what it needs is the key to making it better. As with any relationship, sometimes—no matter how hard you try—things just don't work out. You can always try again by making another batch, but without good dough, there isn't a single topping in the world that will make your pizza taste any better. Great dough is what makes great pizza.

After working with Matteo, I paid more attention to the dough every time I made pizza. I also paid more attention to the people eating it. Even though Bella Blu was wildly different from either Rizzo's or Granita, all three restaurants drew huge crowds of people for their pizzas. The pizza was just that good. After working at Bella Blu, I knew that one day I would open up my own place. I started imagining Pizzeria Vetri, and it dawned on me that a pizzeria is not only a place where people go to eat pizza but also a place where people go to experience something incredible *together*. The relationship that you develop with your dough is something you also share with everyone who eats your pizza. It's the care and attention that draw people in. There's just something special about handmade food. People travel for hours or even days to obscure little corners of the world just to marvel over a pizza that someone has created. Children get so excited when you ask them if they want pizza tonight. Neighborhood families have the times of their lives grazing on the local tomato pie made by hand. Pizza is not just a plate of delicious food. It's meant to be shared; it's an invitation to gather around the table for community and conviviality. Pizza brings people together. That's why I put communal tables in my pizzeria. When people are enjoying a slice near each other, they say things like "Ooh, that looks good. What is it?" and "Here; try a slice." I love that. It's something you don't see enough in restaurants.

It may sound corny, but I truly believe that is why pizza is now one of the most popular foods on the planet. Every culture around the world has been putting stuff on bread and baking it for thousands of years. But a big, flat pie, cut for everyone to share? That's a little different. It's hard to say who made the very first pizza. Maybe it was the ancient Etruscans or Romans. Or maybe it was some kind of focaccia made by the Genoese in Liguria. Who knows? When tomatoes came to Italy in the late 1500s, tomatoes ended up on the bread. In Naples and Rome, that combo took off and—boom!—pizza was born.

In Naples, pizza was sold mostly from street carts and folded up so you could take it with you.

When visitors went to Naples and Rome and tasted pizza, they couldn't get enough. Later, when Italians immigrated to America, they brought pizza to cities like New York, Boston, and Philadelphia. At that point, it was mostly an Italian thing. But then, during World War II, American soldiers in Italy couldn't get enough pizza, and when they came back home, pizza started spreading across the entire United States—from tomato pie in New Jersey to pizza Napoletana in Connecticut. From there, it just spread everywhere and became more and more popular all over the globe.

It's amazing to me how the whole world fell in love with pizza. But I get it. I fell in love with it, too! It's just so adaptable. Different doughs, different shapes, different toppings. You can make it however you like. And that's exactly what everyone around the world does. And that's what you should do. But this book is not an exhaustive survey of every style out there. I focus on the pizzas that started it all, like round pizza Napoletana that's soft and foldable with a big, puffy rim; round pizza Romana that has a thin, crunchy crust and almost no rim; and rectangular or square pizza al taglio that's baked in a pan with a superthick but light and pillowy crust. Sure, I have some fun with Naples dough and Roman dough. I show you how to make a few things like calzones and rotolo—a Pizzeria Vetri original! I also show you how to make focaccia, the Italian bread that probably kicked off the whole pizza craze in the first place. Just don't go in expecting to find edamame pizza with a fucking cauliflower crust. That is not in this book. You won't find gluten-free pizza either. But you will find gluten-friendly pizza that is thoroughly fermented and made with wheat flour (see page 54 for more detail). Yes, it is possible!

You'll find almost twenty different pizza and focaccia dough recipes and dozens of variations on those doughs. You'll see plenty of pizza toppings, too—from classics like Marinara (page 152) and Margherita (page 112) to some of my new favorites like Zucchine (page 126) and Carbonara (page 133). There are more than forty different toppings and fillings here. Certain toppings go particularly well with certain doughs, and I've pointed these out in the recipes. But, really, you can mix and match the toppings however you like. For me, it's all about nailing the crust. No matter what kind of pizza you make, your dough and your oven will always have the biggest impact on how your pizza turns out.

A lot of pizza books focus on the "one" dough recipe you'll ever need. Or they show you the "best" method for baking pizza. The truth is, there is no "one" pizza dough to rule them all, and there is no "best" method—and acting like there is can lead you astray. It all depends on what you are trying to achieve and the tools you have at hand. Different doughs and different ovens make different pizzas! If you make pizza in a wood-fired oven at 900°F (482°C), you won't get the same results when you bake that same dough in a home oven at 500°F (260°C). It just won't work. My promise in this book is that I will help you make better pizza in *whatever* oven you have with *whatever* dough you want.

Like everything else in today's world, you can get your pizza cheap and easy, or you can seek out better quality. If you're reading this book, I assume you want to go a step above Chuck E. Cheese's. Let's say you've never made pizza

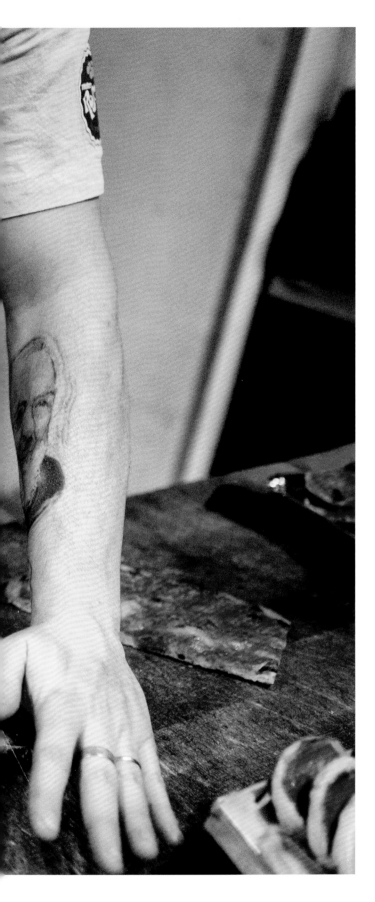

before, and you want to give it a shot. You'll find everything you need here to make great pizza from scratch in your home oven the very first time. Or, maybe you've been at it for a while and you've gotten pretty good at slinging pies. These pages offer lots of opportunity to up your game—from perfecting your dough to getting the most out of your oven, and I bet you'll also pick up a few new toppings to try out.

Either way, the first few chapters take a deep dive into various ovens, different baking methods, types of flour, and the magic that is pizza dough. If you really want to learn about the art and science of pizza, start there. If you just want to eat something delicious, go straight to the recipes. The recipes are set up as a two-stage process. First make one of the Pizza Dough Recipes (page 59), let the dough rest, then shape it and bake it into your choice of Naples Dough Pizzas (page 91), Roman Dough Pizzas (page 135), or Pizza Al Taglio (page 165), and top them with any of the pizza toppings from any of the chapters. I show you how to make soft, chewy and foldable Neapolitan pizza in a home oven as well as in a wood oven, a cast-iron pan, a kamado-style grill, a charcoal grill, and a gas grill. There's even a recipe for frying it in a pan. Or maybe you prefer crispy thin-crust pizza—try the Roman dough pizzas. You'll see how to get a crunchy pizza Romana from whatever oven you have. Or, let's say you're a fan of square pie. Then you've gotta try pizza al taglio (by the slice), a dough that holds a special place in my heart. It's ready overnight, you bake the pizza in a regular home oven, and the crust comes out superlight and fluffy. Plus, it's open to all kinds of interpretation. You can top it with whatever, from potatoes, rosemary, and mozzarella (page 188) to butternut squash, crispy sage, and Taleggio cheese (page 184). My kids absolutely adore this kind of pizza. You'll also find other fun things like Parmesan Fried Dough (page 150) and Home Oven Nutella-Stuffed Pizza (page 235).

Really, it doesn't matter which pizza you make. Put together any one of them and invite some people to come enjoy it with you. You'll make friends in an instant. There's just something magical about hot pizza. No one can resist it. All around the world, pizza brings people together in a way that nothing else can. And that's something we could all use a little more of.

1

BAKING
AT SBANCO

If you can't explain it simply, you don't understand it well enough.
—ALBERT EINSTEIN

I'M NOT OFTEN SURPRISED WHEN EATING PIZZA. Sure, there is good pizza, and there is great pizza, along with shitty pizza, interesting pizza, and totally out-of-the box pizza. But for the most part, I've seen and eaten almost every style of pizza out there. Then I met Stefano Callegari at Sbanco in Rome.

Katie Parla, my friend and colleague who lives in Rome, introduced us. Katie knows pretty much everything about Roman history, culture, and food, including how to give Roman Uber drivers who try to scam her a serious verbal ass kicking—in both Italian and English! She said Sbanco was a can't-miss restaurant on our Rome itinerary, and I trusted her. It was our last day of a pretty intense research trip, and the four of us (including my collaborator David Joachim and photographer Ed Anderson) had already eaten forty-five different pizzas in three days.

We had set aside a good chunk of that afternoon to just talk and make pizza with Stefano at his pizzeria. I was curious because at most of the other places, we had talked with the chefs during service, gazed in their ovens, taken pictures, and eaten tons of pizza, but we hadn't spent hours just making pizza and talking with them while the restaurant was closed. Once Stefano and I started chatting, I understood Katie's motives immediately. There is an authenticity to Stefano that is not easy to find in these days of nonstop self-promotion. He is humble and passionate, and he knows his craft. He's also a big bear of a guy who loves to eat pizza. We chatted about our lives, our obsessions, and what had brought us to where we are in life, all while pressing out pizzas together, first Stefano, followed by me, both of us making simple Neapolitan-style pies and eating, drinking, and talking without a care in the world. Then he showed me the unthinkable.

He put ice on the raw dough. Ice? How does that make sense? Stefano proceeded to load the pizza into his wood-fired oven. My mind started racing, not only with the anticipation of tasting this pizza but also with the infinite possibilities that could be fabricated from such a simple exercise.

It's genius. Ice on pizza . . . the ice melts in the oven, mixes with starch from the dough, and creates a thickening agent right on the dough. When you pull out the pizza, it has a thin layer of starchy water on top, and you can make a kind of sauce on it, the same way you would make a pasta sauce, mixing the starchy liquid with cheese, butter, or whatever you want. I wanted to kiss him! Stefano mixed some pecorino by hand into the starchy water, ground some black pepper over the top, and drizzled on a little olive oil. Boom! Cacio e pepe pizza.

It was amazing. The sauce was creamy, the pecorino was sharp, the pepper tingly, the olive oil aromatic, and the dough chewy in the middle. It tasted like cacio e pepe pasta. All of Stefano's toppings were simple, thoughtful, and slightly edgy for a traditional Neapolitan-style pizzeria. But the cacio e pepe pizza stood out. It truly stretched the parameters of the age-old question: tradition or innovation? This pizza perfectly married the two by juxtaposing a classic Roman pasta dish with a classic Neapolitan pizza.

This is what starts my creative juices flowing. If cacio e pepe can successfully become a pizza, what else can?

BAKING TEMPERATURE AND DOUGH HYDRATION

Stefano's dough turned out to be one of the most alluring representations of Naples-style dough that we ate on that trip—with perfect leopard spotting on the rim, a chewy crust, and a subtle crunch. Two key things made that happen: (1) the high, dry heat of his wood-fired oven and (2) the amount of water in his dough or, the dough's hydration. Yes, the flour makes a huge difference, too, but we'll get to that later. Stefano's dough is almost 70% water (relative to the flour), which is pretty high for Naples-style dough. That amount of water, gives the dough a lot of bubbles and a big lift, which makes Stefano's crust light and airy. His pizza oven is about 800°F (427°C) on the floor, which puffs up the dough pretty fast and makes the bottom crust nice and crisp. His crust is a little crisper than most of the pizzas you find in Naples, and I kinda like it that way.

That brings us to one of the most important points of this book: to get the kind of texture you're looking for in a pizza crust, it helps to balance the heat of your oven with the water in your dough. Think about it. Classic Neapolitan pizza (Vera Pizza Napoletana) is baked at about 900°F (482°C), the dough is pretty low in water (55 to 59% hydration), and the pizza cooks for only 90 seconds (for more on Vera Pizza Napoletana [VPN] standards, see page 97). If you cooked that same dough at only 500°F (260°C), by the time the pizza was done cooking, it would be drier and crisper. To get that same soft and foldable crust on classic Neapolitan

pizza when you're baking at 500°F (260°C), it helps to have more water in the dough because the dough takes longer to bake.

That's why we organized the dough recipes in this book by the amount of water in them. Sure, we have sourdoughs and whole grain doughs, cold-fermented doughs and warm-fermented doughs, and even doughs with fresh-milled flour—my favorite! But first, it's important to pick the dough that bakes best in your oven and results in the kind of pizza you're trying to make. Maybe you want a classic Neapolitan pizza, and you're baking in a blazing wood-fired oven with a cooking surface at 900°F (482°C). You got it. Check out my basic Naples Dough at 60% Hydration (page 61), the one I use most at Pizzeria Vetri. Or, let's say you're making Naples-style pizzas in a home oven on a pizza stone or baking steel at 500°F (260°C). Then try the Old School Naples Dough at 70% Hydration (page 69). The extra water in that dough will help you get the right texture for that pizza when you're baking it at a lower temperature. Or maybe you want to make a thicker, airier, Sicilian-style pizza on a sheet pan in your home oven. Then try the Al Taglio Dough at 80% Hydration (page 80). That pizza is thicker, and the dough has so much water that it's actually easier to bake that kind of dough in the lower temperature of a home oven than in a blazing-hot wood oven. The home oven's lower temp helps the thicker, wetter pizza dough bake completely through before burning on the outside.

Does this mean that all wet pizza doughs above 75% hydration should *always* be baked at lower temperatures? And that all dry doughs below 60% hydration should *always* be baked at higher temperatures? Of course not. It all depends on the type of pizza you want to make. If you want a thin, crispy pizza like a cracker, you can roll Old School Naples Dough at 60% Hydration (page 67) very thinly and bake it at a relatively low temperature of 400°F (204°C) for a relatively long amount of time . . . say, 10 to 15 minutes. The low temp and long baking time will definitely dry out the dough. The pizza you end up with just won't be a classic soft and foldable pizza Napoletana. It will be a thin, crisp pizza. When it comes to pizza, there are no hard-and-fast rules. It just helps to know the relationship between baking

How Domed Wood Ovens Work

To bake the best possible wood-oven pizza, it helps to know how heat moves through the oven and to the pizza.

- A wood fire is lit near the center of the oven floor and then pushed to one side.
- Air enters the oven through the mouth, supplying the fire with oxygen, which keeps the fire burning.
- Heat and smoke exit the oven through the vent or chimney.

- The oven's masonry construction absorbs heat from the fire.
- Heat retained in the oven floor is conducted to the bottom of the pizza, crisping up the bottom crust.
- Heat retained in the oven dome is radiated directly to the top and sides of the pizza, cooking the toppings and rim.
- Convection currents and rolling flames speed heat transfer to the top of the pizza.

temperature and dough hydration so you can achieve your overall goals. Hotter ovens cook dough more quickly, giving water less time to evaporate, resulting in a softer overall texture in pizza. Cooler ovens cook dough more slowly, giving water more time to evaporate, resulting in a crisper overall texture in pizza.

Working your oven and perfecting your dough are what really step up your pizza game. The toppings are simple. They change with the seasons, and you can choose what you like. But playing around with different doughs and baking temperatures to fit your particular situation, and tweaking the variables to get the results exactly the way you want them—from a thick puffy crust that's chewy and moist to a thin crunchy crust that's crisp and dry—that's the real magic of mastering pizza.

OVENS

The bottom line in all this is that your oven is one of the most important factors determining how your pizza turns out. Hotter ovens cook pizza faster and puff up the dough more, giving it more char. Cooler ovens cook pizza more slowly, and you get less puff, less char, and a more golden brown crust. Simple; right? A lot of it comes down to baking temperature. That alone makes a huge difference in what your pizza is going to look like and taste like when it's cooked.

But the size and shape of your oven—and the materials used to construct it—also make a difference. The size of your oven determines how long it takes for it to heat up, how much fuel it needs to stay hot, and how many pizzas you can bake at once. Big ovens take longer to get hot and need more fuel to stay hot. The shape influences how the heat moves through the oven. Rounded or domed ovens get these rolling convection currents that deliver heat very efficiently to food, making it cook faster. In square ovens, convection currents move more slowly because they bump into the corners, so square ovens cook a little more slowly. And what is the oven actually made of? Is it ceramic? Stone? Metal? They all heat differently! And how thick is the material? That determines how much heat the oven can hold and how fast it sends heat to your pizza. Ceramics hold heat really well, especially thick ceramics, but they don't give up their heat as fast as metals like steel. Ceramics have another useful characteristic, though. Unlike metals, unglazed ceramics are porous, which helps water vaporize quickly. That's a big plus for getting things nice and crisp in the oven. When you bake pizza in a ceramic (or brick) oven, the ceramic helps moisture from the crust evaporate. Along with the high heat, that crisps up the pizza. That's one reason why pizza stones help to make better pizza in a home oven. Which brings us to the actual cooking surface. Sometimes it's made of a different material than the oven itself. In some ovens, like wood ovens and deck ovens, the pizza goes right on the oven floor, which is usually firebrick or ceramic stone. In others, like home ovens, your cooking surface could be a baking stone or baking steel, or a baking sheet—and they all heat a little differently, affecting how crisp and brown your pizza will get.

And then there's the small matter of where the heat is coming from. Is it a wood-fired oven? Coal? Charcoal? Gas? Electric? They all heat differently, too! So much to consider. But let's make it easy. Let's look at the most common ovens used to bake pizza, what to expect from each, and how to get the best pizza you can from your oven.

Wood Ovens

Ovens that burn wood are actually part of a larger category called masonry ovens. In fact, the very first ovens were masonry ovens. Going way back, they were clay pots with lids that were put over a wood fire. Today's Dutch ovens are direct descendants of those original primitive ovens. A lot of today's wood-burning masonry ovens are still made of clay, but it's a special type of fire clay that you can heat up and cool down day in and day out without the clay cracking. Clay isn't the only material. Masonry ovens can be made of fire-brick, concrete, stone, or even cob, a kind of dense, fireproof soil. They can be heated with wood, coal, gas, electricity, or a combination. The building materials and the fuel all make a difference in how the oven cooks. Some coal-fired pizza ovens have a separate firebox from the cooking chamber. Coal ovens can also be three times as big as wood-burning ovens. They get hotter, too—upward of 1000°F (538°C). But square coal ovens don't get the high, rolling flame and convection heat currents of a domed wood-fired oven, so pizzas bake a little differently in them.

Most wood ovens have a classic dome or igloo shape, and that's the type I'll be discussing here. Back in 1991, my very first experience baking pizzas was on this type of oven at Wolfgang Puck's Granita in Los Angeles. It was the restaurant's showpiece—a domed wood-fired oven right in the center of the room. Everyone would watch us loading pizzas in and out of the oven. I have to admit: it was pretty awesome. And talk about an education in heat control. A domed wood oven is radically different from a square electric oven or gas oven. I learned how to stoke the fire, rotate the pizzas, use the hot spots, and cook different foods when the oven was at different temperatures. It was a great foundation for a young cook to build on.

GET TO KNOW YOUR OVEN

These days, a lot of people have wood-fired pizza ovens in the backyard or right in the kitchen. Every wood oven is a little different in size, shape, and the materials used to construct it. Each one has its own idiosyncrasies, so if you have a wood oven, get to know it. Bake different foods in it at different temperatures. Getting a feel for your oven is the single most important thing you can do to make better pizza. Wood ovens are very traditional and considered by many to be the best for pizza. But like everything else—it depends. If you're making pizza in a sheet pan, such as pizza al taglio, wood ovens are trickier to work with. I prefer an electric oven for that kind of pizza, because it heats more evenly. But you can make it work in a wood oven. And, yes, for Naples-style pizza, a wood oven is the bomb. The high heat, the round shape, the dry heat of the wood, and the masonry itself all combine to cook a fantastic round pizza Napoletana. You see the most "leopard spotting" on pies baked in wood ovens because the initial blast of high, dry heat forces steam out of the dough so quickly, leaving behind tiny spots of char.

At Pizzeria Vetri, we use a wood oven with a gas burner on the side. The wood heat is mostly what cooks the pizza, but it's nice to have the gas to keep the temperature steady. It's a domed brick oven with the traditional igloo shape, and that sends flames from the wood fire right up the dome and over the pizza, where it licks the top of the pie. We use oak in our oven because it burns hot and lasts longer. The wood is split and seasoned (dried) to about 20% moisture. A lot of American brick-oven pizzerias use ash wood. You can also use beech or maple or fruitwoods like cherry and apple. Some places even use compressed bricks of sawdust. Any hardwood will work.

ADVANTAGES OF WOOD OVENS

Some people think smoke and smoke flavor are the reasons to use wood as fuel. I've had countless arguments with chefs about wood vs. gas vs. sawdust. The fact is that smoke rises to the dome in a wood-fired oven and sits way above the pizza. You hardly get any smoke flavor at all in wood-oven pizza. The best thing about a wood oven is the high, dry heat and the oven's ceramic material and round shape. Those are primarily what give you a nice, crisp pizza crust. When you load pizza into a hot wood oven, the masonry (both the walls and the firebrick floor) transfer heat to the pizza so fast that the dough immediately starts to puff up; this is known as oven spring. The instant heat causes bubbles in the dough to expand right away, giving you a nice, airy crust with some big holes in the rim. The oven's shape also

How to Fire Up a Wood Oven

Everyone has a different method of building a fire. Just make sure your wood oven is cured before you start baking pizzas, or it could crack. Curing means that you remove any leftover moisture in the firebrick or clay, usually by lighting a few slow fires over a period of a couple days and letting each fire burn out naturally. Just follow your oven manufacturer's instructions. When dried and cured, the inside of the oven should go from looking black on the dome and floor to looking white or dull gray.

Once your oven is cured, then you can fire it up for real. To do that, light a wood fire on the oven floor directly where you will be cooking pizza. For smaller wood ovens, build the fire right in the middle. For bigger ovens, build it a little closer to the mouth of the oven so you can easily reach the cooking area with a pizza peel. Build a small pyramid (teepee) or crosshatch pattern of thin branches and/or dry kindling on the bottom. Then add a layer of slightly larger branches or kindling, making sure you leave lots of space for oxygen to flow. No oxygen = no fire. Use a long lighter to light the thin branches or dry kindling in a few places and then let everything burn. You can also use other kinds of fire starters if you prefer them.

Either way, if your oven has a damper or top vent, make sure it's open to get the air flowing. You'll get some smoke at first. Just give it more air, and when the fire is burning steadily, throw on a slightly larger branch or small log. When adding new logs, position them perpendicular to the burning ones to let the air flow freely. The goal is a steady burning, hot fire that takes up about 2 square feet of space, depending on the size of your oven. Feed the fire until the oven comes up to temperature. For me, that means an ambient temperature of 650° to 700°F (343° to 371°C). It usually takes an hour or two to get a wood oven up to temperature, depending on how big it is.

When the oven is up to temp, push the coals and burning logs to one side, containing the fire in a neat pile near the edge. Then brush the cooking surface clean where the fire was. Let the fire burn for a few minutes, making sure it has good oxygen flow. Now, you're ready to bake pizzas. Just remember to stoke the fire and brush the cooking surface clean between pies. You don't want a sooty bottom crust. A few long-handled tools make this whole process a snap: a fire poker, a stiff cleaning brush, and an ash shovel.

helps speed along the baking process. The low dome and round shape make the fire creep up the dome, rolling the heat around the entire pie and helping to cook the whole pizza—especially the top—superfast. That's part of what creates the big, puffy rim on pizza Napoletana. Neapolitans love that rim so much they call it the *cornicione,* or the cornice, the "crown molding" of your well-crafted masterpiece.

For Naples-style pizzas, there's no doubt that wood heat and masonry construction are a slam-dunk combination. But I gotta say, this idea that every pizza has to cook at a blistering 900° or 1000°F (482° or 538°C) is nonsense. It depends on what you're trying to achieve. I was doing a Neapolitan pizza pop-up dinner recently in Boulder, Colorado, and I had to actually lower the heat in their wood oven. They keep the oven at 950° to 1000°F (510° to 538°C), which is traditional for Vera Pizza Napoletana (see page 97). But I prefer to bake Naples-style pizzas at 650° to 700°F (343° to 371°C). It might surprise some people, but that's the sweet spot for my Naples dough. Any hotter, and the dough cooks too fast. Well, after I brought the oven heat down, it got a little too low. How did I know the heat was too low? No leopard spots on the crust. The first one came out with a browned rim and bottom crust but no little spots of char. I love those. So I stoked the fire to bring up the temp a bit. It's pretty cool to see how even a slight change in temperature makes a big difference in how pizza dough cooks. You'll have to experiment to find your own sweet spot with your oven.

GETTING THE MOST FROM YOUR WOOD OVEN

Now, let's say I were baking a calzone instead of a pizza in that same wood oven. I would have started it out in a hot part of the oven and then looked for a cooler spot. That first blast of heat is great for puffing up the crust. But calzones are thicker and need a little more time to cook through before they burn on the outside, so it's good to move them to a cooler spot after the initial puff. The same goes for rotolos, which are like big pizza rolls. The dough is thicker, so it takes even longer for the heat to get to the center. But you want that initial blast of heat. The point is—you should adjust the heat of your oven to match whatever it is you're baking. Basic; right?

Simply put, a wood oven is a tool. Get a feel for this particular tool. Once you get a sense of what it can do, then use it in different ways to achieve the results you want. For Neapolitan-style pizza, my basic method is to build a wood fire in the center of the oven, and when it's going strong, I shove the fire to one side. I feed the fire with more logs until the ambient temperature in the oven is between 650° and 700°F (343° and 371°C). Then I brush the oven floor clean. The floor and dome are usually a bit hotter than the ambient temperature. If you want to check the floor and dome temperature, you can use a laser thermometer (see page 25). Right before sliding a pizza onto the floor, I usually toss an extra piece of wood on the fire to stoke it up. That gives the pizza an initial blast of heat and helps puff it up quickly. In a wood oven, most of the heat comes from the wood fire to the side of the pizza, so you have to watch the pizza and spin it around with a long metal pizza peel, moving it toward or away from the fire, making sure the pizza cooks evenly. If you need to cook the toppings or the rim a little more, you "dome" the pizza or lift it closer to the oven's dome, where it's also a little hotter. My Naples-style pizzas cook in about 3 minutes. The crust gets beautiful leopard spots of char, and the bottom is nice and crisp, yet the pizza is still soft enough to fold.

If you're baking pizza in a wood oven—and I hope you are—the recipes in this book take you through the whole process step by step. See the recipes for Wood Oven Neapolitan Pizza (page 93) and Wood Oven Pizza Romana (page 138). But I can't stress enough how important it is to know your particular oven and how to work it. Wood ovens are very hands-on, but that's also exactly what gives them the most potential for turning out mind-blowing pizzas.

Deck Ovens and Convection Ovens

Certified "true" pizza Napoletana or Vera Pizza Napoletana (see page 97) must be baked in a wood oven. But you see some very good Neapolitan-style pizza coming out of other types of ovens—such as coal. And commercial pizzerias use a variety of different ovens, depending on their goals. The most common pizza oven you see in America is the deck oven. These relatively shallow ovens are stacked in a deck

so they take up less space and allow you to cook more pizzas at once. A lot of Roman pizzerias bake in deep deck ovens, too. These ovens are usually powered by gas or electricity, and you bake the pizza directly on the floor of the deck, which is made of ceramic baking stone or sometimes steel. The oven heats pretty evenly and predictably, so you don't have to watch the pizza as much as you do in a wood oven. Most deck ovens run at about 550°F (288°C), so the pizzas bake in about 6 to 8 minutes, a little longer than it takes in a hot wood oven. The lower temperature and longer bake time mean you don't often get that nice leopard spotting you see on wood-oven pizzas. The rim comes out more browned than charred, like the crust on your typical New York–style pizza.

Other pizzerias use convection ovens. These cook boxes are similar to home ovens but with more sophisticated fans for blowing hot air throughout the oven. The convection itself allows you to lower the baking temperature because the hot air delivers heat to the pizza more efficiently than in a deck oven. Convection ovens usually have a bunch of oven racks, each fitting a couple pizzas, depending on the oven's size. You load the pizza on a pizza pan or screen and bake it on the rack with the convection heat constantly circulating all around it. These ovens typically aren't meant for turning out a high volume of pies. But when you add a conveyor belt to a convection oven, then you can speed up production. That's the kind of oven the big commercial pizza companies use—the Domino's and Papa John's of the world. With a convection conveyor oven, you basically set and forget it. Put the pizza on a pizza pan or screen, lay it on the conveyor, and it cooks in 4 to 5 minutes with absolutely zero attention required. You can hire cheap labor and automate your whole pizza-making process, cranking out dozens of pies in no time. That sounds like heaven to some pizza makers. To me, it defeats the whole purpose. I prefer the taste and look of handcrafted food. I want someone fussing over my pizza.

The good news is that you can bake some amazing handcrafted pizzas without a wood oven or any other commercial pizza-making equipment. You just need a home oven or even a grill.

Home Ovens

Modern home ovens are typically square boxes made of steel. The standard 30-inch (76 cm) model is pretty small, so it heats up quickly. As far as materials go, steel is a better heat conductor than ceramic, providing quicker, more precise temperature control, which is important for baking different foods at different temperatures, as you do in a home oven. But the superior heat transference of steel means that the oven uses up more fuel. Why? Because the walls of the oven are constantly giving up their heat. That's why your home oven makes your kitchen so hot. A square oven also heats less efficiently than a round one because the convection currents are not as robust. Sure, you can turn on the convection fan in a home oven, but it doesn't get nearly as good at delivering heat all around the pizza as a domed, wood-fired oven.

In a home oven, the heat itself comes from gas or electricity. Gas releases some moisture as it heats, so gas ovens tend to be a bit more humid inside than electric ovens. Gas ovens also have to be vented to allow combustion gases like carbon dioxide to escape. Even though gas is popular on cooktops (and for good reason: instant heat control), among ovens, electric outsells gas by two to one. I'm not sure why, really. Maybe people think it's safer to have electric coils inside the cook box instead of burning flames. Yes, electric heat is drier than gas, but otherwise, gas and electric ovens both heat pretty evenly and offer decent control. You can thank your thermostat for that. Make sure it's calibrated!

COOKING SURFACES

Now let's take a look at what you are actually cooking your pizza on in a home oven. The floor is most likely made of thin steel, but it's not meant to be baked on directly. So what's the best cooking surface for home oven pizza? A baking stone? A baking steel? A baking sheet? It depends on what kind of pizza you're making. For pizza al taglio, a baking sheet is perfect. It helps to create the square pizza shape, and you can put the baking sheet right on the oven rack. It's even better if you put the baking sheet on a hot baking stone or baking steel. A stone or steel will deliver more heat through the baking sheet to the bottom of the pizza, helping to crisp up the bottom crust.

And what about a Naples-style pizza? What cooking surface is best for that? You might think a stone is best because it's closest to the cooking surface of the wood oven used for traditional pizza Napoletana. It's true that a baking stone retains heat really well, gives it up to the pizza crust nice and steady, and helps water vaporize from the dough, all of which create a pretty crisp crust. But you have to take into account the fact that a home oven maxes out at 500° to 550°F (260° to 288°C). There just isn't as much heat in the oven for the stone to deliver to the pizza. When testing recipes for this book, we found that a baking steel actually gives you a better bottom crust. Steel delivers heat to the pizza faster, helping it get hotter in less time. We tested dozens of pies on ¼-inch (0.6 cm)-thick steel, and they all had darker bottom crusts than the same pies baked on various ½-inch (1.3 cm)-thick baking stones.

But you know what? We found something even better: a cast-iron skillet. Cast-iron is well known for its searing ability. It heats very evenly and conducts heat even better than steel. The key is using thick cast-iron because thicker metals have more total heat capacity. Some cast-iron "pizza pans" are too thin and end up being less effective at transferring heat than ¼-inch (0.6 cm)-thick baking steel. But a regular old cast-iron skillet works great. Side by side, a

¼-inch (0.6 cm)-thick cast-iron skillet consistently gave us faster baking, deeper browning, and a crisper crust than a ¼-inch (0.6 cm)-thick baking steel. The only downside, of course, is that cast-iron is heavy. But if you really want an amazing bottom crust on a Naples-style pie baked in a home oven, give it a try. See the recipe for Cast-Iron Neapolitan Pizza (page 98).

THE BROILER METHOD

And what about the top crust? Here's where home ovens have an ace up the sleeve. They have their own sort of "dome"—the broiler. With a stone, steel, or cast-iron cooking surface on the bottom and the oven's broiler on top, your home oven can do a decent job of re-creating the intense bottom and top heat of a domed wood-fired oven. Just make sure your broiler is clean! When testing recipes in my home ovens, we used an oven one day that hadn't been heated up in a while. We preheated the oven, turned on the broiler, then loaded in the pizza, and closed the oven door. Well, guess what? We came back to a blazing fire! I must have broiled some steaks or something in there because whatever fat was on the broiler ignited, and I had to pull out the fire extinguisher to keep the house from burning down. Word to the wise: keep your broiler clean. And keep a fire extinguisher on hand just in case!

Anyway, here's the basic procedure I recommend for a kick-ass Naples-style pizza in a home oven. Preheat your oven to its max, usually 500° to 550°F (260° to 288°C). Set a baking steel or stone on the upper rack of the oven, about 4 to 6 inches (10 to 15 cm) below the broiler for electric ovens or 6 to 8 inches (15 to 20 cm) below the broiler for gas ovens. If you're using a cast-iron skillet, skip the steel or stone. And if your broiler is separate from the oven itself, you'll love this cast-iron method. You can preheat the skillet on a burner right on your stovetop instead of in the oven. Get the cast-iron pan smoking hot just as you would when searing a steak.

Either way, you want your oven fully preheated, especially if a steel or stone is in there. Make sure that your cooking surface is superhot. If you shoot a laser thermometer on the cooking surface, it should read somewhere around 500°F (260°C).

Then, just before you shape and top your pizza, switch on the broiler. For some electric ovens, you may have to crack open the oven door for 10 seconds or so. Some ovens won't turn on the broiler if the oven is already at max temperature. Cracking open the door lets some heat escape and lowers the oven temperature slightly. If you have one of these "smart" ovens, you might have to sort of trick it into turning on the broiler.

After you get the broiler preheating, shape your pizza dough. For the cast-iron skillet method, slide the shaped dough round into the hot skillet, cut the burner heat to low under the pan, quickly add your toppings, and then put the pan under the broiler. For the baking steel or stone method, add your toppings to the dough round and then slide the topped pizza onto the hot cooking surface under the broiler. Close the oven door and cook the pizza until the rim is puffed, the dough blisters and chars in spots, and the bottom is crisp. With the hot cooking surface below and the broiler above, the effect is the closest you'll come to the top and bottom heat in a traditional wood-fired pizza oven.

If you want a little extra poof in the crust, add a splash of water to the oven floor then quickly close the oven door. Water transfers heat faster than air, so the steam helps bring heat to the pizza faster, improving the initial "oven spring" and puff in the crust.

The one drawback we found with these broiler methods is that soft cheeses like fresh mozzarella can overcook and separate from the long cooking time under the broiler. The fat in the cheese starts to leak out from the milk protein. Depending on your total bake time and how far your pizza is from the broiler, you may want to add soft cheeses halfway through the bake time. No big deal, really. You need to open the oven at least once to check the pizza anyway. Just try not to keep the oven door open too long, or you'll lose a lot of heat. That's another reason why I love the skillet method. If you need to, you can just pull the skillet from the oven, close the oven door, quickly add the cheese to the pizza, and then slide the skillet back under the broiler.

Since the baking steel/stone method and the cast-iron skillet method are a little different from each other, we wrote separate recipes for each. See the recipes themselves for complete step-by-step details, beginning on page 93.

And what if you have no broiler at all? No problem. Make your own top heat. Preheat two baking stones or steels on separate racks in your oven—one below as your cooking surface and one 4 to 6 inches (10 to 15 cm) above as your "dome." Load the pizza onto the bottom stone or steel (or just on the oven rack if you're baking in a cast-iron skillet), and heat will radiate from the top steel or stone to cook the top of the pizza. Easy! Two stones or steels are also useful if you want a little extra crispness on your bottom crust when you use the broiler method. After the first stone or steel gives up its heat to the pizza, move the pie to the second stone or steel to give it an extra blast of heat.

Grills

If you want pizza in the summertime, a grill makes a great option. Who wants to heat up the kitchen when it's 90°F (32°C) outside? Grills offer some distinct advantages, too. If you have a big grill area, you can grill a big pizza, like Gas-Grilled Pizza al Metro (page 104). That's something you can't really do in a small home oven with a small baking steel or stone. And if you have a charcoal grill, you'll get a nice crisp crust from the high, dry heat of the charcoal. Better yet, if you have a kamado-style grill, like a Big Green Egg, you'll also get the advantage of baking in a superhot ceramic oven with top heat that radiates from the oven dome to cook your toppings. Depending on your grill, the baking technique for each type of grilled pizza is slightly different.

KAMADO-STYLE GRILL

These grills are modeled on the ancient Japanese kamado and the Indian tandoor. They are essentially ceramic ovens that you can also use for grilling directly over the heat source, which is typically charcoal. Big Green Egg, Primo, Broil King, and Komodo Kamado all make this type of grill. They are very fuel-efficient because ceramic retains heat so well. Once you get the grill up to temp, you don't need to add much charcoal to maintain the temperature, so they're pretty cheap to run. Plus, they get really hot. You can get the ambient temperature in most ceramic kamados over

700°F (371°C). That's pretty much where I keep my wood-fired pizza oven. Modern versions of these grills are rounded or egg-shaped, which also provides those efficient rolling convection heat currents. And the ceramic lid stores up heat and sends it to the top of the pizza like the dome in a wood oven. With a ceramic baking stone in there as your cooking surface, a kamado is basically as close as you're gonna get to a wood-fired pizza oven. It's just smaller. And one other big difference: the heat comes from below. For that reason, you need some kind of heat diffuser to redirect the heat around the pizza so it doesn't just hit the bottom. Most heat diffusers are ceramic or metal plates that sit between the fire and the food. Most kamados come with a heat diffuser for this type of cooking, which is often called indirect grilling. Once you fire it up, baking pizza in a kamado is pretty similar to baking pizza in a wood oven. You preheat the oven (with the heat diffuser and baking stone in place). Shape and top the dough, and then load the pizza onto the hot stone. One advantage here is that you don't even need to rotate the pizza during baking because the oven disperses the heat so evenly. Plus, the grill's dome blisters the rim of the pizza and cooks the toppings in just a few minutes.

You might be thinking, "Why not use a baking steel instead of a stone in there?" Steel holds and transfers more heat than ceramic, and more heat = crisper crust; right? Well, the temperature difference matters! Steels are great for baking at 500° to 550°F (260° to 288°C). But when you're baking at 700° or 800°F (371° or 427°C), you've got a lot more heat overall, and steel is transferring all that heat to the pizza faster. It turns out that a ¼-inch (0.6 cm)-thick piece of steel in a Big Green Egg blazing away at 700°F (371°C) burns the shit out of whatever you put on it. It's like sticking a piece of steel in your raging hot wood oven. It's overkill. When you're baking at temperatures over 650°F (343°C), stick with a baking stone. The ceramic holds on to the heat a bit longer and delivers it more gradually to the pizza, crisping it up perfectly. For a fully detailed recipe, see Kamado-Grilled Neapolitan Pizza on page 101.

CHARCOAL GRILL

Like kamados, these grills also get heat from hot coals below, but the grill itself is usually constructed of metal, not ceramic. That makes a huge difference because the metal is constantly transferring heat away from the grill. A metal grill won't hold as much heat inside. And even though most backyard charcoal grills have a lid to trap heat, it's still not enough heat to cook the top of the pizza. You can buy inserts like KettlePizza that have a baking stone and sometimes a cover assembly to trap heat and help cook the toppings. But then you're retrofitting your metal grill to make it more like a ceramic oven. What you end up with is not really grilled pizza. It's pizza baked on a grill.

Honestly, if I'm working with a grill, I prefer to just grill the dough right on the grate. Grilled pizza is a very different animal than baked pizza. You grill both sides of the dough instead of just one. That makes the crust nice and crisp on the bottom and the top, but the pizza toppings don't seep into the dough as the pizza cooks. The overall texture ends up being crunchier. If you like a crisp crust, you might like this kind of pizza better. The method is dead easy. Just light up your coals and preheat the grill with the grate in place for 20 minutes or so. When you're ready to grill the pizza, adjust the coals and the vents (if you have them) for medium heat in the grill. Brush the grates clean and then rub an oily paper towel over the grates. You want clean, hot, well-lubricated grill grates to transfer heat efficiently to the dough. Then slide the shaped pizza dough—without any toppings—right onto the grates and close the lid. It helps to use slightly stiffer dough, so it doesn't slump into the gaps between the grill grates. I usually use Old School Naples Dough at 60% Hydration (page 67). With the dough on the hot grates and the lid down, the crust starts firming up in seconds. It also gets grill marks on the bottom. To keep the marks from getting too dark, rotate the dough about 45 degrees after it's firm enough to move, maybe a minute or two into the cooking. Just use tongs and a large spatula to grab and rotate the dough. Then close the lid and grill the dough until the bottom is crisp and the top of the dough is almost dry, another minute or two. Grab the pizza crust with tongs, transfer it to your pizza peel, and close the lid to keep the heat in the grill. Then flip the dough over on the pizza peel. You want the grilled side facing up. Quickly add your toppings to the grilled side, and then slide the topped pizza back onto the grill. Close the lid and close the vents a little to bring down the heat in the grill. You want to lower the heat a little so there's time for the heat to reach the toppings and cook the top before the crust burns on the bottom. It also helps to rotate the pizza again for even browning on what is now the bottom crust. After a few minutes with the lid down, the toppings cook through, and the bottom crust gets nice and crispy. Boom! Grilled pizza. See the recipe for Charcoal-Grilled Neapolitan Pizza (page 106).

GAS GRILL

The method here is essentially the same as for charcoal-grilled pizza. The big difference is the fuel. It's much easier to control the temperature in a gas grill—just turn the knobs up or down. Gas does release some moisture as it burns, so your pizza crust may not come out quite as crisp as it does in the drier heat of a charcoal grill. Size matters, too. If you have one of those big backyard gas grills, you can put a couple dough balls together, shape them into a big rectangle, and grill a big pizza al metro for a party. Check out the recipe for Gas-Grilled Pizza al Metro (page 104).

USEFUL TOOLS

As you can see, your oven is critical—no matter what kind you have. Each is a little different, so get to know yours. Other tools are important, too. Every carpenter I know tells me to "buy good tools." It's good advice. To smooth out the entire process of making pizza, it's important to have reliable tools that feel good when you use them. Here are some of my preferences in order of use from dough making to pizza baking—but try different tools to find out what works best for you.

Digital scale. For any kind of dough making, there is just no getting around an accurate scale. This is a definite necessity! Volume measurements are too imprecise. Pick up a digital scale that can handle a few pounds of flour and be easily reset to zero (tare) when you're weighing ingredients. Also, I call for some very small amounts of dry yeast in a few dough recipes. For these, it's helpful to have a second, smaller, pocket- or palm-sized scale that measures to the hundredth of a gram (0.01 grams). Let's say you want to make only a single dough ball for pizza tonight. Then you only need about 0.03 grams of dry yeast, which is impossible to measure by volume. It comes out to something like $\frac{1}{128}$ of a teaspoon. Digital scales are pretty inexpensive. Consider them essential for any kind of baking.

Mixing bowls. I use a variety of mixing bowls. At home, glass and stainless steel bowls are great for mixing up starters and doughs. They're easy to clean, and it's helpful to see starters working their magic through the side of a glass bowl. I keep a few different sizes on hand. But when I'm going old school and mixing up dough by hand, there's nothing better than a wooden mixing bowl. Wood is porous and lets the dough "breathe." It seems to encourage more robust fermentation. A lot of old-school pizzaiolos like Franco Pepe mix their dough in wood. When I mix and ferment dough in wooden bowls, I feel a deeper connection to the entire history of pizza making, and that alone means something to me.

Stand mixer. This piece of equipment isn't absolutely necessary. Pizza dough was originally mixed by hand. But it's nice to have a stand mixer if you make a lot of Naples Dough (pages 61 and 64). If you don't have one, use your hands and my recipes for Old School Naples Dough (pages 69 and 72) and no-knead Al Taglio Dough (page 80).

Bench knife. You'll find yourself using this baker's tool for all kinds of tasks: scooping up flour, cutting and portioning dough, even shaping loose, wet doughs into balls on your work surface. A straightedge metal bench knife or dough cutter is a workhorse, and restaurant supply stores sell them cheaply. You could even use a large spackle knife or putty knife from the hardware store.

Dough scraper. Pick up a round-edge plastic dough scraper, too. The round edge and flexible material make it easy to scrape dough from a proofing bowl to your work surface. You can also use it to help fold no-knead doughs like Al Taglio Dough (page 80) right in the bowl.

Proofing boxes. A lot of people ferment their dough on half-sheet pans with parchment paper underneath and plastic wrap over the top. But the plastic always sticks to the dough, and when you try to pull it off, the dough tears. If you make a fair amount of pizza, pick up a dough proofing box from a restaurant supply store. They're cheap. You can also use a deep glass dish or a plastic tray with a lid. To take it to the next level, find an old wooden proofing box at an antique store—or have one made for you by a local carpenter. I found a wooden proofing box years ago and use it all the time for fermenting dough balls. The wood seems to help the dough reach its full potential.

Rolling pins. When it comes to dough, I'm a rolling pin fanatic. They are my favorite baker's tool to buy. I like wood rolling pins that have a uniform diameter and don't taper at the end. They're like big logs that roll out big pieces of dough. For me, the longer, the better. I have superlong ones for rolling out pasta, too . . . but that's another book. For rolling out a single ball of pizza dough (about 8.8 ounces/250 grams), a 12-inch (30 cm) rolling pin works just fine.

Dough docker. This thing looks like a medieval torture tool. It's like a little log with spikes all over it and has a short handle. You roll it over your pressed-out dough to "dock" it, or poke holes all over the dough. Docking helps air escape and keeps the dough from puffing up too much in the oven, if that's what you're going for. I use a docker to make Home Oven Stuffed Pizza (page 146). Just buy a cheap one from a restaurant supply store or baker's supply store, or use a fork to poke the holes by hand.

Pizza peels. This may sound hokey, but wood makes me happy. When I make risotto, I love using olive wood spoons. And when I make pizza, I prefer using wooden pizza peels. Build your pizza on the peel and then shake it into the oven. I even like the *swoosh* sound you get when pizza slides off the wood. It connects me to the pizza more! You can get wooden peels in all different sizes. Look for one that's at least 14 to 16 inches (35 to 40 cm) in diameter. For handle length, go by the depth of your oven. Short handles are best for home ovens, and longer ones are essential for wood ovens. If you have a wood oven, pick up a metal peel as well. This tool is like a round spatula you use to rotate the pizza toward or away from the fire so the pizza cooks evenly. You can also use a metal peel to move embers or logs that roll from the fire to your cooking area.

Baking steels and stones. As I mentioned previously, a ¼-inch (0.6 cm)-thick baking steel delivers heat to your pizza really fast in a home oven. Half-inch-thick steel works even better because it can hold and deliver more heat. But it's super heavy and expensive. A ¼-inch-thick steel is more practical. One that's at least 16 by 14 inches (40 by 35 cm) in size will easily accommodate a 12-inch (30 cm)-diameter pizza. If you're planning on making Home Oven Personal Pizza al Metro (page 142), get one that's a bit bigger, about 22 by 14 inches (56 by 35 cm). Baking stones come in the same sizes, but they are usually about ½ inch (1.3 cm) thick. Even so, a baking stone is less durable than a baking steel. After repeated thermal cycling (constant heating and cooling), the stone weakens and becomes more prone to cracking. If you already have a functional baking stone and you're considering buying a steel, I highly recommend it. It's actually useful to have both—especially if you don't have a broiler or if you want to get your bottom crust even crisper. For details on using both stones and steels in a home oven, see page 18.

Cast-iron skillet. This was a nice surprise during the recipe testing for this book. Cast-iron wins again! Cast-iron conducts heat better than either steel or ceramic. It makes a nice, dark pizza crust. Plus, cast-iron is cheap and durable—and will get lots of use beyond just making pizza. Look for your standard, heavy cast-iron skillets or griddles. These are thicker than some cast-iron pans sold as "pizza pans." That thickness makes all the difference in the amount of heat that gets to your pizza. Cast-iron skillets and griddles average about ¼ inch (0.6 cm) in thickness. A pan that's 12 inches (30 cm) in diameter is good if you already have one, but a 14 incher (35 cm) is even better so you have more room for a slightly bigger pizza. You can also use a rectangular cast-iron griddle (about 16 by 8 inches/40 by 20 cm) to make an oval-shaped Home Oven Personal Pizza al Metro (page 142).

Sheet pans. If you like square pie, sheet pans are the way to go. Look for half-sheet pans (18 by 13 inches/45 by 33 cm) so you can make Home Oven Pizza al Taglio (page 172). You'll love how easy it is to make this kind of pizza. You shape the dough right in the pan and then bake it. Most sheet pans are aluminum, which transfers heat pretty well, but they tend to be kinda thin, so the heat capacity is low. Thin pans also warp more easily. Look for thicker-gauge aluminum sheet pans—at least 18 gauge. Remember: as the gauge number goes down, the thickness goes up. So 13-gauge aluminum is thicker (about ¹⁄₁₆ inch/1.5 mm thick). At Pizzeria Vetri, we use "blue" steel sheet pans instead of aluminum. They're about ¹⁄₃₂ inch (0.8 mm) thick and are more durable than aluminum, so they warp less. But thick-gauge aluminum works just fine.

Parchment paper. I like loading pizzas directly onto the hot cooking surface. But shaking a pizza—especially a big one—off a pizza peel can be tricky. If you're nervous about sliding the pizza into the oven, a piece of parchment will help it along. Build the pizza on the parchment and then slide both the parchment and pizza onto your cooking surface. It's like training wheels. Start there if you need to. Eventually, you should be able to shake the pizza off the peel with a quick jerk of your hand.

Pizza cutter. I love cutting pizza with a pizza wheel. Wood-handled ones with metal wheels are my favorites. Some people use these big pizza cutting knives, but that's not my style. If it's yours, though, go for it. I'll stick with old-fashioned pizza wheels. And scissors. In Rome, it's traditional to cut pizza al taglio (which means "by the cut") with scissors. Just pick up a pair of offset scissors so you can cut into a 3-inch (7.6 cm)-deep square pie. Once you add the toppings, that's how deep some al taglio pies get!

Thermometers. If you don't have an infrared (IR) thermometer, you might want one. They're fun! They're like a laser gun that you point and shoot into your oven. Although they're not 100% accurate, you'll get a good sense of the temperature of your cooking surface, whether it's the floor of your wood oven or the steel, stone, or cast-iron pan in your home oven. If you have a wood oven, look for an IR thermometer that goes to at least 900°F (482°C). For home ovens, you might not have to spring for an IR thermometer, but it helps to have a good thermometer inside it. Home ovens are not always calibrated correctly, and the temperature readout on your dial or screen is probably not 100% accurate. Bi-metal dial thermometers are not very reliable. Have your oven calibrated and stick a decent digital oven thermometer inside to get a more accurate reading of the oven's ambient temperature.

Cooling rack. To keep your bottom crust really crisp, slide the baked pizza onto a cooling rack. The pizza will be steaming hot, and cutting boards or pizza pans will trap the steam and soften the crust. It's not absolutely necessary, but most people already own one of these. I like to let the pizza cool off for a minute or two on the cooling rack and then cut it on a cutting board or pan.

Mandolines. These cutting tools are so handy for slicing vegetables and garlic paper thin really fast. You don't need a giant metal French-style mandoline—although they are very versatile if you cook a lot. Just buy an inexpensive handheld model. If you don't have one, a thin-bladed knife and a very steady hand also work.

Tongs. Now here's something most chefs can't live without. Need to grab something hot without getting burned? Grab the tongs! They're useful for pulling hot pizzas from the oven, flipping vegetables on a sheet pan, and so many other tasks. Get a pair of spring-loaded tongs with scalloped edges; about 12 inches (30 cm) is a good length for most cooks.

PRACTICE

As I said earlier, the number one thing you can do to bake better pizza is to get to know your oven. That means practice. Like doing yoga or handling a bike, making good pizza takes some time. At first, you will mess up a few. Don't worry. Keep at it. Failure is a stepping-stone on the road to success. Or as chefs say, "When you burn things, you learn things!" Once you have a good feel for your oven and how it delivers heat to the pizza, then you can start experimenting with the pizza itself. That's exactly what led Stefano Callegari to toss a handful of ice cubes on his raw dough. He knew what would happen in his wood-fired oven. He knew the ice would melt, and the water would mix with starch from the dough and create a creamy sauce so he could make something like cacio e pepe pasta, but as pizza right inside his oven. That's the kind of experimentation I love. I hope the rest of this book gives you everything you need to experiment and create your own signature pizzas.

2

GRAIN AT PEPE IN GRANI

*We have neglected the truth that a good farmer
is a craftsman of the highest order, a kind of artist.*
—WENDELL BERRY

THERE IS NO BEST OF ANYTHING, NO ABSOLUTE IDEAL OF PERFECTION.
I truly believe that. But at any moment, you can stumble upon your own
experience of perfection. You remember every detail, every nuance, every
taste of these special moments. You don't need to take any pictures or write
anything down because it is all written on your soul. That's what it was like
the first time I tasted Franco Pepe's pizza. There were five of us, and we
had been eating great pizza all day at places like 50 Kalò and Da Attilio in
Naples. We pretended to relax with some espresso and rum baba by the
water. But inside, we were all so excited to drive up to Caiazzo that night
and eat pizza at Pepe in Grani.

I remember the first bite: fried pizza with mortadella and ricotta. We had been chatting away at the table. Then that pizza—perfectly cut in five slices—was laid down in front of us. An eerie silence came over the table. It didn't look like anything new or innovative. It looked like a piece of fried dough with some mortadella and ricotta on top. That all changed when we tasted it. We stared at each other, gazing in amazement, our mouths full of happiness. Then we hungrily kept eating. One slice each . . . that's all we got. Franco knew we had about ten more pizzas to go.

That night, we had pizza with shaved celery, melted onions, mozzarella di bufala, and tuna from the Amalfi Coast; pizza scarpetta with aged tomato passata and a beautiful crema of Grana Padano; the most amazing margherita pizza I have ever tasted; and a calzone stuffed with escarole, olives, capers, and anchovies. Every pizza was incredible. Each one told a story of Franco's ingredients from the ricotta cheese

made with local buffalo milk to the tomatoes grown in nearby mineral-rich soil.

But it was the pizza crust that really grabbed me. You know how sometimes you eat pizza and maybe skip the crust, just leaving it there on the plate? That never happens at Pepe in Grani. We ate every scrap of all ten pizzas. After finishing the toppings and getting down to the rim of each pizza, all these new flavors emerged . . . flavors in the crust itself. It was mostly the flavor of Franco's wheat. You could taste minerals, grass, flowers, butter, hazelnuts, and popcorn. In pizza crust. It was sick!

Not many people talk about the flavor of wheat. But the truth is, wheat has flavor, and different wheat varieties have different flavors. They're sort of like wine grapes. Wheat gets different flavors from the variety, the soil, and the climate it's grown in, and those flavors end up in your flour and in your pizza. Chefs spend hours sourcing the best possible ingredients, forming relationships with produce farmers and getting to know the difference between heirloom vegetables like Green Zebra and Cherokee Purple tomatoes. But we have so much to learn about wheat. Do you know what's in that bag of 00 flour you grab for your pizza dough? What wheat variety is it? How was it milled into flour—and when? And where was it grown—in what kind of soil? Like every other ingredient you cook with, whether you cook at home or in a professional kitchen, it makes a difference. Even freshness matters. A lot. As with other foods, fresh flour has more flavor than flour that's been sitting around for months. It's that simple.

So I asked Franco where he gets his wheat. Turns out most of it comes from just outside Bergamo. The mill is called Molino Piantoni, and the Piantoni family business goes back five generations. In the fall, Franco also gets a small amount of flour milled locally from an ancient wheat variety that isn't widely grown in the region anymore. But the farmer he works with still grows that wheat to preserve the food traditions of Campania. Franco made us a "pizza del territorio" with that flour because he wants to preserve the local traditions, too. All of Franco's ingredients have stories like this. He puts all his efforts into regional ingredients to honor the history of Campania and to preserve the customs of his fellow craftsmen— the farmers, the millers, the butchers, and the cheese makers. He respects the old way of doing things. He knows who grows and mills his wheat. He mixes his dough by hand in a wooden bowl and ferments it with no refrigeration. And he makes his pizza from start to finish with no machinery whatsoever. Just a wood-fired oven. Franco Pepe is laser-focused on quality at every step. That's what makes his pizza taste so ethereal, and his flour is a huge part of that.

WHITE FLOUR

If you think about it, when you eat pizza, you're eating mostly flour. A typical Neapolitan pizza is about 60% dough by weight, and pizza dough itself is about 60% flour by weight. That's why your flour makes such a big difference in the taste of your pizza. Pizza made with white flour isn't all bad—just look at how many people love it. I'm just saying that your

pizza could just be soooo much better by using better flour. The crust is the foundation of any pizza, and the sad truth is that the vast majority of wheat flour in most pizza crusts has had most of the dynamic wheat flavors milled away.

Modern grain mills are designed to remove the most flavorful—and nutritious—parts of the wheat kernel, the germ and the bran. That leaves behind only the endosperm, the starchy white center of wheat that is ground into white flour. In the mid-1800s, the "roller" mills that removed the bran and germ were considered revolutionary. They broke the wheat kernels into separate pieces instead of just grinding the whole grain. Roller mills made quick work of separating out the bran and germ so that huge volumes of refined white flour could be milled in less time.

It's true that roller mills are efficient, but they can create a lot of friction in the process, and that heats up the wheat, destroying some valuable enzymes and subtle flavors in the flour. Today's American all-purpose flour, bread flour, and even most tipo 00 flours from Italy are ground in roller mills. They all taste mild and vaguely "earthy," the familiar taste of bland wheat flour. Why have we grown accustomed to such flavorless food? Because it's profitable for the grain industry! Refined white flour lasts longer on the shelf. That's because the germ in a kernel of wheat is high in oil, and when you grind the germ along with everything else in the grain, the oil makes the flour go rancid faster. Removing the germ and bran extends the shelf life, so the flour can be kept and sold for more time at the market. But what are we sacrificing in the process? Flavor and nutrition!

The good news is that people are starting to demand more and more flavor and more and more nutrients from real, whole, minimally processed foods. Finally! This demand has fueled a big movement that is reviving heritage wheat varieties and whole-grain flours, ones that taste better—and are better for us—than the flours you find in most markets. These flours, especially fresh milled, can make a big difference in the taste of your pizza dough. So why aren't more people using them on a regular basis? It's complicated. A lot of things came together to put those familiar bags of white flour on the shelves, and no one tells the story of our current situation more simply and beautifully than Dr. Stephen S. Jones (see page 31).

STONE-GROUND FLOUR

As Dr. Jones explains, better-tasting pizza can be as simple as adding fresh-milled, whole grain flour to your dough. You might think, "Why not just add some store-bought whole wheat flour?" Well, store-bought whole wheat flour gives you the nutrition but not the flavor—because it's not fresh! For flavor *and* nutrition, fresh-milled stone-ground flour is the way to go.

Stone milling has been around since, well, the Stone Age. Stone mills differ from roller mills and other mills in one very important way: they grind the whole grain—bran, germ, endosperm, and all. When operated at low speeds, they also tend to generate less friction and less heat than big industrial roller mills. That's how stone milling can preserve some of the heat-sensitive enzymes and subtle flavors in the wheat kernel. All in all, stone-ground flour comes out less processed. I guess wheat is just like every other food. The less processed, the better!

The next time you make pizza dough, look for fresh stone-ground flour at a local farmers' market or mill. Check out the list of regional US stone mills on page 33. Better yet, mill some flour yourself. It's not hard. Milling your own flour or having it ground in a community mill used to be the norm. In fact, Roman soldiers milled their own flour on the go with small portable hand mills—and they ate better in battle than many of us eat at home today.

Home Milling

Think of wheat like coffee. If you grind the beans and brew the coffee right away, your coffee tastes better. Many people get that, and they have coffee grinders at home. Well, it's the same with grains. For better-tasting baked goods like pizza, grind some fresh flour.

You can buy an inexpensive grain mill and make fresh flour at home. It's easy. The two main types of home mills use steel or stone to grind the grain. Steel mills are high speed and produce more friction and heat, which we already know can destroy enzymes and vitamins—and flavor. My advice: go for a small stone mill. They operate at lower speeds, produce less friction, less heat, and help preserve the vitamins, enzymes, and delicate flavors you're trying to get from fresh flour in the first place. A stone mill is basically a hopper and two little stones that rub up against each other to crush the grains that you put in it. It's not gonna break. For a couple

New Flour

Dr. Stephen S. Jones is a renowned wheat breeder and director of The Bread Lab at Washington State University. He enthusiastically agreed to explain the many benefits of using fresh-milled whole wheat flour in this brief essay.

"Yeah, sure, fresh-milled whole wheat flour is great, but what is the shelf life?" I hear this question at least twice a week. My response varies, but usually it is something like, "What is the shelf life of an egg?"

Flour was one of the first foods that we industrialized. Up until the nineteenth century, most community mills were stone mills. With the advent of large-scale roller milling in the late 1800s, we started producing mounds and mounds of shelf-stable white flour in fewer areas of the country. The result? We lost about 25,000 regional stone mills. That's a lot of shelf life. It's also a lot of communities that lost access to good jobs and good-quality regional food—flour—all in the name of a whiter and whiter product with a longer and longer shelf life that, ultimately, has done little more for us than help build an over-efficient, overprocessed, and over-predictable food system that benefits everyone but us, the consumer.

What did we lose in this methodical quest for the ultimate shelf-stable ingredient—white flour? We lost 25% of the wheat kernel, which is discarded in the process. As a result, we also lost flavor, fiber, minerals, genetic diversity, and the understanding of flour as a living food like any other plant food.

What do we need to do to capture all those things back? Nothing. That is the beauty and the irony. All we have to do is grind every bit of the wheat kernel into flour. It is amazingly simple. Use the whole grain.

Want flour and baked goods that taste like something new? Use fresh-milled whole wheat flour, perhaps even some from a local grain grower that you milled yourself. And unless you are filling the larder for a clipper ship, learn to use reasonable quantities of flour that make sense for your scale and frequency of baking. By doing so, you are helping to reclaim one of our most important historic foods—fresh flour.

What can you expect from fresh flour? More flavor, to start. Within a few days, milled grains lose much of their flavor nuance. But fresh flour tastes grassy, nutty, clean, and bright. Fresh flour may be a bit weaker than aged flour, but that's actually good for pizza dough. With fresh flour, your dough will be more extensible and easier to shape instead of snapping back.

One easy way to start using fresh-milled flour is to mill your own with a small home mill (there are several good ones on the market). Just throw a handful of fresh flour into any one of your favorite recipes instead of the flour you usually use. A handful of fresh-milled flour will add nice nuances of flavor, color, and texture. Once you get comfortable with a handful of fresh-milled flour, start ramping up the amount. Remember that fresh-milled whole grain flour absorbs more water than store-bought refined white flour, so add a bit more water as you go.

Want a simple way to improve the taste of your pizza dough? Add some fresh-milled flour. Want shelf life? Buy canned peas.

—Dr. Stephen S. Jones, wheat breeder and director of The Bread Lab at Washington State University

hundred bucks, you can get a stone mill that grinds plenty of flour to whatever fineness you like. Small stone mills like the Mockmill attach right to your stand mixer. They're perfect for making a couple pounds of pizza dough with fresh flour. If you use lots of flour for other kinds of baking, something like the KoMo mill is a slightly bigger countertop version that still costs less than most espresso machines. If you really love pizza, think of it as an investment. Grab a grinder and start making fresh flour for your pizza dough. If you chill your grains and grind them cold, they'll heat up even less when you mill them, and they'll retain even more flavor. Either way, you'll love the sweet, nutty, complex taste of fresh flour.

I have gotten so excited about fresh flour over the past few years that I have a few different stone mills at home and at my restaurants. For some breads, I just mill the grains and mix up the dough with 100% whole grain flour. For other things like pancakes on Saturday morning, I might mix white flour and stone-ground flour fifty-fifty, so the pancakes don't come out too heavy from all the bran and germ. There are so many variations—that's part of the fun of playing around with fresh-milled flour.

For pizza dough, I recommend starting with 10 to 20% fresh-milled stone-ground flour. Just replace 10 to 20% of the bread flour called for in any of my recipes. You can use whole grain wheat, spelt, emmer, einkorn, sprouted flour, or any other flour you like. I usually grind the grains and then sift the flour once through a fine-mesh sieve. It's just a typical metal sieve for home kitchens that I got at Whole Foods Market. The sieve removes some of the larger bran flakes that can weigh down the pizza dough. But don't throw out the bran—save it for other things like sprinkling on yogurt.

Flour Extraction

If you start milling flour at home or buying fresh flour at a farmers' market, you might hear the term "extraction rate." That's basically the amount of grain that ends up in the flour after milling and sifting. If you mill whole grains and don't sift the flour at all, you get 100% extraction because you're keeping 100% of the bran, germ, and endosperm. If you mill whole grains and then sift the flour a little, you get what's called high-extraction flour. You're still extracting a high percentage of the whole grain in the flour. When testing fresh flour for the pizzas in this book, we milled on the finest setting of our home mills. For every 1,000 grams (2.2 pounds) of flour we milled, we sifted out about 100 to 200 grams of bran/germ flakes. That's an 80 to 90% extraction rate, which

Local Grain Mills

Here's a list of sources for whole grains and high-extraction flours milled at stone mills around North America. Many of these farmers and mills use heritage varieties of wheat. Some also make spelt flour, rye flour, and oat flour. If you want stone-ground heritage wheat flour from Italy, check out Mulino Marino in Piedmont. They mill heirloom grains for a lot of Italian bakers in Rome and Naples, and you can buy their flours online. Their buratto flour makes fantastic pizza dough.

NORTHEAST
- Castle Valley Mill, Doylestown, PA
- Small Valley Milling, Halifax, PA
- Beiler's Heritage Acres, Lebanon, PA
- Weatherbury Farm, Avella, PA
- Champlain Valley Milling Corporation, Westport, NY
- Farmer Ground Flour, Trumansburg, NY
- Maine Grains, Skowhegan, ME
- Elmore Mountain Bread, Wolcott, VT

MID-ATLANTIC
- Next Step Produce, Newburg, MD
- Seylou, Washington, DC

SOUTHEAST
- Bellegarde Bakery, New Orleans, LA
- DaySpring Farms, Danielsville, GA
- Independent Baking Company, Athens, GA
- The Comerian, Comer, GA
- Carolina Ground, Asheville, NC
- Anson Mills, Columbia, SC
- Boulted Bread, Raleigh, SC
- Louismill, Louisville, KY
- Weisenberger Mill, Midway, KY

MIDWEST
- Whole Grain Milling Company, Welcome, MN
- Lonesome Stone Milling, Lone Rock, WI
- Breadtopia, Fairfield, IA

SOUTHWEST
- Barton Springs Mill, Dripping Springs, TX
- Hayden Flour Mills, Queen Creek, AZ
- BKW Farms, Marana, AZ
- Blue Grouse Bread, Norwood, CO
- Mountain Mama Milling, Monte Vista, CO
- Grateful Bread, Golden CO

NORTHWEST
- Nash's Organic Produce, Sequim, WA
- Northwest Mills, Skagit Valley, WA
- Fairhaven Organic Flour Mill, Burlington, WA
- Island Grist, Lopez Island, WA
- Bluebird Grain Farms, Winthrop, WA
- Camas Country Mill, Junction City, OR
- Lonesome Whistle Farm, Junction City, OR
- Nootka Rose Milling, Metchosin, British Columbia, Canada

WEST
- Grist and Toll, Pasadena, CA
- The Mill, San Francisco, CA
- Capay Mills, Rumsey, CA
- Community Grains, Oakland, CA

is high-extraction flour. Anything above 75% is considered high extraction.

What about store-bought all-purpose flour? That has a lower extraction rate of about 70%. Much less of the wheat kernel ends up in all-purpose white flour. Bread flour, the kind used in most pizza dough, tends to be a little higher. It hovers around 72% extraction. And what if you pick up a bag of fresh-milled bread flour from the farmers' market or a mill—what kind of extraction rate will it have? Probably 70 to 75%. But it could be higher. Ask. Honestly, don't worry too much about the exact extraction rates in your flour. It only tells you what percentage of the wheat kernel ends up in the flour. Just grind some flour nice and fine at home, sift it once through a sieve, and use it to make pizza dough. It will work fine. More importantly, it will taste awesome because it's fresh!

Other Milling Terms

If you really start getting into fresh milling, you might come across a couple other milling terms. They're good to know, but don't worry too much about them unless you're deep into making different kinds of bread dough.

Ash content. This is the flour's mineral content. A lot of it comes from the soil and where the wheat is grown. Ash content is calculated by incinerating the flour, which leaves behind the mineral residue that is then measured. Most of the minerals (like selenium, manganese, phosphorus, copper, and folate) are in the bran and germ. That's one reason why whole grain flours are so much healthier for you—they contain so many minerals. High-extraction flours also retain more of the bran and germ and have a higher ash content and more minerals. These flours are good for yeast growth, too, because yeast needs minerals to grow. Look for flour with a high ash content if you want robust yeast activity in your pizza dough.

Falling number. This number measures the flour's enzyme activity. Falling number is calculated by mixing the flour with water to make a slurry. The slurry gets heated in a test tube to release starch from the water, and then a plunger is placed on top of the tube. The number of seconds it takes the plunger to fall to the bottom of the test tube is the falling number. During that time, enzymes in the flour are converting the starch to sugar. Remember: the higher the falling number, the lower the enzyme activity. If it takes 300 to 600 seconds (5 to 10 minutes) for the plunger to fall, that's generally considered a high falling number, and that means the flour has low enzyme activity. If it takes less than 200 seconds (3.3 minutes), that's considered a low falling number, and that means the flour has high enzyme activity. Essentially, falling number measures how much the grains have sprouted before being milled. That number can be a factor when you're making pizza dough. Enzymes help along the fermentation process, and if the flour has low enzyme activity (high falling number), the dough fermentation will be less robust. On the other hand, flours with high enzyme activity (low falling number) lead to more robust fermentation. Higher enzyme activity also means that the protein in the flour will degrade or weaken sooner. Both sprouted flours and fresh-milled flours tend to be high in enzyme activity.

FLOUR FINENESS

We should discuss flour texture a little. Some people like their flour milled superfine for pizza. It makes the crust feel soft and silky when you bite into it. That's what's recommended for Vera Pizza Napoletana (page 97). In Italy, that means type 00 flour, which is ground as fine as baby powder.

I used to use 00 flour for pizza. Years ago, when I opened Osteria and started making pizza, we used Caputo tipo 00 flour in the red bag. A lot of good pizzerias use that kind. We used it for 6 months, and it worked great. Then something happened in Italy, and we couldn't get the flour for a month. That's Italy for you! So we started using King Arthur Sir Galahad bread flour instead. American bread flour isn't ground quite as fine as 00, but it worked great, and the dough felt really good when you handled it. We actually liked the King Arthur flour a little better. Then the Caputo 00 became available again and when we switched back, we said, "Hey, it's not as nice." Is it because I like a slightly coarser texture in my pizza crust? Or is it because the King Arthur flour has a little less protein than the Caputo 00? Maybe the flour was fresher? Hard to say! And that's just me. If you like the texture of talcum powder, go for the Caputo.

Just keep in mind that finer flour absorbs less water. If you use 00 flour in a dough recipe that calls for American bread flour, it will be a little looser because the flour doesn't absorb as much water. It's not a big deal. You can just work in a little more flour if you want. But it's good to know. The water absorption of fine flour is also why I recommend that you start by subbing in only 10 to 20% of fresh-milled flour for the bread flour called for in my pizza dough recipes. I have no idea just how finely milled your flour will be, but 10 to 20% won't make a huge difference. As long as you use some kind of bread flour as your main flour, you could use fine or coarse flour along with it, and the dough will still make a nice crust on your pizza.

WHEAT GLUTEN

That brings us to one final facet of wheat flour that's really important: protein. You can play around with different flours, but for bread and pizza, I primarily use high-protein bread flour. There are different wheat varieties out there, but bread wheats are generally hard wheats high in protein. When milled, they make what is called strong flour because the flour is high enough in protein that the dough you make with that flour will be strong enough to hold a shape. When you mix bread flour with water, the protein in the wheat absorbs the water. And then something magical happens. The flour and water rearrange themselves into the largest composite protein in the world, gluten. Gluten is what makes bread flour strong. Gluten is also what makes bread hold its shape. Gluten forms long, stretchy sheets of protein that you can fill with air like a balloon. Gluten is what makes pizza dough elastic and allows it to rise. Gluten is what develops and strengthens when you mix and knead the dough. Gluten is the key to pizza dough! In fact, the protein content and gluten qualities of any particular variety of wheat are the two biggest factors determining how the flour will behave in your pizza dough. Play around with different flours. But if you want pizza dough to rise and puff up nice and big in

the oven, stick mostly with flours that have strong gluten qualities. Check out the chart on page 36 for a snapshot of different modern and ancient wheat varieties, their protein content, and gluten qualities.

Wheat Flour Protein Content and Gluten Quality

In any wheat flour, the protein content and gluten quality determine how the flour will behave in pizza dough. Most of my dough recipes call for bread flour. But you can sub in at least 20% of another flour with a similar protein content and gluten quality without drastically affecting how the dough behaves. You may even be able to mix the flours half-and-half, depending on the particular flour you use. For the best results, use whole-grain flour that is freshly milled! Keep in mind that there is some overlap among these flours and their gluten qualities. Flour is a living food with multiple variables affecting its baking qualities. Use this chart as a general guideline.

WHEAT FLOUR PROTEIN, STRENGTH, AND ELASTICITY			
WHEAT FLOUR	**PROTEIN % BY WEIGHT**	**GLUTEN STRENGTH**	**ELASTICITY**
Einkorn	16–17	Weak	Low
Farro (emmer)	16–17	Moderate	Low
Spelt, whole grain	15–16	Moderate	Moderate
Durum	14–16	Strong	Low
Whole wheat	12–14	Strong	Moderate
Stone-ground (wholemeal)	12–14	Strong	Moderate
Semolina	12–13	Moderate	Low
Tipo 00 for pizza	12–13	Strong	Moderate
Hard red spring	11.5–16	Strong	High
Bread	11.5–14	Strong	High
Hard red winter	11–13	Strong/Moderate	Moderate
Unbleached all-purpose, northern US	11–12	Strong	Moderate
Hard white	10–16	Moderate/Strong	Moderate
Unbleached all-purpose, national US	10–12	Strong	Moderate
Bleached all-purpose, national US	10–12	Moderate	Moderate
Bleached all-purpose, southern US	8–10	Moderate	Moderate
Soft red winter	8–11	Weak	Moderate
Soft white	8–10	Weak	Low
Tipo 00 for pasta	8–10	Moderate	Moderate
Pastry	8–9	Weak	Low
Cake	6–8	Weak	Low

Sources: USDA Food Composition Database; thefreshloaf.com; caputoflour.com; *On Food and Cooking* by Harold McGee; The Bread Lab at Washington State University

WHOLE GRAIN FLOURS

Betcha didn't know wheat was so complex. And we've barely scratched the surface!

I wish I could tell you to just use *all* fresh-milled stone-ground whole grain or high-extraction flours for the pizza dough recipes in this book. But what is the particular wheat variety in the flour you are using? Will it make good pizza dough? What's the protein content? Is it strong enough to form a gluten network that will hold bubbles and puff up the crust during baking? What's the falling number? There are just too many variables to make sure that the dough recipe will work.

The most important thing to take away from all this is that you should start using at least *some* fresh whole grain or high-extraction flour in your dough. Maybe you want to try spelt flour. Go for it! Lots of people with wheat sensitivities say spelt is easier to digest. It makes soft, light-tasting pizza crust, too. Or maybe you want to throw in some sprouted flour. Do it! Sprouted flours are also more digestible and make light doughs with a subtle sweet flavor. Sprouting jump-starts the fermentation process, too, so your pizza dough will ferment faster.

But I digress. The point is that the spelt and sprouted wheat flours on the market today tend to be *whole grain flours*. A lot of other whole grain flours are available now, and I encourage you to try them. Whole grain flours have more flavor than store-bought white flour. Just remember that any whole grain flour will make your pizza dough feel a little looser. The extra bran and germ in whole grain flour weaken the gluten network a little, so you may need to work the dough a bit more to strengthen the network. Even if you do work the dough more, whole grain dough may be a little less elastic and less likely to snap back. But that also makes it easier to stretch, which is great for shaping pizza. Handle whole grain pizza dough with a little more care. Be gentle.

The truth is, you can experiment with replacing 10 to 20% of the bread flour in my dough recipes with *any* other flour you like, whether it's fresh-milled, whole grain, sprouted, gluten-free . . . whatever. Find or make some fresh flour and toss it in your dough. When I started experimenting, I did the same thing that Franco Pepe did. I partnered with a local mill that grinds local grain. At Pizzeria Vetri, we use Redeemer, a heritage variety of hard red winter wheat grown locally in Pennsylvania. It's stone milled at Castle Valley Mill, a short car ride from Philadelphia. We use 10 to 20% of this fresh whole grain wheat in our pizza dough, and it adds such amazing flavor.

I hope you make a similar discovery. Ask around, check the sources on page 33, and find a local farmer or mill with a heritage variety of wheat that's grown and milled near you. Support your region's food traditions and make your own signature pizza dough. If you mix 20% of that local flour into your dough and like the taste and texture of the pizza, then bump up the amount from there. The more whole grain flour you add, the looser the dough will become. You may have to add a bit more water. But that's dough for you. It's all about flour and water!

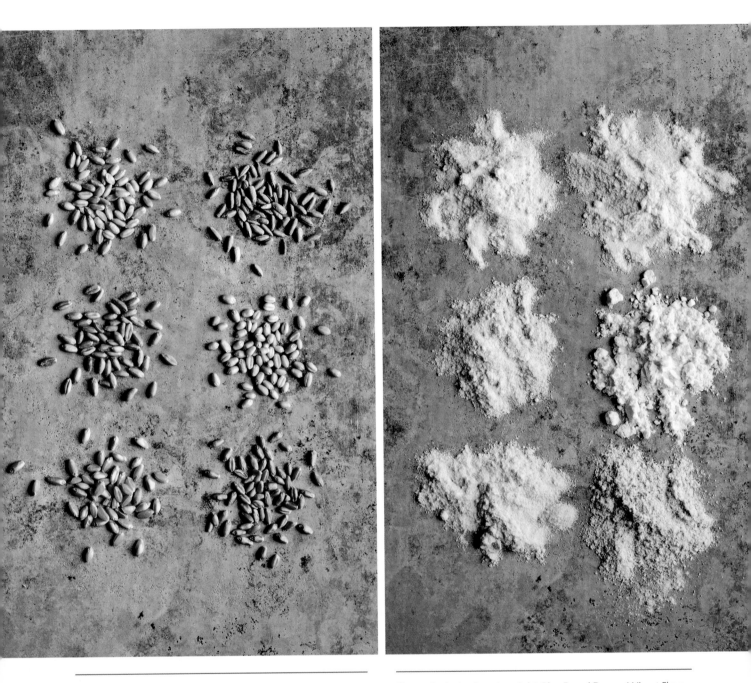

Grains clockwise from top right: Rye, Sonora Hard White Wheat, Redeemer Hard Red Wheat, Khorasan-Kamut, Spelt, Blue Beard Durum Wheat.

Flours clockwise from top right: Blue Beard Durum Wheat Flour, Tipo 00 Wheat Flour, Rye Flour, Silted Redeemer Hard Red Wheat Flour, Whole-Grain Sonora Hard White Wheat Flour, Whole Grain Redeemer Hard Red Wheat Flour.

Protein in Other Whole Grain Flours

Think of these whole grain flours as flavors to add to your pizza dough. Each flour will complement the wheat flavor. You'll also get some healthy fiber, vitamins, and minerals by using the whole grain. My pizza dough recipes generally call for bread flour, which is high in protein and has strong gluten qualities that form the structure of the dough. Most of the flours listed below do not contain gluten (the few that do are marked). When experimenting with these flours, start small by replacing only 10% of the bread flour with one of these flours. You might get a little less lift and poof in the pizza crust, but for some flours, you may be able to use up to 20% to add more of that flour's flavor to your pizza. The protein in these whole grain flours will also give you some chew in the crust.

WHOLE GRAIN FLOURS	PROTEIN % BY WEIGHT
Oat	15–17
Quinoa	14
Rye, dark (contains gluten)	13
Buckwheat	13
Amaranth	13
Teff	12
Sorghum	10
Barley (contains gluten)	10
Kamut (contains gluten)	10
Millet	7
Brown rice	7
Corn	7–10

Source: Data from USDA Food Composition Database.

3

DOUGH AT BONCI

Fermentation may have been a better discovery than fire.
—DAVID RAINS WALLACE

OVER THE YEARS, I'VE HONED MY PIZZA DOUGH RECIPES PRETTY WELL. But I've also learned that it's important to keep experimenting and keep searching for better, more flavorful wheat and more effective methods to improve the dough. It's a matter of constant innovation.

This point was driven home while eating at Gabriele Bonci's Pizzarium in Rome. Bonci loves to innovate, and he breathes new life into square pizza, a type of pizza that's often relegated to second-class status. His dough has big bubbles and complex flavors. He uses a mix of fresh-milled, stone-ground wheat flour and whole grain farro or spelt flour. He mixes a ton of water into the dough, so it's really loose, wet, and bubbly. And he doesn't knead it. He just folds the dough a few times and then sticks it in the fridge for a long, slow fermentation period. Then he presses the dough into sheet pans and bakes it in electric ovens at 450° to 500°F (232° to 260°C).

The result? You taste clean water, minerals, meadows, mushrooms, wildflowers, green apples, grapefruit, musk, butterscotch, and heavy cream. In pizza dough! The texture is equally incredible. Bonci's crust is light and airy with a ton of marble-size holes. It gets crisp and deeply browned on the bottom. At 1 inch (2.5 cm) thick, this crust is the total opposite of heavy, dense Sicilian pizza. And that's just the crust. The toppings are what truly bring Bonci's pizza to the next level. They're always seasonal, often whimsical, and never fail to impress. In spring, you might find his pizza topped with speck and asparagus on a base of fava puree. Summer might bring an unfussy combo of buffalo ricotta and borage flowers. In the fall, maybe rabbit, roasted grapes, and fennel seed. Bonci has a great sense of flavors. At Pizzarium, his pizzas are sold by the cut (*al taglio*), and you can taste them all by getting a slice of this and a slice of that.

If you are truly passionate about understanding pizza making, then this is the single most important chapter you will read. That's not hyperbole. Understanding and cultivating a relationship with your dough is the key to everything you want to learn. Dough is about 60% of what you eat when you eat pizza, and it's the foundation of knowledge that will take your pizza to the next level. I will give you pizza dough recipes that will work. But recipes are just guidelines. They are meant to be altered and adapted to your particular situation. That's especially true with yeast dough because it is alive. Making pizza dough is like caring for a pet. You can just set out some food and water, and your pet will survive, but it will be a lot happier if you give it some old-fashioned TLC. Every batch of dough you make is a living, breathing, bubbling foam of growing yeast and beneficial microorganisms. To help it thrive, the ingredient amounts, the mixing, and the fermentation methods described in any given recipe may need to change according to the dozens of variables that can affect the dough, such as the flour you are using, the type of yeast and the total amount, how much water you use and its mineral content, the humidity in the air, the temperature of your kitchen, and your ideal end result—just to name a few!

Think of it this way: making dough is like dancing. You may be the lead dancer, but you're not the only one on the dance floor. The ingredients and other variables bring their own moves, especially when you dance with natural wild yeasts to make sourdough. You are never in total control of pizza dough. Give up that notion. The best dancers allow their dance partners to shine. What you want to do is hold onto them loosely and let the dance happen. You are more like a maestro who's aware of the flour over here, the water over there, the yeast, the humidity, the temperature, and the time, and you work with it all to deftly bring everything together to create amazing taste and texture. That's how you dance your way to great pizza dough.

I find it incredibly gratifying—and humbling—to be involved in this very traditional, very natural process. You are helping raw ingredients come alive. The dough is born in your own hands, and you nurture it into one of the most beautiful and delicious foods on the planet—pizza. It's magical! I encourage you to develop a relationship with your dough. You could even give your dough a name. Personalize it. Then hold the dough in your hands and be sensitive to its needs. Have some fun with it.

If you've never made pizza dough before, I highly recommend starting with Bonci-style Al Taglio Dough (page 80). I've fallen in love with this kind of dough recently, and the basic recipe in this book couldn't be simpler. It calls for dry yeast and store-bought bread flour. You don't need a mixer. Just stir everything together in a bowl with a spoon. You don't knead it. Just stretch and fold it over itself in the bowl a few times. Then you let it sit in the fridge overnight. The next day, you press the dough into a rimmed baking sheet, and bake it in your home oven at 500°F (260°C) with whatever toppings you like. Boom! Pizza al Taglio (page 165).

But you should definitely experiment with different doughs beyond al taglio dough. The best pizza dough for you depends on what kind of pizza you like best. Making your pizza dough better is really a matter of understanding how all the variables work together: the flour, the water, the yeast, and the salt (and maybe some oil and sugar), along with the less obvious variables of time and temperature. Be open, flexible, and responsive to your dance partners. Adjust as you go. Even your own body temperature and energy level can impact your dough. Get a feel for what makes your pizza dough tick. Here's a brief look at how it all works.

FLOUR

Flour is so important to pizza dough that I devote an entire chapter to it. Here's the overview, but for the full picture, you really should read chapter two, "Grain at Pepe in Grani" (page 27). The bottom line is that wheat is like any other food. Whoever grows it and wherever it's grown make a big difference in how it tastes. The particular variety of wheat also determines its flavor and how much structure it will give to your pizza dough. Some of the world's top pizza makers seek out farmers and millers so they can dial in the specific wheat variety and type of flour that will work best for their particular style of pizza. Gabriele Bonci buys organic flour from Mulino Marino, a small mill in the Piedmont region of Italy. Franco Pepe, who makes out-of-this-world Naples-style pizza, also gets most of his flour from northern Italy, at Molino Piantoni, just outside of Bergamo. To find fresh-milled flour near you, see the list of regional US stone mills on page 33.

Milling and freshness are two important facets of flour. If your flour has been sitting around for months, it's not fresh. And it tastes like it. If you have an old bag or container of white flour on hand, go ahead and put some on your tongue. Tastes kinda bland, doesn't it? Well, it doesn't get much better when it's cooked. Now, put some fresh-milled flour on your tongue. Notice a difference? Fresh flour tastes grassy, nutty, and has a ton of other flavors, depending on the particular wheat variety from which it was milled. Within a few days, though, most of those subtle flavors are gone. Fresh-milled flour just tastes better than flour that has been sitting around for a long time. Like every other food, if you want the most complex and robust flavors, use the freshest ingredients. To keep your flour as fresh as possible, store it in tightly sealed containers in the freezer, refrigerator, or lastly, in a cool, dry place at 65°F (18°C) or less. Dry basements work pretty well.

Keep in mind that fresh flour is a little weaker than store-bought flour. That means pizza dough made with fresh flour will feel looser, and its structure won't be quite as strong. That's not a big deal for pizza. Fresh flour makes pizza dough easier to stretch out and shape. If you really want supertight structure in the dough, then start out with only a handful of fresh flour. In future batches, bump up the amount. You'll notice that even a small burst of fresh flavor will make a big difference in how your dough tastes.

Want even more flavor? Choose whole grain flour. Whole grain flour includes all three parts of the grain—bran, germ, and endosperm—and a lot of the subtle wheat flavors are in the bran and germ. White flour tends to taste bland because it's been processed to remove almost all of the bran and germ. That makes the flour last longer on the shelf, but it doesn't do it any other favors. Choose flavor. Use at least some whole grain flour in your dough—preferably fresh milled. The extra bran and germ in whole grain flour will absorb some water, so you might have to add a bit more water if you're used to using white flour. Again, it's not a big deal. Also keep in mind that whole grain flour can weaken the strength of pizza dough. The extra bran and germ interrupt the gluten network in the dough, making it feel softer and looser. That's why whole grain breads are sometimes less airy than white-flour breads. The weaker gluten structure just can't hold in as many of the leavening gases produced by the yeast. When the dough expands in the oven, more of those gases escape, and the crust doesn't puff up as much. But the taste of whole grain bread is so much more complex. And the flat shape of pizza is so forgiving that there is a lot of room for experimentation.

To help balance out the gluten-weakening effect of whole grain flour, use higher-protein flour. High-protein or "strong" flour is what creates the sturdy gluten structure of bread and pizza dough. As a baseline, choose flour with at least 12% protein (see page 39). Or, if you're using whole grain flour in the dough, go even higher. Spelt flour has 15 to 16% protein and makes fantastic whole grain pizza that doesn't taste heavy. Either way, protein and gluten strength are the keys to sturdy, elastic dough that puffs up big in the oven and holds in all the leavening bubbles that the yeast created when you fermented the dough. That combination of whole grain flour and high-protein flour with strong gluten qualities is partly how Gabriele Bonci manages to create a light, airy, whole grain pizza dough that's riddled with beautiful holes. He uses a fifty-fifty mix of whole grain spelt or farro flour plus high-protein flour called buratto. By the way, buratto means buttery, and that's exactly what you taste when you taste his flour!

If you want everything to work without a hitch the first time you make pizza dough, just follow the basic recipes in this book. They all start off with high-protein bread flour from King Arthur, a widely available brand. But after that, play around. Find your own signature combination of flours. Start incorporating more and more fresh-milled whole grain flour. You can check your local farmers' market for fresh-milled, stone-ground flour. Or better yet, make it yourself with an inexpensive home mill and some whole grains. Grinding wheat is no more difficult than grinding coffee beans for better-tasting coffee. Mill some flour at home and use it in your pizza dough. It's simple, and your pizza dough will taste amazing because it has fresh flour in it. In all of my dough recipes, you can follow the "Options" for subbing in 10% of any fresh-milled, whole grain flour. If it works well with the flour you choose, then bump up the amount to 15 or 20%. For Al Taglio Dough (page 80), you can use an even higher percentage of fresh whole grain flour. Al taglio pizza is shaped in a pan and doesn't need quite as much structure as Naples-style round pizza. Either way, you should feel free to experiment and try different flours.

WATER

After flour, water is the second most important ingredient in pizza dough. Water gets absorbed by the flour, swells up the flour's starches, and makes the dough sticky. Water also triggers the formation of gluten, which creates the firm structure in pizza dough. Water activates the yeast, too, so it can begin to grow. Obviously, you add water to flour to make dough, but flour also absorbs water from the air. A humid environment will make your dough wetter. Either way, more water makes pizza dough loose, wet, and sticky. Less water makes it stiff and dry. Basic, right?

Professionals call this hydration. That's the amount of water in the dough relative to the flour by weight. If you mix together 100 grams of flour and 60 grams of water, the dough hydration is 60%. The average hydration among all yeast breads is about 65%. That's typical for a loaf of sandwich bread and for a classic baguette. For pizza, the hydration varies. And you should switch it up to get the kind of pizza you want. Vera Pizza Napoletana (page 97) has a pretty low hydration of 55 to 59%. Pizza al taglio, on the other hand, has a high hydration of 80%. Why do these two pizza doughs have such radically different amounts of water? A lot of it comes down to baking temperature and the desired end result. Vera Pizza Napoletana bakes on the hot floor of wood ovens at a blistering 900°F (482°C). That pizza dough cooks in just 90 seconds. There's less water in the dough, and the water evaporates quickly at that high temperature: the dough firms up fast, creating a nice, crisp yet foldable crust. At the other end of the spectrum, pizza al taglio usually gets baked in electric ovens at a much lower temperature of 450° to 500°F (232° to 260°C). Al Taglio Dough at 80% Hydration (page 80) has so much water and bakes at such a low temperature that it takes 20 to 30 minutes for the crust to cook through and get crisp. A bake time of 1 to 2 minutes vs. 20 to 30 minutes is completely different! The dough hydration is a big part of that. You can adjust the hydration and baking temperature to achieve the kind of pizza you want to make.

Baking temperature is partly why I organized the dough recipes in this book by hydration. That helps you choose the kind of dough that will bake best in your oven and create the kind of pizza you're going for.

The amount of water in your dough also affects how much puff you get in the crust. More water = more puff. When the water heats up in the oven, it creates steam, especially when the pizza first goes in the oven. Steam helps transfer heat to the dough faster, giving it an initial blast of heat that puffs up the dough quickly. That's called oven spring. More water in the dough gives it better oven spring. You can also inject some steam into the oven. Some professional ovens are steam injected. In my home oven, I just toss a cupful of water on the oven floor. But it's the water inside the dough that really creates the hole structure in your pizza crust. In high-hydration doughs, all that steam building up inside the hot dough expands the bubbles, creating an airier structure in the finished crust. Higher-hydration doughs have more bubbles in them. Lower-hydration doughs have fewer bubbles. More bubbles in the dough will also stretch the gluten network thinner, and that eventually makes the baked pizza crust crispy on the surface. So high-hydration pizza doughs tend to get nice and crisp on the outside. And what about the size of the holes? That depends partly on how strong the gluten network becomes when you mix everything together. A stronger gluten network holds the bubbles in tighter so they don't get as big. A looser gluten network lets the bubbles swell up like balloons throughout the dough. The size of the holes also depends on the heat of your oven. A hotter oven and a shorter bake time sets the dough before the bubbles expand too big, while cooler ovens allow the bubbles to expand more before the dough sets.

And you thought water just made the dough wet! Keep in mind that higher-hydration doughs (upward of 70%) will mix easier in a countertop stand mixer like a KitchenAid. These wet doughs are just looser and easier to mix. On the other hand, lower-hydration doughs, like my Old School Naples Dough at 60% Hydration (page 61), are stiffer and make stand mixers work a little harder. If you're mixing up a lower-hydration dough and your machine seems to be straining, do it in two batches. Mix everything together first, then separate the dough into two piles so there's a smaller volume of dough in the mixer. Mix and knead each batch separately and then recombine the batches at the end of the process. Or just make less dough in the first place.

As you might guess, wet doughs are so loose that they don't always hold a shape very well. They're like edible water balloons. When you poke them, they actually wobble like Jell-O. Don't worry about it. I give detailed shaping directions in each pizza dough recipe. Just don't be surprised if you ball up a high-hydration dough, and then it flattens out some as it sits. It's the water spreading out. It's okay. You'll be stretching out the dough when you shape your pizza anyway.

One other very important factor of your water: its temperature. Water temperature can make the dough rise faster or slower. Warm water, above 80°F (27°C), gets the yeast going right away and kick-starts the whole fermentation process. Cold water, below 50°F (10°C), slows down the process so it happens more slowly. Really hot water, above 140°F (60°C) kills the yeast, and your dough won't rise at all. Don't kill the yeast! You can, however, play with the water temperature to speed up or slow down the rising process. Let's say you want pizza dough for tomorrow. When you mix up the dough, you can start off with warm water to get the yeast going right away. After a couple hours, you can stick the dough in the fridge to cool things off so fermentation happens nice and slowly, and you can get deeper flavors in the pizza crust. That's how I make my Al Taglio Dough (page 80). Or, let's say you have a little more time and want a really flavorful crust for Naples-style pizza. You can start off with cold water, let the dough sit overnight at room temperature, and then ferment the dough in the fridge for an even longer, slower fermentation period of 3 days. That's how I make my Naples Dough (pages 61 and 64). The bottom line in both of these examples is that longer fermentation times will give your pizza dough deeper and more complex flavors.

Oh, and one last thing: what's in your water? That can have an effect on yeast fermentation and the texture of your dough. Hard water is rich in minerals, usually calcium and magnesium. It turns out that, like every other living thing, yeast needs minerals to grow, and mineral-rich hard water can make yeast grow faster. The minerals in hard water also firm up pizza dough because the gluten proteins form strong bonds with the calcium and magnesium in the water. Want stronger, stiffer dough? Use hard water. On the flip side, soft water can make for slow-rising dough with a weaker gluten structure. Just so you know, pure water is considered neutral and has a pH of about 7. That means it's neither acidic (low in minerals) nor alkaline (high in minerals). Most tap water ranges from 6.5 to 8 on the pH scale and works fine for pizza dough. But if you're having trouble with your dough, check your water. And if you normally filter your tap water before drinking it, use that same filtered water in your pizza dough. You can also use bottled still water.

Clockwise from top: Whole Grain Sourdough Starter at 100% Hydration (page 84); compressed fresh cake yeast; active dry yeast.

YEAST

It really helps to think of pizza dough like a big balloon filled with smaller balloons. The flour and water create the balloon walls. But yeast is what inflates it all. Yeast is a tiny, single-celled organism, a fungus actually, and it's the driving force in your pizza dough. Yeast is alive, and like all living things, it has the basic functions of respiration and reproduction. Yep. Yeast breathes and makes little baby yeasts. There are hundreds of yeast species. Some like to feed on grapes. Some like to eat wheat. And they all love sugar. That's their main food. That's also why yeasts are harder to find in wintertime. There isn't as much sugar around when plants go dormant. Like other fungi, yeasts like it warm and wet, too. A warm, wet environment makes yeast grow faster. Under warm, wet conditions, you can cultivate all kinds of yeasts. Different yeast species produce different flavor profiles in bread and pizza dough, and you can look for various yeast strains to make signature breads and pizzas.

The species of yeast that was domesticated thousands of years ago to make beer and bread is called *Saccharomyces cerevisiae*. This species is now widely cultivated on molasses and preserved in various forms for baking. In the late 1800s, baker's yeast was only available fresh. Then, during World War II, the Fleischmann's company developed active dry yeast for the US Army. Now, dried yeast is more common than fresh, and fresh is hard to get. Dry yeast has had up to 90% of its moisture removed to slow down its activity so it lasts longer at room temperature. Most of the recipes in this book call for active dry yeast because it's consistent, predictable, and widely available. This kind of yeast is a little slow to wake up, which I like, because it gives pizza dough a long, slow fermentation time, and that helps build flavor. I don't use quick-rise or rapid-rising yeast. Those types are meant primarily for bread machines. But you can use Saf-Instant® yeast in place of active dry yeast in any of my recipes. Just substitute it one for one. This type of dry yeast gets going a little faster than active dry yeast, but no other adjustments are really necessary. The only thing I've noticed is that instant yeast sometimes gives pizza crust a slightly more "yeasty" taste after it's baked. So I prefer active dry yeast.

You used to have to dissolve dry yeast in warm water, and packets of active dry yeast still say to do that. But it really isn't necessary. Active dry yeast now comes in smaller granules that help the yeast grow even when added directly to dry ingredients. If you're used to dissolving dry yeast in water first or if you have any doubts about whether your yeast has expired, it's fine to keep doing that. If not, you can just skip that step and add the yeast directly to the flour. Either way, I highly recommend measuring yeast—and everything else in pizza dough—by weight instead of volume. Some of my recipes use tiny amounts of dry yeast that measure out to less than ⅛ teaspoon. Just pick up a cheap digital pocket scale that measures to the hundredth of a gram (0.01 grams). It's more precise.

All that being said, when it comes to yeast—and everything else—I prefer using fresh over dried. Fresh yeast just seems to create more leavening gases, better flavors, and

Using Sourdough Starter in Place of Commercial Yeast

For every 500 grams of flour called for in any of my dough recipes, you can use about 200 to 250 grams of active Whole Grain Sourdough Starter at 100% Hydration (page 84) instead of the yeast that's called for. To account for the flour and water already in the starter, reduce the flour and water in the recipe by 100 to 125 grams each. For instance,

my Al Taglio Dough at 80% Hydration (page 80) calls for 4 grams (about 1¼ teaspoons) active dry yeast. To use starter instead, replace the dry yeast with 200 grams active Whole Grain Sourdough Starter at 100% Hydration (page 84). Then reduce the amount of flour in the recipe from 500 to 400 grams and the amount of water from 400 to 300 grams.

more robust and mature pizza dough. Fresh yeast has had only 25 to 30% of the water removed. You might see it called wet yeast or compressed cake yeast—if you see it at all. Fresh yeast is not available everywhere, and some retailers only stock it during the fall and winter when more home cooks are baking. That's partly because it's so perishable. It has to be kept refrigerated. If you use fresh compressed yeast, crumble it up and swish it around in the water in your recipe to help disperse it. That's how I mix fresh yeast into all my pizza doughs. If you can't find fresh yeast, use dry yeast and convert the weight of fresh to dry by multiplying by 0.4. In other words, 10 grams fresh yeast x 0.4 = 4 grams active dry yeast. Don't worry—this isn't a math quiz! All these

conversions appear in my recipes so you can use either type of yeast, and I tested all the recipes with both types.

Now, let's say you really want to go all out for the most complex flavor in your pizza dough. Then, go wild! Wild yeasts give pizza dough incredible layers of flavor. Italians call wild yeast *lievito naturale* (natural yeast). The fact is, yeast is everywhere. It's on your hands and on bread flour, and you can capture yeast and then use it to make pizza dough. When captured in flour and water, it's called *lievito madre* (mother yeast). You might know it better as sourdough starter. It's called sourdough because natural, wild yeasts have a symbiotic relationship with various bacteria that give off different acids, and those acids give sourdough bread and pizza a sour taste. If you want to make sourdough pizza, get some sourdough starter from a friend. Or make it yourself. It's not hard. See the recipe for Whole Grain Sourdough Starter at 100% Hydration (page 84). You can use this kind of starter to replace any other yeast called for in my pizza dough recipes (beginning on page 59). I'll be the first to admit that wild yeast is not as predictable as active dry yeast. But if you can get a handle on it, it makes some damn fine pizza!

Whether you use fresh, dry, or wild yeast, it starts working whenever you mix up a batch of pizza dough. Mostly it inflates the dough. As flour absorbs water, the water activates enzymes in both the flour and the yeast, and the enzymes start converting large starch molecules in the flour to smaller, simple sugars. Then, the yeast feeds on those sugars and passes gas. It's true! After metabolizing the sugars, yeast gives off carbon dioxide gas (CO_2). That gas makes its way to air bubbles in the dough and inflates them like balloons. The more the yeast eats, the more it passes gas, and the bigger the balloons get. The dough rises. If you add more yeast, the dough rises faster.

This process is the basis of yeast fermentation. As it continues, the expanding bubbles act like a natural form of kneading, too. The yeast fermentation actually helps to strengthen the gluten network in the dough. The bubbles stretch the dough and cause the flour and water to form even more gluten, helping to firm up the dough's structure.

Yeast fermentation also creates flavor in pizza dough. When the yeast and other microorganisms convert large starch molecules in the flour into smaller amino acids, these smaller acids bring flavor to the dough. You know all those alluring flavors and aromas that people love in bread and pizza? The process of yeast fermentation is a big part of what creates them.

Yeast fermentation creates another important by-product in pizza dough: alcohol. And when yeast fermentation goes too far, too much alcohol gets produced. If that happens, the dough gets too acidic, and the extra acid weakens both the yeast and the gluten network. With too much acid, the dough rises too high, and then it falls. That's one reason why you don't want to add too much yeast to your dough. A smaller amount of yeast slows down the CO_2 and alcohol production

and allows the dough to ferment and rise nice and slow, so the structure stays strong. About 5 grams of active dry yeast for every 500 grams of flour is plenty to raise pizza dough in only a few hours. But you'll get even more flavor out of the yeast if you use less. You can use only 0.5 grams of active dry yeast for every 500 grams of flour. With that small amount of yeast, you can let the dough take all night to ferment. To slow down the fermentation process even more, you can stick the dough in the fridge. The cold temperature "retards" or slows down the yeast and gives it even more time to develop complex flavors in the dough. Less yeast and more time generally make for better-tasting pizza dough. Flavor is really what I'm after when I mix up a batch of dough.

SALT

Flavor is also the biggest reason to add salt to pizza dough. Salt amplifies the taste of everything. I usually use kosher salt in cooking, and I love finishing pizzas with big flakes of crunchy Maldon salt. But in pizza dough, I prefer fine sea salt. It disperses better, and it's easy to measure in small amounts. I especially like sea salt for baking because it has more minerals in it than kosher salt and table salt. No matter what salt you use, salt also helps tighten the gluten structure in pizza dough. The sodium interacts with gluten proteins in the flour, causing the gluten to contract. With sea salt, the additional minerals like calcium and magnesium help tighten the gluten network even more. More minerals = stronger dough. Sea salt is particularly helpful for firming up sourdough pizza doughs because the acids in these doughs can damage gluten formation. Mineral-rich salt helps minimize the gluten-damaging effect of those acids.

I usually use about 1.5% fine sea salt for most pizza doughs. That's relative to the weight of everything else. It's important to keep in mind that salt slows down yeast, and salt can kill the yeast altogether. Mind the yeast! That's why I usually mix salt into pizza dough after the yeast gets going a little. That's especially true if I'm fermenting the dough in the fridge, where the cold temperatures slow down the yeast even more. That's how I do it for my basic Naples Dough (pages 61 and 64). For that dough, I make a starter of flour, water, and yeast with no salt at all; this gives the yeast a chance to get active. Then, the next day, I mix the starter with more flour, water, and yeast, and then, finally add in the salt. Adding the salt last protects the yeast.

Sometimes I do it differently, though. There are no rules! You can add salt early in the process if you want to slow down the yeast *on purpose*. I usually do it that way when I'm fermenting pizza dough at warmer temperatures. Yeast grows faster when it's warm, and you don't want it to work too fast because you won't get as much flavor out of it. Adding salt early slows down the yeast so it will last longer even when warm. That's how I mix up my Old School Naples Dough (pages 67 and 69). I like that dough to ferment completely at room temperature with no refrigeration at all. I just dissolve the salt in some water and then mix the yeast right into the salt water. Then I mix in the flour by hand. Adding the salt early retards the yeast so it works more gradually at room temperature and has time to develop deep flavors in the dough.

See how complex it all is? In pizza dough—as in life— everything is related to everything else. If you're already confused, just keep this one basic principle in mind: pizza

The Ritual of Making Dough

Mix flour, water, yeast, and salt. Knead. Rest.

Everybody who has ever made pizza goes through the same motions, the same process. Making dough, shaping it, and cooking it are a human ritual. This ritual is the same as it's always been for centuries. And it's a big part of why so many people find making pizza dough—or any kind of dough—so therapeutic.

As your hands go through the motions, your mind is free to wander. You handle the dough, feel its warmth on your skin, and your thoughts meander, just like the millions of people who have handled dough before you and the millions of people who will handle dough after you. Making pizza connects you to human history.

This happens when you make pasta dough, and so it goes when you make pizza. The ritual is good therapy, good practice. Like every other human ritual, proceeding through the movements, and doing them mindfully, connects you to an entire culture—even different cultures. The simple process of mixing, kneading, and shaping dough allows you to transcend space and time and dwell in the same world as millions of other cooks throughout history around the globe.

Even more magical is the fact that each time you make it, you make it your own. Without even trying, you personalize the ritual just by using your own hands to perform the requisite actions. Your dough will bear the warmth and imprint of your fingertips, and the pizza you shape and bake will be completely unique. The heat of your oven will transform the raw ingredients into something greater, and that pizza will never exist again in exactly the same way. When you share the pizza with others, you will give to them a unique part of yourself and a unique moment in time. Passing a slice will also connect them to the age-old ritual of making and sharing bread that unites all humanity.

As quickly as your pizza rose, it will disappear. The pizza will be gone in seconds. After you and your guests enjoy what you made, only crumbs will be left behind, minuscule traces of the human ritual that produced it. Yet these traces are enough to remind you that the ritual will never change. It's a constant fertile process that will always remain the same. And that's what inspires you to make it, enjoy it, and share it, again and again.

Mix flour, water, yeast, and salt. Knead. Rest. Shape. Bake. Eat pizza. Forever.

dough that rises really quickly doesn't develop as much flavor as pizza dough that rises really slowly. Long, slow rising gives everything more time to develop deeper, fuller, more complex flavors. With time comes flavor.

OIL

Most pizza dough consists of just flour, water, yeast, and salt. In fact, oil is forbidden from the dough in Vera Pizza Napoletana (see page 97 for details). I don't add any oil to my Naples dough. But I do add it to some other doughs, like Roman dough. Why? Oil makes the dough richer, softer, and easier to stretch thin. It also makes the crust crunchier. That's what I'm going for in a crisp pizza Romana (pages 138 and 140). Here's how oil makes pizza dough more tender: the fat coats protein molecules in the flour. With a coat of fat, the flour can't absorb as much water, and that inhibits gluten formation, which makes the dough less tough and more tender. Fat actually shortens the chains of gluten. That's why fat is called shortening in baking. Usually, there isn't much fat in pizza crust, so there isn't much of that shortening effect. But let's say you want the best of both worlds. Let's say you want sturdy dough with a strong gluten network, but you also want some oil in there for richness. In that case, mix and knead the dough without any oil to develop the gluten network first, and then knead in the oil at the end. That's exactly how I make panettone, the classic holiday sweet bread riddled with dried and candied fruit. I mix the dough like hell at first to develop enough structure for the dough to hold in lots of air and make the panettone light and fluffy. Then, after the dough is strong, I mix in a ton of butter to enrich the whole thing.

SUGAR

Some bakers add sugar or malt or even milk to feed the yeast in their pizza dough. Any form of sugar will sweeten up the dough. It also gives you a more deeply browned crust. At Forno Roscioli in Rome, they add 10% milk to their dough because they use dry yeast instead of wild yeast. The milk helps the dry yeast get going by feeding it some extra sugar.

The milk also helps their dough brown up more at a lower baking temperature (usually 450° to 500°F/232° to 260°C). The only kind of pizza dough that I add sugar to is Roman dough (page 76 and 78). Along with the oil, a little sugar in that dough softens it and makes it easy to stretch. Just like fat, sugar also inhibits gluten development. Sugar attracts water and prevents the flour from absorbing as much water, and without as much water, the gluten doesn't get as strong. I like some of that softening effect in Roman dough. It makes the dough so easy to press out by hand or just roll out with a rolling pin. For Naples dough, though, I like a little more chew, a little stronger gluten network. I don't add sugar to that dough. If you want to, though, go for it. Just choose the kind of dough and the kind of pizza you want to make. If you do add sugar, keep in mind that it will make the yeast grow faster. And watch your baking temperature. Sugar burns while you're not looking!

MIXING AND KNEADING

The simple act of mixing together flour and water is the first step in the dance of making dough. When those two ingredients first touch, one of the most magical natural processes unfolds. Protein in the flour absorbs water, and both ingredients transform into the longest composite protein on earth: gluten. There are actually two smaller proteins in wheat flour called glutenin and gliadin. Water causes these smaller proteins to shift and change shape, and then they bond together and create a larger protein, gluten. Gluten is what allows pizza dough to trap air and swell up like a balloon. Gluten is what makes pizza possible. For more details on gluten and different types of flour, read the chapter on grains, particularly pages 35 and 36.

Mixing or applying any kind of force to pizza dough develops the gluten. Manipulating the dough stretches and folds all those chains of gluten over one another. The strands of gluten get longer and stronger, forming a tighter and tighter network. As you mix, the dough's texture goes from wet and sticky to firm and smooth. The exact same thing happens with pasta dough (minus the yeast). Mixing and handling the dough firm it up. Every time you pass pasta dough through the rollers, you develop the gluten structure, and the dough gets firmer and more elastic.

The recipes in this book show you several different methods for mixing up pizza dough, including machine mixing, hand mixing, and just using a plain old wooden spoon. Each method has a different effect. All mixing methods will incorporate some air into the dough, but vigorous mixing and kneading incorporate more air. As you mix and knead—or even fold—you also disperse those air bubbles more widely throughout the dough's gluten network. Vigorous kneading creates lots of small bubbles held tightly within the network. After baking up that sort of dough, the strong gluten structure leaves behind a tight crumb with several small, evenly distributed holes. That's pretty much what happens in my Naples Dough (page 61 and 64) and in my Roman Dough (page 76 and 78). I mix both of these doughs completely by machine for 12 to 15 minutes; this gives them the kind of texture and chewiness I like in Naples-style pizza and pizza Romana.

But I encourage you to use your hands to mix up pizza dough, especially if you're new to the process of making dough in general. Mixing by hand gives you such a better feel for the dough and for what's happening in it as everything comes together. With your hands in the dough, you can actually feel the flour absorbing the water and getting sticky. You can feel the gluten starting to firm up and the dough getting smoother. If you stretch out a handful of dough like bubblegum, you can see how the gluten structure gets longer and stronger, and you can see all the bubbles right through the dough. You can even feel the dough warm up from your body heat and the friction of mixing. I love that! That's why I prefer to mix and knead my Old School Naples Dough (pages 67 and 69) and Whole Grain Sourdough Pizza Dough (pages 86 and 88) completely by hand. Like Franco Pepe says, mixing and kneading pizza dough without a machine is like watching a creature being born in your own hands. It's magic!

But, really, you don't even need to knead. Flour and water will eventually form a gluten structure all on their own. That's how no-knead doughs work. Instead of using your hands or a machine to force water into the flour and develop the

gluten, you just give the flour and water more time. You simply stir everything together in a bowl and let it sit. Gently stretching and folding the dough now and then will create a loose, delicate gluten network. The stretching incorporates air and spreads out the air bubbles nice and wide throughout the dough; this gives you even more puff when the pizza is baked—especially when you use high-hydration dough. With gentle folding, you get a less chewy, more tender crust with fewer yet bigger bubbles. That's the kind of open, airy hole structure you see in no-knead artisan breads. And that's the method I prefer for Al Taglio Dough at 80% Hydration (page 80). When you press that loose high-hydration dough into a big rectangle in a sheet pan, you elongate the gluten chains and air bubbles even more, giving you a nice, big, airy crumb. It makes fantastic Pizza Al Taglio (page 165). I use the same dough for a similar hole structure and texture in Pizza Bianca (page 170) and Home Oven Pizza Rossa (page 169).

It's all about what you're trying to achieve. You can mix and knead the dough, or you can stretch and fold it. Either way, when it's ready to be set aside to ferment and rise, the dough should look less rough than when you started. It should look smoother on the surface. It should also feel somewhat springy when poked. Those are signs of gluten strength. There's a simple "windowpane" test you can do, too. It will tell you whether your dough has been mixed, kneaded, or folded enough to rise and puff up in the oven. Just grab a small piece of dough in your hands and slowly press and stretch it into a thin sheet—like making a mini-dough round. It should stretch paper thin without tearing and hold the round shape. It should also be translucent enough to see light through the dough, like a windowpane. If the dough tears or doesn't let in much light, the gluten isn't developed enough, and the dough is most likely underkneaded. Give it some more kneading or folding to strengthen the gluten. Or just give it more time to rise. Keep in mind that when you use whole grain flour in pizza dough, it helps to knead the dough a little more to firm up the gluten network. That's because the bran and germ in whole grain doughs interrupt the gluten network, making the dough softer. A little more kneading helps firm it up. Is it possible to overknead dough? Yes. Overworked dough will just stretch and stretch and not hold a shape very well. Think of the kneaded dough like a bungee cord. Ideally, when you test a ball of kneaded dough by stretching it, the dough will slowly spring back into its original shape like a bungee cord. If it's underkneaded, instead of stretching, the dough just rips. If it's overkneaded, instead of coming back into shape, the dough just keeps stretching and stretching. Don't worry. Once you start making dough, you'll get a better feel for it. But the bungee cord analogy helps. You'll know whether your dough is strong enough to hold air just by looking at it and feeling it.

FERMENTATION

If you're into fermented foods like pickles, then you're on your way to understanding pizza. Pizza is fermented food. Fermentation is a completely natural process and part of what makes pizza taste so good. It also makes pizza good for us. When you mix flour, water, yeast, and salt together, that is just the beginning. Then the real fun begins. The dough grows!

Yeast is what kicks off the fermentation in pizza dough. Enzymes in the yeast break down starches in the flour into sugars. The yeast feeds on those sugars, and then the yeast gives off carbon dioxide gas, which puffs up the dough like a balloon. The yeast also gives off alcohol. Yeast fermentation is actually called alcoholic fermentation. Well, guess what? There's a second kind of fermentation going on in your pizza dough: lactic acid fermentation. Alcohol triggers it, but lactic acid bacteria are really what drive lactic acid fermentation. Lactic acid bacteria are among the good bacteria in your digestive system, and they are found in many common foods, like *Lactobacillus acidophilus*, the kind found in probiotic yogurt. In bread and pizza dough, various other species of beneficial lactic acid bacteria show up, like *L. brevis*, *L. pontis*, and *L. sanfranciscensis*. That last one is named after San Francisco, where it was first discovered in sourdough bread. *L. sanfranciscensis* bacteria aren't exclusive to San Francisco. They were just named there.

Why does all this matter? Because lactic acid fermentation brings incredibly complex flavors to pizza dough. If you want next-level flavors in your dough, you want to encourage lactic acid fermentation. The yeast works on one level. It creates flavor by transforming large starch molecules in the flour into smaller components that are more detectable by our senses—more flavorful. Lactic acid fermentation works on another level. It transforms large protein molecules in the flour into smaller, more flavorful components. This process of breaking down wheat proteins is called proteolysis, and it brings all kinds of amazing flavors to pizza dough, including the aromas of cooked potatoes, ground cloves, fresh cucumbers, and vanilla.

Proteolysis also makes pizza dough more digestible. Yes, you read that right. Digestibility is a big deal for pizza lovers. It's one of the biggest compliments you hear among Italian pizzaiolos: "Your pizza is so digestible." As if that were high praise. But it is! It means that your dough is so completely and fully fermented that you can eat lots of pizza without feeling bloated or weighed down. It may sound weird, but fully fermented dough is sort of "predigested" by the yeast and bacteria, making it easier on our own digestive systems. On one of our research trips to Italy for this book, we traveled around Naples and Rome, and four of us ate 45 different pizzas in 3 days. That's 11 pizzas each! We enjoyed every bite, and not a single one of us felt the slightest bit bloated. I know that's just a personal anecdote, but it turns out that lactic acid fermentation is a key factor in making pizza dough more digestible. Proteolysis breaks down the tough gluten proteins in wheat flour and makes pizza easier for us to digest. For people with gluten intolerance, it may help to seek out breads and pizzas made with fully fermented dough.

How do you encourage lactic acid fermentation in yeast dough? Give it some time! You can also adjust the temperature to bring different acids and flavors into play. If you stick your dough in the fridge, the cold temperature radically slows down yeast fermentation, but lactic acid fermentation continues. Cold temperatures tend to bring more acetic acid and sharper, brighter flavors to pizza dough. Acetic acid is essentially the sharp taste of vinegar. Warm temperatures, on the other hand, bring more lactic acid and mild, buttery

flavors to pizza dough. Lactic acid is more like the pleasantly sour tang of yogurt. Depending on the balance of lactic acid and acetic acid in your dough, your pizza will taste different. You can play with your dough fermentation temperature to get a different balance of these acids. Be careful, though. Too much acid overall can weaken the gluten structure.

Here are some examples of how I play with the fermentation temperature to bring different flavors into the dough. For my Old School Naples Dough (pages 67 and 69), I let the dough sit out entirely at room temperature for about 9 hours to bring those mellow lactic acid flavors. That's very similar to the kind of fermentation recommended for Vera Pizza Napoletana (page 97). The pizza comes out tasting almost buttery. At Pizzeria Vetri, though, I use a slightly different kind of Naples Dough (pages 61 and 64). For that one, I start the fermentation at warm room temperature to get the yeast and lactic acid flavors going—for a good 12 hours. Then I stick the dough in the fridge to slow everything down and bring other flavors—and extract as much flavor as possible—over a long, cold fermentation period of 2 to 3 days.

When I really want lactic acid fermentation to kick into high gear, I make Whole Grain Sourdough Pizza Dough (pages 86 and 88). I'm tellin' ya: go wild! The simple fact is that wild yeast cultures (sourdough starters) attract a much greater diversity of beneficial bacteria than doughs made with commercial dried yeast. That's partly because sourdough starters also attract different yeast species like *Candida milleri* and *C. holmii*. Capturing and using these yeasts isn't as predictable as using dry yeast. But they bring awesome flavors to pizza dough! It helps to use fresh-milled stone-ground flour, too. In general, fresh whole grain flour attracts more yeasts and beneficial bacteria than store-bought white flour. Once again, the freshest ingredients bring the deepest flavors. Are you intrigued? Do you want the ultimate flavor and the most digestible pizza? Make Whole Grain Sourdough Starter at 100% Hydration (page 84) and then use that starter instead of dry yeast to make your favorite pizza dough. That's exactly how Gabriele Bonci makes his dough for the awesome-tasting pizzas at Pizzarium in Rome. He uses natural wild yeast, a mix of organic whole grain and high-extraction flours, a lot of water, and a long fermentation time at both warm temperatures and cold temperatures to extract as much flavor as possible from all of his ingredients. Pizza made with that kind of deeply fermented dough has got it going on! Try it—it's not hard to make. It just takes time.

PIZZA AND JAZZ

After reading all this, you might be feeling overwhelmed. Don't. Yeast dough is something that people have been making for thousands of years. You don't have to geek out on all these details. Don't sweat the small stuff! Just mix up some dough and let it ferment nice and slow. To get a handle on all the ingredients and the fermentation, maybe think of pizza dough like a jazz band. Flour is like the drummer in the band. It's the foundation, pounding out the pulse and keeping everything else together. Water is the bass, meshing with the drums, fleshing out the rhythm, and tying the whole rhythm section to the other instruments. Yeast and bacteria are the piano and guitar in the band. Those instruments are really what sing the melody, pushing the band here, pulling

it there, raising up the band, and taking the whole combo to unimaginable heights of harmony. And the salt? That's the saxophone, punctuating the song with tasty licks and keeping everyone tight. Just fold all these ingredients together and give them a place to do their thing. They'll start bubbling away and make some beautiful music in your pizza dough. And, like jazz, it'll be a little different every time, which is part of what makes it so amazing!

Just remember this one thing: pizza is not fast food. Pizza dough, in particular, is not fast food. It takes time. Like a jazz band, pizza dough does not come bursting onto the stage playing its best stuff right away. It has to warm up a little. Give your dough the time it needs. Give all the players—the flour, water, yeast, and salt—a chance to get to know each other. Eventually, they'll get comfy, and then your dough will start to grow. It will come alive. It will pulse and sing. Have you ever smelled pizza dough while it's rising and fermenting? It smells like pure sex! And then after you bake it, the smell of freshly baked pizza? It's out of this world! If there is any such thing as the music of the spheres, pizza is singing some of those heavenly songs!

Test Your Dough Fermentation

No matter what kind of dough you make or how you ferment it, you might be wondering, "How do I know when it's ready to bake?" There is a simple test. After all the mixing, kneading, folding, fermenting, and shaping, your dough should be looking pretty plump. It should also feel somewhat relaxed. Poke a finger about ¼ inch (0.6 cm) deep into the dough. The dent you make should remain in the dough or fill in slowly. That's a sign that the dough is mature yet relaxed. If the dent springs back right away, the dough needs more fermentation time. Underfermented or "underproofed" dough doesn't rise as much in the oven. And overproofed dough can taste unpleasantly sour because the yeast gives off too much alcohol. Just give your pizza dough a poke before you bake it. If it's mature, it will look plump but feel relaxed.

Time, Temperature, and Moisture

I can't tell you how many times it's been 90°F (32°C) outside, and inside my restaurants the AC is set to 77°F (25°C)—and the staff thinks that lowering the AC to 65°F (18°C) is going to make it cool down faster. It doesn't work. Central air conditioners work at a constant pace. Lowering the AC doesn't make it work any faster. It just keeps the AC on longer until the room reaches the lower temperature that you set it to. And then people in the restaurant complain that it's too cold. The moral is: no one understands temperature. No one understands humidity either. Moisture, temperature, and time are key variables in pizza dough. The temperature of your kitchen and fridge, the temperature of your water, even the heat of your hands . . . they all make a difference. The humidity in the air is equally important. As the humidity changes, the flour in your dough will absorb more or less water, making the dough wetter or drier. That's why Italy's master pizzaiolo Franco Pepe ferments his pizza dough as close to 86% humidity as possible. That way, he knows how wet his dough will be. Time is another critical factor. Pizza dough is alive, and like all living things, it gets more complex and mature as time passes. Long, slow rising times tend to create the deepest flavors. Keep in mind that it takes more time for a big batch of dough to change temperature than it does for a smaller batch. Time and temperature go hand in hand. Here's a brief synopsis of how time, temperature, and moisture can affect your pizza dough. Get to know these variables. Then manipulate them to get the kind of dough you want in the kind of time you have.

MORE TIME
- Requires less yeast
- Creates larger bubbles
- Creates more complex flavors

LESS TIME
- Requires more yeast
- Creates smaller bubbles
- Creates less complex flavors

HIGHER TEMPERATURE
- Speeds up yeast
- Decreases fermentation and rising time
- Brings more lactic acid

LOWER TEMPERATURE
- Slows down yeast
- Increases fermentation and rising time
- Brings more acetic acid

MORE WATER
- Speeds up yeast
- Increases fermentation and rising time
- Brings more lactic acid
- Creates more bubbles
- Creates more steam

LESS WATER
- Slows down yeast
- Decreases fermentation and rising time
- Brings more acetic acid
- Creates fewer bubbles
- Creates less steam

4

PIZZA DOUGH
RECIPES

EVEN THE BEST OF US SOMETIMES MAKES A CRACKER. It does happen. A few years ago, the Philadelphia Eagles were in the playoffs, and I decided to make pizza for the game. My wife and kids went out to run a bunch of errands. I was busy with phone meetings that day, but I promised that when we were all home for the game, we'd have hot, fluffy tomato pie. I had mixed up some Al Taglio Dough (page 80) the night before and had let it ferment all night in the fridge. Then that morning when I took out the dough, my heart sank. The dough looked as if it was going nowhere—no bubbles. But sometimes, you gotta just go with it. It was a January day, and I thought, well, it's a little colder out, and even though the dough didn't rise much in the fridge, I'll just leave it out at room temperature for a while to get it going. After a while, it did start to relax and stretch out a bit. But I wasn't seeing those big, beautiful bubbles. After I got off the phone about an hour later,

I finally saw a few bubbles in the dough. I thought—whew—I'll just give it a little more time. I went with it. Of course, I knew . . . deep down, I knew. It wasn't gonna work.

When my kids got home, their smiling excited faces kept my hopes alive. I stretched out the dough in a sheet pan, spread on a layer of San Marzano tomatoes, and doused the whole thing with olive oil and rock salt. It sure looked good. My kids' faces lit up. Into the hot oven it went. My wife and kids went into the living room to watch the game, and after a couple minutes, I took a peek at the pizza in the oven. It wasn't happening. No bubbles . . . no lift, just the hardening of flour, water, salt, and dead yeast. I started prepping them early on. "Hey guys . . . I'm making something different tonight . . . a pizza cracker!" They got so excited. "Really, Dada?" my kids said. "A pizza cracker? That sounds so cool." I said, "Oh, just you wait . . . it's gonna be awesome!"

When I brought it in, my wife, Megan, bit into it, laughed, and said, "Nice pizza, Dada." She knew. I looked at her and said, "What? It's a pizza cracker." "Yeah, right," she said. The kids had my back. They thought it was good. But in the end, we all agreed that, despite my efforts to make something new, it was probably best not to have pizza crackers anymore. I gotta tell you, though, I ate them . . . and enjoyed them. Because in the end, pizza is like sex. Even when it's bad, it's still pretty good!

When you make pizza dough, don't worry if something goes wrong. It happens. Some things are just out of your control. If you want to know about all the variables (like the dead yeast in my pizza cracker), read chapter three, "Dough at Bonci" (page 41). There's a ton of information there, and it will help you make better pizza dough.

What's the best kind of pizza dough? The kind that makes the pizza you like best! Do you like thick, fluffy square pie? Then try Al Taglio Dough at 80% Hydration (page 80). Do you like round Margherita pizza with a big poofy rim? Make Naples Dough at 60% Hydration (page 61). And what kind of oven do you have? It makes a difference. If you have a really hot, wood-fired oven and want Naples-style pizza with a big, puffy, charred rim, go for the Naples Dough at 60% Hydration (page 61). It's perfect. If you have a home oven that only goes up to 500°F (260°C), try the Al Taglio Dough at 80% Hydration (page 80). That dough is perfect for that oven. You see, to get the kind of pizza you're going for, it helps to balance out the heat of your oven with the amount of water in your dough—this is known as the dough's hydration. That's because hotter ovens cook pizza faster, and the water in the dough evaporates faster. Cooler ovens cook pizza more slowly, and it takes more time for the water to evaporate.

I organized all the dough recipes here by hydration because that will help you achieve the kind of results you want from the oven you have. Start there—with your oven—and then play around with the dough recipes. If you want to know more about your oven and how to bake great pizza in it, read the chapter on "Baking at Sbanco" (page 9). Or just pick a dough from this chapter that looks good to you and follow the recipe. Then make pizza with it. Everything you need to do is explained in the recipes. The doughs are all here, while complete shaping and baking directions appear in each pizza recipe.

You'll find cold-fermented doughs, warm-fermented doughs, sourdoughs, whole grain doughs, and doughs made with fresh-milled flour. Some are mixed and kneaded in an electric mixer. Some are mixed and kneaded by hand. Some are no-knead doughs that you just fold a couple times. Some are ready the same day. Some are ready the next day. And some take a few days. Some use dry yeast. Some use sourdough starter. Some make 1 dough ball and others make 3, 5, or 6 dough balls. So many options. Choose the dough recipe that looks as if it'll work for your particular pizza situation.

Whatever dough you choose, I strongly encourage you to work in at least a little fresh whole grain flour when you make it. We all want food that tastes awesome and is good for us. Naturally fermented yeast dough made with stone-ground whole grain flour is just that—great tasting and good for you. We've been thriving on this kind of food for thousands of years. In fact, human civilization was founded on yeast bread. Once you get a feel for making pizza dough, tossing in a handful of fresh whole grain flour will become second nature. And don't be surprised if things don't always work out every time. No big deal. The more pizza you make, the more you learn. Even if you make a pizza cracker, it will still be good to eat!

NAPLES DOUGH AT 60% HYDRATION

MAKES 6 DOUGH
BALLS, EACH ABOUT
250 GRAMS/8.8 OUNCES

Flour, water, salt, yeast. Period. There is something magical about perfecting what's simple. This is the style of pizza dough that started it all and made the whole world fall in love with pizza. It's the dough we use most often at Pizzeria Vetri. A couple days of fermentation give it great flavor, but it only takes 20 minutes of hands-on time. Then on Day 3, you can make pizzas. It is 60% hydration dough, and we bake it in our wood ovens with an ambient temperature of around 700°F (371°C).

STARTER

354 grams (2⅔ cups)
King Arthur bread flour

354 grams (1½ cups) water
at 45°F (7°C)

0.8 grams (¼ teaspoon) fresh
yeast or 0.3 grams (scant
⅛ teaspoon) active dry yeast

DOUGH

241 grams (1 cup) water
at 55°F (13°C)

1.3 grams (½ teaspoon) fresh
yeast or 0.6 grams (generous
⅛ teaspoon) active dry yeast

638 grams (4⅔ cups)
King Arthur bread flour

20 grams (3½ teaspoons)
fine sea salt

DAY 1: For the starter, mix everything together in the bowl of an electric mixer, crumbling in the yeast if it's fresh or sprinkling the dry yeast over the water. Mix just long enough to make sure all the flour is wet. The starter will be wet and sticky. Cover tightly with plastic wrap and let rest at room temperature (about 70°F/21°C) for 24 hours.

DAY 2: By this time, the starter should be bubbly and smell like sex. For the dough, pour the water into a small bowl, crumble in the yeast, and whisk them together until no lumps remain; or, if using dry yeast, you can just sprinkle the yeast over the starter.

TO MIX AND KNEAD: Add the water (or water/yeast mixture) to the starter and then add the flour and then the salt. Attach the dough hook and mix on low speed until the dough comes together, about 1 minute. This dough will be fairly stiff during mixing and kneading in the mixer. If your mixer is less than 600 watts, remove half of the dough and mix it in 2 batches to avoid burning out your mixer motor. Recombine the dough at the end of mixing both batches. Either way, mix and knead each batch of dough in the mixer on low speed for 7 minutes. Then switch to medium-low speed and mix for another 4 minutes. The dough should look smoother and feel somewhat resilient when poked.

TO FERMENT: Cover tightly and let the dough ferment in the refrigerator until it proofs and almost doubles in size, at least 2 hours or up to 24 hours for more flavor. You could also let the dough ferment at room temperature for 5 to 6 hours if you're pressed for time.

TO BALL UP AND FERMENT AGAIN: When finished fermenting, divide the dough into 6 equal pieces, about 250 grams (8.8 oz) each. Make a tight ball out of each piece using your dry hands and a dry work surface: pick up a piece of dough and make the smooth side the top, tucking the rough bottom side into itself to swell up the top. It's like stuffing a sock into itself (see the photos on page 63). When all the loose dough is tucked into the ball, firmly squeeze the ball near the bottom to get out any big air pockets. The top should swell up like a balloon and be smooth like a baby's bottom. Gently roll the bottom under your palm on a dry work surface, using a circular motion to close the bottom and smooth it out. Ideally, the dough ball will be tight and smooth all over.

Place the dough balls evenly in a proofing box or on a wide tray, making sure they are separated and not touching. I don't dust them with flour. They get plenty of flour when

CONTINUED

you shape them. Cover tightly and refrigerate for 24 hours. Or leave at room temperature for up to 12 hours.

DAY 3: After the dough balls have rested, use them immediately or chill them for up to 36 hours after that (until the evening of Day 4). Let the dough rest at room temperature for 1 hour before using to take the chill off. That will make the dough easier to shape. Complete shaping and baking directions appear in each pizza recipe.

OPTIONS

If you can't find King Arthur bread flour, look for another bread flour that has about 12.7% protein.

To freeze the dough balls, dust them lightly with flour, place each one in a quart-size zipper-lock bag, suck out the air, seal, and freeze for up to 1 month. Thaw the dough in the refrigerator, and then let it warm up at room temperature for 1 to 3 hours before using.

WHOLE GRAIN NAPLES DOUGH AT 60% HYDRATION: Replace some of the bread flour with any whole grain flour, preferably fresh milled. It can be whole grain wheat, spelt, einkorn, emmer, sprouted flour, or any other flour you like. When I mill it myself, I like to sift the flour through a fine-mesh sieve (a typical metal sieve for home use) to remove some of the larger bran flakes. You can use the sifted-out bran for another purpose—it makes a great yogurt topping! Sifting will create "high-extraction" flour because you will retain about 80% of the whole grain in the sifted flour. The more fresh-milled high-extraction flour you use, the more germ, bran, and earthy flavor you'll get in the crust. The raw dough will also feel a little softer and looser. It may help to mix and knead a little longer to strengthen the gluten network and firm up the dough. Handle it carefully when shaping it. For dough with 10% whole grain flour, use 35 grams whole grain flour plus 319 grams bread flour in the

starter; then use 64 grams whole grain flour plus 574 grams bread flour in the dough. For dough with 20% whole grain flour, use 71 grams whole grain flour plus 283 grams bread flour in the starter; then use 127 grams whole grain flour plus 511 grams bread flour in the dough. If you experiment with higher percentages of fresh-milled whole grain flour, you'll need to add slightly more water because whole grain flour absorbs more water. The extra fiber can give the dough a heavier texture as well, so you may want to use a little more yeast for extra lift. Either way, dough made with fresh-milled whole grain flour is so much more flavorful. It's also more perishable, so use the mature dough balls within a day or two.

BLACK NAPLES DOUGH AT 60% HYDRATION: Want to turn some heads with really dark dough? Use grano arso (burnt grain) bread flour. Or, when you mix up the dough, add 10 to 15 grams vegetable carbon powder, which you can get online. It will give the pizza dough a grayish black color. You can also make vegetable ash yourself. Here's a method using eggplant from my friend Shola Olunloyo, who runs the pop-up dinners at Philadelphia's Studio Kitchen, a culinary event space. Heat a grill, preferably charcoal, or a broiler for high heat. Grill a whole eggplant (about 1 pound) directly over the heat, or 4 to 6 inches (10 to 15 cm) under the broiler on a baking sheet, until the skin is blackened and charred all over, about 30 minutes total, rotating for even charring. When it's completely burnt all over, put the eggplant in a small bowl, cover tightly with plastic wrap, and let it steam until cooled, 15 to 20 minutes. Cut the cooled eggplant in half lengthwise and scoop out the softened flesh (use the flesh in caponata or toss it with cooked pasta). Transfer the eggplant skin to a dehydrator set to 115°F (46°C) or an oven set to 175°F (79°C) with convection and let it dry completely, 10 to 15 hours. Then just crush the dried eggplant skin into small pieces and grind them to a powder in a spice grinder. Store the powder in an airtight container for up to 1 month.

NAPLES DOUGH AT 70% HYDRATION

MAKES 6 DOUGH BALLS, EACH ABOUT 270 GRAMS/9.5 OUNCES

This dough is essentially the same as the previous one but with more water. It's meant to be baked at 500° to 600°F (260° to 316°C) as you would in a home oven. We found that a little more water in the dough helps create a classic Neapolitan crust that's soft, foldable, and delicately crisp on the bottom when you're baking at this lower temperature. The extra water makes the dough a bit looser, so this recipe has slightly different directions for shaping it into a ball.

STARTER

354 grams (2⅔ cups) King Arthur bread flour

354 grams (1½ cups) water at 45°F (7°C)

0.8 grams (¼ teaspoon) fresh yeast or 0.3 grams (scant ⅛ teaspoon) active dry yeast

DOUGH

340 grams (1½ cups) water at 55°F (13°C)

1.3 grams (½ teaspoon) fresh yeast or 0.6 grams (generous ⅛ teaspoon) active dry yeast

638 grams (4⅔ cups) King Arthur bread flour

20 grams (3½ teaspoons) fine sea salt

DAY 1: For the starter, mix everything together in the bowl of an electric mixer, crumbling in the yeast if it's fresh or sprinkling the dry yeast over the water. Mix just long enough to make sure all the flour is wet. The starter will be wet and sticky. Cover tightly with plastic wrap and let the starter rest at room temperature (about 70°F/21°C) for 24 hours.

DAY 2: By this time, the starter should be bubbly and smell like sex. For the dough, pour the water into a small bowl, crumble in the yeast, and whisk them together until no lumps remain; or, if using dry yeast, you can just sprinkle the yeast over the starter.

TO MIX AND KNEAD: Add the water (or water/yeast mixture) to the starter and then the flour, and then the salt. Attach the dough hook and mix on low speed for 8 minutes. Switch to medium-low speed and mix for another 4 minutes. The dough should be somewhat loose, since it has a fair amount of water in it. But if your mixer is less than 600 watts and the mixer is straining, remove half of the dough and mix the dough in 2 batches to avoid burning out your mixer motor. Recombine the dough at the end of mixing both batches.

TO FERMENT: Cover tightly and let the dough ferment in the refrigerator until it proofs and almost doubles in size, at least 2 hours or up to 24 hours for more flavor. You could also let the dough ferment at room temperature for 5 to 6 hours if you're pressed for time.

TO BALL UP AND FERMENT AGAIN: Lightly flour your hands and a bench knife (the bigger the better). Resist the temptation to dust the dough or your work surface with more flour; that will just make the dough stiffer. You want to keep the dough soft. Use your hand to scrape and dump the mass of dough onto a dry work surface. Use the bench knife to cut and divide the dough into 6 pieces, each about 270 grams (9.5 oz). Just cut and scrape away a 270-gram piece from the dough, transferring the piece to a scale to weigh it (at least weigh the first piece so you can eyeball the rest). The dough will be loose, wet, and sticky—especially if you use some fresh-milled whole grain flour. Handle it with authority. Scoop it up with the bench knife and scrape it off with your fingers. Transfer the 270-gram piece to a 2-foot-square area on the dry work surface. Then scrape and shape the dough into a ball. To do that, position the bench knife at one edge of the dough and then push the dough in the opposite direction, scraping and pushing the dough at least a foot or two away from you. It will swell up and form an oval shape. Remove the bench knife (using your fingers if necessary), reposition the knife on the pointy end of the dough, and proceed to push the dough in a direction perpendicular to the first, tilting the knife down a bit and scraping the dough with some pressure, swelling up the dough again. Repeat this process of pushing, repositioning, and scraping the dough in opposite directions all around the 2-foot square until the dough goes from a loose oval shape to a more organized round one. It's almost like shaping a water balloon, so it's a somewhat delicate operation. You want to gently squeeze all around the balloon to swell it up into a round ball, always increasing the surface tension. When the dough becomes a somewhat organized round ball, use the bench knife to quickly transfer the dough ball to a proofing box or a wide tray with a tight-fitting lid. It will flatten out quite a bit, so leave room for the other dough balls. Repeat the process with each lump of dough, transferring the dough balls to the container and leaving several inches between each—you don't want the balls reconnecting themselves. I don't dust them with flour. They get plenty of flour when you shape them. Cover tightly and refrigerate for 24 hours. Or leave at room temperature for up to 12 hours.

DAY 3: After the dough balls have rested, use them immediately or chill them for up to 36 hours after that (until the evening of Day 4). Let the dough rest at room temperature for 1 hour before using to take the chill off. That will make the dough easier to shape. Complete shaping and baking directions appear in each pizza recipe.

OPTIONS

If you can't find King Arthur bread flour, look for another bread flour that has about 12.7% protein.

To freeze the dough balls, dust them lightly with flour, place each one in a quart-size zipper-lock bag, suck out the air, seal, and freeze for up to 1 month. Thaw the dough in the refrigerator and then let it warm up at room temperature for 1 to 3 hours before using.

WHOLE-GRAIN NAPLES DOUGH AT 70% HYDRATION: Replace some of the bread flour with any whole grain flour, preferably fresh milled. It can be whole grain wheat, spelt, einkorn, emmer, sprouted flour, or any other flour you like. When I mill it myself, I like to sift the flour through a fine-mesh sieve (a typical metal sieve for home use) to remove some of the larger bran flakes. You can use the sifted-out bran for another purpose—it makes a great yogurt topping! Sifting will create "high-extraction" flour because you will retain about 80% of the whole grain in the sifted flour. The more fresh-milled high-extraction flour you use, the more germ, bran, and earthy flavor you'll get in the crust. The raw dough will also feel a little softer and looser. It may help to mix and knead a little longer to strengthen the gluten network and firm up the dough. Handle it carefully when shaping it. For dough with 10% whole grain flour, use 35 grams whole grain flour plus 319 grams bread flour in the starter; then use 64 grams whole grain flour plus 574 grams bread flour in the dough. For dough with 20% whole grain flour, use 71 grams whole grain flour plus 283 grams bread flour in the starter; then use 127 grams whole grain flour plus 511 grams bread flour in the dough. If you experiment with higher percentages of fresh-milled whole grain flour, you'll need to add slightly more water because whole grain flour absorbs more water. The extra fiber can give the dough a heavier texture as well, so you may want to use a little more yeast for extra lift. Either way, dough made with fresh-milled whole grain flour is so much more flavorful. It's also more perishable, so use the mature dough balls within a day or two.

OLD SCHOOL NAPLES DOUGH AT 60% HYDRATION

MAKES 3 DOUGH BALLS, EACH ABOUT 270 GRAMS/9.5 OUNCES

Before there was electricity and refrigeration, there were bare hands and old-fashioned chutzpah! This dough is mixed by hand and fermented at room temperature. Start this dough first thing in the morning and you can have pizza tonight. Or stick the dough balls in the fridge if you want pizza the next day. This dough is fairly low in hydration, about 60%, because it's typically cooked in blazing hot ovens at about 900°F (482°C) for only 90 seconds. If your oven is that hot, you'll love this dough.

13 grams (2⅛ teaspoons) fine sea salt

300 grams (1¼ cups) water at 55°F (13°C)

0.3 grams (1/16 teaspoon) fresh yeast or 0.1 grams (1/32 teaspoon) active dry yeast

500 grams (3⅔ cups) King Arthur bread flour

Remove any rings from your fingers. You'll be getting sticky!

TO MIX AND KNEAD: Dissolve the salt in the water in a large (about 6 quart) wooden mixing box or heavy ceramic bowl, swishing it around with your hands. You'll be kneading and folding in the box or bowl, and something heavy will stay put. After the salt dissolves, swish in the yeast, stirring it around until it disperses. Gradually mix in the flour by hand until the little beads of water-coated flour begin to feel soft and dispersed throughout the mixture. Continue adding flour and mixing until there is no more loose flour in the box or bowl. As you continue to mix, knead the dough like a cat would, pressing your hands and fingers into it. It will be wet and sticky at first. Scrape the dough from your fingers with the opposite hand now and then. Observe the beauty of the dough as it comes together in a ragged mass. Yeast is a living thing, and you are giving it food (the flour) and helping it grow.

As the dough begins to firm up and take shape, periodically fold it over itself. Handle it gently. It is alive yet young, like a creature being born in your own hands. You will feel it start to spring back a bit as you knead it. With every knead and fold, you will create a stronger gluten network, and the dough will become stretchier. The dough will also begin to feel less wet because the flour will continue to absorb the water. Knead and fold the dough for a total of 10 to

15 minutes. At that point, the dough will hold together in a lump and start to feel somewhat plump and resilient when poked. Scrape as much dough from your hands as possible, rubbing your palms together and patting the loose bits into the mass of dough in the box or bowl.

TO FERMENT: Cover the box or bowl tightly with wood (a large cutting board works well) or a clean kitchen towel and let the dough ferment at room temperature (about 70°F/21°C) for 6 hours.

TO BALL UP AND FERMENT AGAIN: After 6 hours, divide the dough into 3 pieces, each about 270 grams (9.5 oz). At this point, the dough will feel even more plump and resilient. Make a tight ball out of each piece using your dry hands and a dry work surface: pick up a piece of dough and make the smooth side of the dough the top, tucking the rough bottom side into itself to swell up the top. It's like stuffing a sock into itself (see the photos on page 63). When all the loose dough is tucked into the ball, firmly squeeze the ball near the bottom to get out any big air pockets. The top should swell up like a balloon and be smooth like a baby's bottom. Gently roll the bottom under your palm on a dry work surface, using a circular motion to close the bottom and smooth it out. Ideally, the dough ball will be tight and smooth all over.

CONTINUED

Place the dough balls evenly on wooden or plastic trays, making sure they are separated and not touching. I don't dust them with flour. They get plenty of flour when you shape them. Cover and let rest at room temperature for 3 hours. At that point, the pizza dough will be plump, mature, and ready to shape. Complete shaping and baking directions appear in each pizza recipe.

OPTIONS

Instead of mixing by hand, you can mix and knead the dough in a stand mixer on low speed for 15 minutes.

To freeze the dough balls, dust them lightly with flour, place each one in a quart-size zipper-lock bag, suck out the air, seal, and freeze for up to 1 month. Thaw the dough in the refrigerator, and then let it warm up at room temperature for 1 to 3 hours before using.

You can easily double this recipe. If you are mixing in a stand mixer with less than 600 watts and the mixer is straining, avoid burning out your motor: remove half of the dough and mix it in two batches, recombining the two portions of mixed dough at the end of mixing both batches.

To hold the dough longer and get a little more flavor, you can ferment it in the refrigerator instead of at room temperature. For instance, you can ferment the bulk dough in the fridge for up to 24 hours (instead of 6 hours at room temp), and then hold the dough balls in the fridge for 8 hours (instead of 3 hours at room temp). Adjust the time and temperature to suit your schedule.

WHOLE GRAIN OLD SCHOOL NAPLES DOUGH AT 60% HYDRATION: Replace some of the bread flour with any whole grain flour, preferably fresh milled. It can be whole grain wheat, spelt, einkorn, emmer, sprouted flour, or any other flour you like. When I mill it myself, I like to sift the flour through a fine-mesh sieve (a typical metal sieve for home use) to remove some of the larger bran flakes. You can use the sifted-out bran for another purpose—it makes a great yogurt topping! Sifting will create "high-extraction" flour because you will retain about 80% of the whole grain in the sifted flour. The more fresh-milled high-extraction flour you use, the more germ, bran, and earthy flavor you'll get in the crust. The raw dough will also feel a little softer and looser. It may help to mix and knead a little longer to strengthen the gluten network and firm up the dough. Handle it carefully when shaping it. It will stretch very easily. For dough with 10% whole grain flour, use 50 grams whole grain flour plus 450 grams bread flour. For dough with 20% whole grain flour, use 100 grams whole grain flour plus 400 grams bread flour. If you experiment with higher percentages of fresh-milled whole grain flour, you'll need to add slightly more water because whole grain flour absorbs more water. The extra fiber can give the dough a heavier texture as well, so you may want to use a little more yeast for extra lift. Either way, dough made with fresh-milled whole grain flour is so much more flavorful. It's also more perishable, so use the mature dough balls within a day or two.

SOURDOUGH OLD SCHOOL NAPLES DOUGH AT 60% HYDRATION: For the complex flavor of wild yeast, replace the yeast with 200 grams active Sourdough Starter (page 84). To account for the flour and water already in the starter, reduce the flour and water in the dough by 100 grams each. In other words, use 200 grams water and 400 grams flour. Ferment the bulk dough in the refrigerator for 24 hours, ball up the dough, and then chill the dough balls for 8 to 12 hours. If you're pressed for time, you can let the dough balls ferment at room temperature for 4 to 6 hours.

BLACK OLD SCHOOL NAPLES DOUGH AT 60% HYDRATION: When you mix up the dough, use grano arso (burnt flour) or add 5 to 10 grams vegetable carbon powder, which you can get online. Or make vegetable ash yourself (see "Options" on page 62). It will give the pizza dough a grayish black color.

OLD SCHOOL NAPLES DOUGH AT 70% HYDRATION

MAKES 3 DOUGH BALLS, EACH ABOUT 270 GRAMS/9.5 OUNCES

This dough is similar to the previous one but with a little more water. At 70% hydration, I like baking this one at 500° to 600°F (260° to 316°C). The dough ferments in a single day at room temperature, so if you want pizza from your home oven tonight, try it!

13 grams (2⅛ teaspoons) fine sea salt

350 grams (1½ cups) water at 55°F (13°C)

0.3 grams (1/16 teaspoon) fresh yeast or 0.1 grams (1/32 teaspoon) active dry yeast

500 grams (3⅔ cups) King Arthur bread flour

Remove any rings from your fingers. You'll be getting sticky!

TO MIX AND KNEAD: Dissolve the salt in the water in a large (about 6 quart) wooden mixing box or heavy ceramic bowl, swishing it around with your hands. You'll be kneading and folding in the box or bowl, and something heavy will stay put. After the salt dissolves, swish in the yeast, stirring it around until it disperses. Gradually mix in the flour by hand, until the little beads of water-coated flour begin to feel soft and dispersed throughout the mixture. Continue adding flour and mixing until there is no more loose flour in the box or bowl. As you continue to mix, knead the dough like a cat would, pressing your hands and fingers into it. It will be wet and sticky at first. Scrape the dough from your fingers with the opposite hand now and then. Observe the beauty of the dough as it comes together in a ragged mass. Yeast is a living thing, and you are giving it food (the flour) and helping it grow.

As the dough begins to firm up and take shape, periodically fold it over itself. Handle it gently. It is alive yet young, like a creature being born in your own hands. You will feel it start to spring back a bit as you knead it. With every knead and fold, you will create a stronger gluten network, and the dough will become stretchier. The dough will also begin to feel less wet because the flour will continue to absorb the water. Knead and fold the dough for a total of 10 to 15 minutes. At that point, the dough will hold together in a lump and start to feel somewhat plump and resilient when poked. Scrape as much dough from your hands as possible, rubbing

your palms together and patting the loose bits into the mass of dough in the box or bowl.

TO FERMENT: Cover the box or bowl tightly with wood (a large cutting board works well) or a clean kitchen towel and let the dough ferment at room temperature (about 70°F/21°C) for 6 hours.

TO BALL UP AND FERMENT AGAIN: Lightly flour your hands and a bench knife (the bigger the better). Resist the temptation to dust the dough or your work surface with more flour; that will just make the dough stiffer. You want to keep the dough soft. Use your hand to scrape and dump the mass of dough onto a dry work surface. Use the bench knife to cut and divide the dough into 6 pieces, each about 270 grams (9.5 oz). Just cut and scrape away a 270-gram piece from the dough, transferring the piece to a scale to weigh it (at least weigh the first piece so you can eyeball the rest). The dough will be loose, wet, and sticky—especially if you use some fresh-milled whole-grain flour. Handle it with authority. Scoop it up with the bench knife and scrape it off with your fingers. Transfer the 270-gram piece to a 2-foot-square area on the dry work surface. Then scrape and shape the dough into a ball. To do that, position the bench knife at one edge of the dough and then push the dough in the opposite direction, scraping and pushing the dough at least a foot or two away from you. It will swell up and form an oval shape. Remove the

CONTINUED

bench knife (using your fingers if necessary), reposition the knife on the pointy end of the dough, and proceed to push the dough in a direction perpendicular to the first, tilting the knife down a bit and scraping the dough with some pressure, swelling up the dough again. Repeat this process of pushing, repositioning, and scraping the dough in opposite directions all around the 2-foot square until the dough goes from a loose oval shape to a more organized round one. It's almost like shaping a water balloon, so it's a somewhat delicate operation. You want to gently squeeze all around the balloon to swell it up into a round ball, always increasing the surface tension. When the dough becomes a somewhat organized round ball, use the bench knife to quickly transfer the dough ball to a proofing box or a wide tray with a tight-fitting lid. It will flatten out quite a bit, so leave room for the other dough balls. Repeat the process with each lump of dough, transferring the dough balls to the container and leaving several inches between each—you don't want the balls reconnecting themselves. I don't dust them with flour. They get plenty of flour when you shape them. Cover tightly and let rest at room temperature for 3 hours. At that point, the pizza dough will be mature and ready to shape. Complete shaping and baking directions appear in each pizza recipe.

OPTIONS

Instead of mixing by hand, you can mix and knead the dough in a stand mixer on low speed for 15 minutes.

To freeze the dough balls, dust them lightly with flour, place each one in a quart-size zipper-lock bag, suck out the air, seal, and freeze for up to 1 month. Thaw the dough in the refrigerator and then let it warm up at room temperature for 1 to 3 hours before using.

To hold the dough longer and get a little more flavor, you can ferment it in the refrigerator instead of at room temperature. For instance, you can ferment the bulk dough in the fridge for up to 24 hours (instead of 6 hours at room temp), and then hold the dough balls in the fridge for 8 hours (instead of 3 hours at room temp). Adjust the time and temperature to suit your schedule.

WHOLE GRAIN OLD SCHOOL NAPLES DOUGH AT 70% HYDRATION: Replace some of the bread flour with any whole grain flour, preferably fresh milled. It can be whole grain wheat, spelt, einkorn, emmer, sprouted flour, or any other flour you like. When I mill it myself, I like to sift the flour through a fine-mesh sieve (a typical metal sieve for home use) to remove some of the larger bran flakes. You can use the sifted-out bran for another purpose—it makes a great yogurt topping! Sifting will create "high-extraction" flour because you will retain about 80% of the whole grain in the sifted flour. The more fresh-milled high-extraction flour you use, the more germ, bran, and earthy flavor you'll get in the crust. The raw dough will also feel a little softer and looser. It may help to mix and knead a little longer to strengthen the gluten network and firm up the dough. Handle it carefully when shaping it. It will stretch very easily. For dough with 10% whole grain flour, use 50 grams whole grain flour plus 450 grams bread flour. For dough with 20% whole grain flour, use 100 grams whole grain flour plus 400 grams bread flour. If you experiment with higher percentages of fresh-milled whole grain flour, you'll need to add slightly more water because whole grain flour absorbs more water. The extra fiber can give the dough a heavier texture as well, so you may want to use a little more yeast for extra lift. Either way, dough made with fresh-milled whole grain flour is so much more flavorful. It's also more perishable, so use the mature dough balls within a day or two.

SOURDOUGH OLD SCHOOL NAPLES DOUGH AT 70% HYDRATION: For the complex flavor of wild yeast, replace the yeast with 200 grams active Sourdough Starter (page 84). To account for the flour and water already in the starter, reduce the flour and water in the dough by 100 grams each. In other words, use 250 grams water and 400 grams flour. Ferment the bulk dough in the refrigerator for 24 hours, ball up the dough, and then chill the dough balls for 8 to 12 hours. If you're pressed for time, you can let the dough balls ferment at room temperature for 4 to 6 hours.

SINGLE NAPLES DOUGH BALL
AT 60% HYDRATION

MAKES 1 DOUGH BALL,
ABOUT 270 GRAMS/
9.5 OUNCES

Need just 1 dough ball? This down-and-dirty dough is mixed in a mixer and ferments at room temperature so you can have pizza tonight. The fermentation time is short, so you don't get complex flavor, but it works great if you're in a hurry. It's at 60% hydration here, which I like best for baking at 700°F (371°C) or higher.

100 grams (⅓ cup plus 1½ tablespoons) water at 55°F (13°C)

0.1 grams (¹⁄₆₄ teaspoon) fresh yeast or 0.03 grams (¹⁄₁₂₈ teaspoon) active dry yeast

166 grams (1¼ cups) King Arthur bread flour

4 grams (⅔ teaspoon) fine sea salt

TO MIX AND KNEAD: Pour the water into the bowl of a stand mixer. Crumble in the yeast if it's fresh or sprinkle the dry yeast over the water and mix with the flat beater on speed 2, about 30 seconds. With this small volume, it's easiest to mix with the flat beater at first. Add all the flour and mix on low speed until everything is combined, and the dough comes together, 2 to 3 minutes. Add the salt and mix until it disperses, another 30 seconds. Switch to the dough hook and continue mixing on low speed for 12 to 15 minutes. The dough should look smoother and feel somewhat resilient when poked.

TO FERMENT: Cover the bowl and let the dough rest at room temperature (about 70°F/21°C) for 2 hours.

TO BALL UP AND FERMENT AGAIN: At this point, the dough should feel somewhat plump and resilient. Make a tight ball out of the dough using your dry hands and a dry work surface: pick up the dough and make the smooth side the top, tucking the rough bottom side into itself to swell up the top. It's like stuffing a sock into itself (see the photos on page 63). When all the loose dough is tucked into the ball, firmly squeeze the ball near the bottom to get out any big air pockets. The top should swell up like a balloon and be smooth like a baby's bottom. Gently roll the bottom under your palm on a dry work surface, using a circular motion to close the bottom and smooth it out. Ideally, the dough ball will be tight and smooth all over.

Place the dough back in the bowl or in a proofing box or on a tray, cover and let rest at room temperature for 6 to 12 hours. Use the dough within that time window or see the options below. Complete shaping and baking directions appear in each pizza recipe.

OPTIONS

You can easily double or triple this recipe to make dough for 2 or 3 pizzas.

To hold the dough longer and get more flavor, you can ferment it in the refrigerator instead of at room temperature. For instance, you can ferment the bulk dough in the fridge for up to 24 hours (instead of 2 hours at room temp) and then hold the dough ball in the fridge for 8 hours (instead of 6 hours at room temp). Or if you've fermented it all day at room temperature but then decided you want pizza the next night instead, stick the dough ball in the fridge for 24 hours. Adjust the time and temperature to suit your schedule.

WHOLE GRAIN SINGLE NAPLES DOUGH BALL AT 60% HYDRATION: Replace some of the bread flour with any whole grain flour, preferably fresh milled. It can be whole grain wheat, spelt, einkorn, emmer, sprouted flour, or any other flour you like. When I mill it myself, I like to sift the flour through a fine-mesh sieve (a typical metal sieve for home use) to remove some of the larger bran flakes. You can use the sifted-out bran for another purpose—it makes a great yogurt topping! Sifting will create "high-extraction" flour because you will retain about 80% of the whole grain in the sifted flour. The more fresh-milled high-extraction flour you use, the more germ, bran, and earthy flavor you'll get in the crust. The raw dough will also feel a little softer and looser. It may help to mix and knead a little longer to strengthen the gluten network and firm up the dough. Handle it carefully when shaping it. For dough with 10% whole grain flour, use 16 grams whole grain flour plus 150 grams bread flour. For dough with 20% whole grain flour, use 33 grams whole grain flour plus 133 grams bread flour. If you experiment with higher percentages of fresh-milled whole grain flour, you'll need to add slightly more water because whole grain flour absorbs more water. The extra fiber can give the dough a heavier texture as well, so you may want to use a little more yeast for extra lift. Either way, dough made with fresh-milled whole grain flour is so much more flavorful. It's also more perishable, so use the dough within a day or two.

SOURDOUGH SINGLE NAPLES DOUGH BALL AT 60% HYDRATION: For the complex flavor of wild yeast, replace the yeast with 70 grams active Sourdough Starter (page 84). To account for the flour and water already in the starter, reduce the flour and water in the dough by about 35 grams each. In other words, use 65 grams water and 131 grams flour. Ferment the dough at room temperature for 6 to 12 hours.

SINGLE NAPLES DOUGH BALL
AT 70% HYDRATION

**MAKES 1 DOUGH BALL,
ABOUT 286 GRAMS/
10.1 OUNCES**

If you're baking at 500° to 600°F (260° to 316°C) and want a single Neapolitan pizza tonight, try this dough recipe. A stand mixer does all the work. After mixing, you let it sit on the counter for a couple hours, ball it up, and let it sit again until you're ready to make pizza. Simple! You can also double or triple the recipe to make dough for 2 or 3 pizzas.

116 grams (scant ½ cup)
water at 55°F (13°F)

0.1 grams (¹⁄₆₄ teaspoon)
fresh yeast or 0.03 g
(¹⁄₁₂₈ teaspoon) active
dry yeast

166 grams (1¼ cups)
King Arthur bread flour

4 grams (⅔ teaspoon)
fine sea salt

TO MIX AND KNEAD: Pour the water into the bowl of a stand mixer. Crumble in the yeast if it's fresh or sprinkle the dry yeast over the water and mix with the flat beater on speed 2, about 30 seconds. With this small volume, it's easiest to mix with the flat beater at first. Add all the flour and mix on low speed until everything is combined, and the dough comes together, 2 to 3 minutes. Add the salt and mix until it disperses, another 30 seconds. Switch to the dough hook and continue mixing on low speed for 12 to 15 minutes. The dough should look smoother and feel somewhat resilient when poked.

TO FERMENT: Cover the bowl, and let the dough rest at room temperature (about 70°F/21°C) for 2 hours.

TO BALL UP AND FERMENT AGAIN: Lightly flour your hands and a bench knife (the bigger the better). Resist the temptation to dust the dough or your work surface with more flour; that will just make the dough stiffer. You want to keep the dough soft. Use your hand to scrape and dump the dough onto a dry work surface. Use the bench knife to shape the dough into a ball. To do that, position the knife at one edge of the dough and then push the dough in the opposite direction, scraping and pushing the dough at

least a foot or two away from you. It will swell up and form an oval shape. Remove the bench knife (using your fingers if necessary), reposition the scraper on the pointy end of the dough, and proceed to push the dough in a direction perpendicular to the first, tilting the knife down a bit and scraping the dough with some pressure, swelling up the dough again. Repeat this process of pushing, repositioning, and scraping the dough in opposite directions all around the 2-foot square, until the dough goes from a loose oval shape to a more organized round one. It's almost like shaping a water balloon, so it's a somewhat delicate operation. You want to gently squeeze all around the balloon to swell it up into a round ball, always increasing the surface tension. When the dough becomes a somewhat organized round ball, use the bench knife to quickly transfer the dough ball to a proofing box or a wide tray with a tight-fitting lid. It will flatten out quite a bit, which is okay. I don't dust the dough with flour. It will get plenty of flour when you shape it later. Cover tightly and let the dough rest at room temperature for 6 to 12 hours. Use the dough within that time window or see the options below. Complete shaping and baking directions appear in each pizza recipe.

OPTIONS

To hold the dough longer and get more flavor, you can ferment it in the refrigerator instead of at room temperature. For instance, you can ferment the bulk dough in the fridge for up to 24 hours (instead of 2 hours at room temp), and then hold the dough ball in the fridge for 8 hours (instead of 6 hours at room temp). Or if you've fermented it all day at room temperature but then decided you want pizza the next night instead, stick the dough ball in the fridge for 24 hours. Adjust the time and temperature to suit your schedule.

WHOLE GRAIN SINGLE NAPLES DOUGH BALL AT 70% HYDRATION: Replace some of the bread flour with any whole grain flour, preferably fresh milled. It can be whole grain wheat, spelt, einkorn, emmer, sprouted flour, or any other flour you like. When I mill it myself, I like to sift the flour through a fine-mesh sieve (a typical metal sieve for home use) to remove some of the larger bran flakes. You can use the sifted-out bran for another purpose—it makes a great yogurt topping! Sifting will create "high-extraction" flour because you will retain about 80% of the whole grain in the sifted flour. The more fresh-milled high-extraction flour you use, the more germ, bran, and earthy flavor you'll get in the crust. The raw dough will also feel a little softer and looser. It may help to mix and knead a little longer to strengthen the gluten network and firm up the dough. Handle it carefully when shaping it. For dough with 10% whole grain flour, use 16 grams whole grain flour plus 150 grams bread flour. For dough with 20% whole grain flour, use 33 grams whole grain flour plus 133 grams bread flour. If you experiment with higher percentages of fresh-milled whole grain flour, you'll need to add slightly more water because whole grain flour absorbs more water. The extra fiber can give the dough a heavier texture as well, so you may want to use a little more yeast for extra lift. Either way, dough made with fresh-milled whole grain flour is so much more flavorful. It's also more perishable, so use the dough within a day.

SOURDOUGH SINGLE NAPLES DOUGH BALL AT 70% HYDRATION: For the complex flavor of wild yeast, replace the dry yeast with 70 grams active Sourdough Starter (page 84). To account for the flour and water already in the starter, reduce the flour and water in the dough by about 35 grams each. In other words, use 81 grams water and 131 grams flour. Ferment the dough at room temperature for 6 to 12 hours.

ROMAN DOUGH AT 57% HYDRATION

**MAKES 5 DOUGH BALLS,
EACH ABOUT
230 GRAMS/8.1 OUNCES**

Rome is a bustling, convivial city where everyone walks around snacking. Pizza Romana is thinner and crisper than Naples pizza, and a lot of people walk around with it. A little oil in the dough lets you stretch it really thin. This is the first pizza dough I learned how to make and the one I go back to again and again. It's an overnight dough, so it comes together a little faster than my Naples dough. And it's so soft that you can easily shape it by hand into rounds or press it into ovals for a Personal Pizza al Metro (page 142). At this hydration, it's best baked at 700°F (371°C) or higher.

680 grams (5 cups)
King Arthur bread flour

30 grams (2 tablespoons plus
1¼ teaspoons) sugar

385 grams (1½ cups plus
2 tablespoons) water at
55°F (13°C)

54 grams (¼ cup)
extra-virgin olive oil

7.5 grams (2½ teaspoons)
fresh yeast or 3 grams
(1 teaspoon) active dry yeast

15 grams (2½ teaspoons)
fine sea salt

TO MIX AND KNEAD: Put the flour, sugar, water, and oil in the bowl of a stand mixer. Crumble or sprinkle in the fresh or dry yeast. Attach the dough hook and mix on low speed until everything is moist, about 4 minutes, scraping the bowl as needed with a rubber spatula. Switch to medium-low speed and mix until the dough clings to the dough hook, about 4 minutes more. Add the salt and mix until the dough is soft, stretchy and somewhat resilient when poked, another 3 minutes.

TO BALL UP: Scrape the dough onto a dry work surface and cut it into 5 pieces, each about 230 grams (8.1 oz). Make a tight ball out of each piece using your dry hands and a dry work surface: pick up a piece of the dough and make the smooth side the top, tucking the rough bottom side into itself to swell up the top. It's like stuffing a sock into itself (see the photos on page 63). When all the loose dough is tucked into the ball, firmly squeeze the ball near the bottom to get out any big air pockets. The top should swell up like a balloon and be smooth like a baby's bottom. Gently roll the bottom under your palm on a dry work surface, using a circular motion to close the bottom and smooth it out. Ideally, the dough ball will be tight and smooth all over.

TO FERMENT: Place the dough balls evenly in a proofing box or on trays, making sure they are separated and not touching. I don't dust them with flour. They get plenty of flour when you shape them. Cover tightly and refrigerate for 24 hours or up to 3 days. Let the dough rest at room temperature (about 70°F/21°C) for 1 hour before using to take the chill off. That will make the dough easier to shape. Complete shaping and baking directions appear in each pizza recipe.

OPTIONS

To freeze the dough balls, dust them with a little flour, place each in a quart-size zipper-lock bag, and suck out the air, seal, and freeze for up to 1 month. Thaw the dough in the refrigerator and then let it warm up at room temperature for 1 to 3 hours before using.

WHOLE GRAIN ROMAN DOUGH AT 57% HYDRATION: Replace some of the bread flour with any whole grain flour, preferably fresh milled. It can be whole grain wheat, spelt, einkorn, emmer, sprouted flour, or any other flour you like. When I mill it myself, I like to sift the flour through a fine-mesh sieve (a typical metal sieve for home use) to remove some of the larger bran flakes. You can use the sifted-out bran for another purpose—it makes a great yogurt topping! Sifting will create "high-extraction" flour because you will

retain about 80% of the whole grain in the sifted flour. The more fresh-milled high-extraction flour you use, the more germ, bran, and earthy flavor you'll get in the crust. The raw dough will also feel a little softer and looser. It may help to mix and knead a little longer to strengthen the gluten network and firm up the dough. Handle it carefully when shaping it. For dough with 10% whole grain flour, use 68 grams whole grain flour plus 612 grams bread flour. For dough with 20% whole grain flour, use 136 grams whole grain flour plus 544 grams bread flour. If you experiment with higher percentages of fresh-milled whole grain flour, you'll need to add slightly more water because whole grain flour absorbs more water. The extra fiber can give the

dough a heavier texture as well, so you may want to use a little more yeast for extra lift. Either way, dough made with fresh-milled whole grain flour is so much more flavorful. It's also more perishable, so use the mature dough balls within a day or two.

SOURDOUGH ROMAN DOUGH AT 57% HYDRATION: For the complex flavor of wild yeast, replace the dry yeast with 200 grams active Whole Grain Sourdough Starter at 100% Hydration (page 84). To account for the flour and water already in the starter, reduce the flour and water in the dough by about 100 grams each. In other words, use 580 grams flour and 285 grams water.

ROMAN DOUGH AT 67% HYDRATION

MAKES 5 DOUGH BALLS,
EACH ABOUT
250 GRAMS/8.8 OUNCES

Here's the Roman dough with a little more water for baking Pizza Romana at 500° to 600°F (260° to 316°C). Shape it by hand into rounds, ovals, or whatever shape you like. Sometimes I split rounds of this dough in half and make a sandwich of Home Oven Stuffed Pizza (page 146) with robiola cheese inside—or fontina, prosciutto, and arugula. It's also great fried up into Parmesan Fried Dough (page 150).

680 grams (5 cups)
King Arthur bread flour

30 grams (2 tablespoons)
sugar

455 grams (scant 2 cups)
water at 55°F (13°C)

54 grams (¼ cup)
extra-virgin olive oil

7.5 grams (2½ teaspoons)
fresh yeast or 3 grams
(1 teaspoon) active dry yeast

15 grams (2½ teaspoons)
fine sea salt

TO MIX AND KNEAD: Put the flour, sugar, water, and oil in the bowl of a stand mixer. Crumble or sprinkle in the fresh or dry yeast. Attach the dough hook and mix on low speed until everything is moist, about 4 minutes scraping the bowl as needed with a rubber spatula. Switch to medium-low speed and mix until the dough clings to the dough hook, about 4 minutes more. Add the salt and mix until the dough is soft, stretchy, and somewhat resilient when poked, another 3 minutes.

TO BALL UP: Lightly flour your hands and a bench knife (the bigger the better). Resist the temptation to dust the dough or your work surface with more flour; that will just make the dough stiffer. You want to keep the dough soft. Use your hand to scrape and dump the mass of dough onto a dry work surface. Use the bench knife/scraper to cut and divide the dough into 5 pieces, each about 250 grams (8.8 oz). Just cut and scrape away a 250-gram piece from the dough, transferring the piece to a scale to weigh it (at least weigh the first piece so you can eyeball the rest). The dough will be loose, wet, and sticky—especially if you use some fresh-milled whole grain flour. Handle it with authority. Scoop it up with the bench knife and scrape it off with your fingers. Transfer the 250-gram piece to a 2-foot-square area on the dry work surface. Then scrape and shape the dough into a ball. To do that, position the bench knife at one edge of the

dough and then push the dough in the opposite direction, scraping and pushing the dough at least a foot or two away from you. It will swell up and form an oval shape. Remove the knife (using your fingers if necessary), reposition the knife on the pointy end of the dough, and proceed to push the dough in a direction perpendicular to the first, tilting the knife down a bit and scraping the dough with some pressure, swelling up the dough again. Repeat this process of pushing, repositioning, and scraping the dough in opposite directions all around the 2-foot square until the dough goes from a loose oval shape to a more organized round one. It's almost like shaping a water balloon, so it's a somewhat delicate operation. You want to gently squeeze all around the balloon to swell it up into a round ball, always increasing the surface tension. When the dough becomes a somewhat organized round ball, use the bench knife to quickly transfer the dough ball to a proofing box or a wide tray with a tight-fitting lid. It will flatten out quite a bit, so leave room for the other dough balls. Repeat the process with each lump of dough, transferring the dough balls to the container and leaving several inches between each— you don't want the balls reconnecting themselves. I don't dust them with flour. They get plenty of flour when you shape them.

TO FERMENT: Cover the container tightly and refrigerate for 24 hours or up to 3 days. Let the dough rest at room temperature (about 70°F/21°C) for 1 hour before using to take the chill off. That will make the dough easier to shape. Complete shaping and baking directions appear in each pizza recipe.

OPTIONS

To freeze the dough balls, dust them with a little flour, place each in a quart-size zipper-lock bag, and suck out the air, seal, and freeze for up to 1 month. Thaw the dough in the refrigerator and then let it warm up at room temperature for 1 to 3 hours before using.

WHOLE-GRAIN ROMAN DOUGH AT 67% HYDRATION: Replace some of the bread flour with any whole-grain flour, preferably fresh milled. It can be whole grain wheat, spelt, einkorn, emmer, sprouted flour, or any other flour you like. When I mill it myself, I like to sift the flour through a fine-mesh sieve (a typical metal sieve for home use) to remove some of the larger bran flakes. You can use the sifted out bran for another purpose—it makes a great yogurt topping! Sifting will create "high-extraction" flour because you will retain about 80% of the whole grain in the sifted flour. The more fresh-milled high-extraction flour you use, the more germ, bran, and earthy flavor you'll get in the crust. The raw dough will also feel a little softer and looser. It may help to mix and knead a little longer to strengthen the gluten network and firm up the dough. Handle it carefully when shaping it. For dough with 10% whole grain flour, use 68 grams whole grain flour plus 612 grams bread flour. For dough with 20% whole grain flour, use 136 grams whole grain flour plus 544 grams bread flour. If you experiment with higher percentages of fresh-milled whole grain flour, you'll need to add slightly more water because whole grain flour absorbs more water. The extra fiber can give the dough a heavier texture as well, so you may want to use a little more yeast for extra lift. Either way, dough made with fresh-milled whole grain flour is so much more flavorful.

SOURDOUGH ROMAN DOUGH AT 67% HYDRATION: For the complex flavor of wild yeast, replace the dry yeast with 200 grams active Sourdough Starter (page 84). To account for the flour and water already in the starter, reduce the flour and water in the dough by about 100 grams each. In other words, use 580 grams flour and 355 grams water.

AL TAGLIO DOUGH AT 80% HYDRATION

MAKES ABOUT
920 GRAMS/2 POUNDS
TOTAL, ENOUGH FOR
1 HALF-SHEET PAN
(18 BY 13 INCHES/
45 BY 33 CM) PIZZA,
PIZZA ROSSA (PAGE 169),
OR PIZZA BIANCA
(PAGE 170)

There's so much variety among Roman pizzas. Some are round, some are 6-foot-long thin sheets, and others are thicker pizzas cooked in a pan and sold "by the cut" (*al taglio*). Here's the dough we use at Pizzeria Vetri for sheet pan pizza al taglio and for pizza bianca (naked white pizza topped with only olive oil and salt). We bake it between 500° and 600°F (260° and 316°C). Pressed out and baked on a baking steel or stone, it's similar to the pizza bianca at Forno Campo de' Fiori in Rome. On a half-sheet pan, it's similar to what Gabriele Bonci serves at his incredible Pizzarium in Rome. It's super simple. Mix it up with a spoon one day, fold it by hand a few times during the day, and it's ready to make pizza the next day. It is also very wet, 80% hydration, which makes it very soft. You can almost pour the dough into the pizza pan. Handle it gently to keep all the bubbles alive.

400 grams (1⅔ cups) warm water at 90°F (32°C)

4 grams (1¼ teaspoons) active dry yeast

500 grams (3⅔ cups) King Arthur bread flour

15 grams (2½ teaspoons) fine sea salt

TO MIX AND FERMENT: Mix together 350 grams (about 1½ cups) of the water and the yeast in a large bowl. Let sit until the yeast begins to grow, about 10 minutes. Stir in the flour with a spoon until there is no more loose flour and the dough comes together in a shaggy mass. Cover the bowl with a kitchen towel or plastic wrap and let the dough rest for 30 to 40 minutes at room temperature (about 70°F/21°C).

TO FOLD AND FERMENT: After the rest period, "fold" the dough. Instead of kneading by hand or in a mixer, you'll be periodically folding the dough. Here's how: wet one hand to prevent sticking and then dig your hand deep under the dough between the dough and the bowl. Pull up a handful of the dough from the bottom (about one-fourth of the volume of the dough) and then stretch and fold that piece over the center of the dough. This stretch and fold should be pretty aggressive because the yeast hasn't yet created bubbles and lightened the dough. After the first fold, rotate the bowl a quarter turn and then repeat the aggressive stretching and folding. Continue the process until you have gone 360 degrees around the bowl and folded all of the

dough. We call this a 360-degree fold, and it will only take a minute. At that point, cover the bowl and let the dough rest for another 30 to 40 minutes.

Dissolve the salt in the remaining 50 grams (about 3 tablespoons) warm water. Pour the salt water over the dough and use the stretch-and-fold technique to mix it in gently with your wet hands. When the water is incorporated, you should have given the dough at least one more—if not two—360-degree folds. Let the dough rest for 30 to 40 minutes.

Wet your hand and fold the dough one more time. This third fold should be a bit gentler because the dough will have more bubbles in it and feel puffier and more buoyant from the yeast. You don't want to pop the bubbles. They are what puff up the dough and give it a light, airy texture. Cover the bowl and let the dough ferment in the refrigerator for at least 12 hours or up to 36 hours. Then it will be ready to shape. Let the dough rest at room temperature for 1 hour before using to take the chill off. That will make the dough easier to shape. Complete shaping and baking directions appear in each pizza recipe.

Add 30 to 40 grams (2 to 3 tablespoons) extra-virgin olive oil along with the first addition of water for more richness. The extra fat will make the dough softer and more supple.

If you want this dough ready to bake today, use more yeast. You'll sacrifice some flavor because of the shorter fermentation time, but it's your choice. For dough today, use 7 grams (2¼ teaspoons) of active dry yeast, fold the dough as described, then let it ferment in the fridge for at least 6 hours or up to 12 hours. You could also use the same amount of yeast and ferment the dough in the fridge for only 5 to 6 hours, then leave it out at room temperature to ferment for another 4 to 5 hours.

If you want to ferment the dough at room temperature (and bring out more clean and light lactic acid flavors), use only ½ gram (⅛ teaspoon) of dry yeast, fold the dough as described, and then let it ferment at room temperature for 12 hours or up to 36 hours.

WHOLE GRAIN AL TAGLIO DOUGH AT 80% HYDRATION: Replace some of the bread flour with any whole grain flour, preferably fresh milled. It can be whole grain wheat, spelt, einkorn, emmer, sprouted flour, or any other flour you like. When I mill it myself, I like to sift the flour through a fine-mesh sieve (a typical metal sieve for home use) to remove some of the larger bran flakes. You can use the sifted-out bran for another purpose—it makes a great yogurt topping! Sifting will create "high-extraction" flour because you will retain about 80% of the whole grain in the sifted flour. The more fresh-milled high-extraction flour you use, the more germ, bran, and earthy flavor you'll get in the crust. The raw dough will also feel a little softer and looser. It may help to repeat the folding process one more time to strengthen the gluten network and firm up the dough. For dough with 10% whole grain flour, use 50 grams whole grain flour plus 450 grams bread flour. For dough with 20% whole grain flour, use 100 grams whole grain flour plus 400 grams bread

flour. If you experiment with higher percentages of fresh-milled whole grain flour, you'll need to add slightly more water because whole grain flour absorbs more water. The extra fiber can give the dough a heavier texture as well, so you may want to use a little more yeast for extra lift. Either way, dough made with fresh-milled whole grain flour is so much more flavorful.

SOURDOUGH AL TAGLIO DOUGH AT 80% HYDRATION: For the complex flavor of wild yeast, replace the dry yeast with 200 grams (about 1 cup) active Bread Flour Sourdough Starter (page 85). To account for the flour and water already in the starter, reduce the flour and water in the dough by about 100 grams each. In other words, use 400 grams (about 3 cups) flour and 300 grams (about 1¼ cups) water.

PINSA DOUGH AT 80% HYDRATION: This classic Roman dough features a combination of spelt, rice, soy, and wheat flours, giving it a lighter texture. You could use active dry yeast but sourdough starter and a long fermentation time make this pizza even easier to digest. To make it, replace the dry yeast with 200 grams (about 1 cup) active Bread Flour Sourdough Starter (page 85). To account for the flour and water already in the starter, reduce the flour and water in the dough by about 100 grams each. In other words, use 400 grams (about 3 cups) flour and 300 grams (about 1¼ cups) water. For the flour itself, use a combination of 100 grams (about ¾ cup) bread flour, 200 grams (1⅔ cups) spelt flour, 75 grams (about ½ cup) rice flour, and 25 grams (about 3½ tablespoons) soy flour. Also add 30 grams (2 tablespoons) olive oil along with the first addition of water. Fold and ferment the dough as directed, but cover and refrigerate the dough for 48 hours for a long, slow fermentation. Let the dough rest at room temperature for 1 hour before using to take the chill off. To use this dough for a single Pinsa Pizza (page 143), use one-fourth of the total amount, or about 230 grams (8.1 oz).

WHOLE GRAIN SOURDOUGH STARTER AT 100% HYDRATION

MAKES ABOUT 200 GRAMS/7 OUNCES

If you have a friend with active starter, ask for some. It's easier than starting from scratch. But if you need to start one, it's not hard. It just takes time. Basically, you mix flour and water together into a paste and let it sit. That's it! Eventually, the right combination of yeast and beneficial bacteria show up, and the mixture starts to bubble and smell sour, the signs of fermentation. Signs of life! This usually takes about a week. I like to start with whole grain flour because it has the most beneficial micronutrients for yeast and bacteria. Rye flour, especially when fresh milled, has even more of these active enzymes and beneficial microorganisms to help get a starter started. After that, when feeding and refreshing the starter, I usually use wheat flour because that's what I prefer in pizza dough.

TO START:

100 grams (¾ cup) whole grain flour, preferably fresh-milled rye

100 grams (6¾ tablespoons) water at room temperature (about 70°F/21°C)

TO REFRESH:

80 grams (⅔ cup) whole grain flour, preferably fresh-milled wheat

80 grams (5⅓ tablespoons) water at room temperature

TO START: Mix together the flour and water in a 1-quart container with a lid. You need a large container because the starter will grow in volume. A clear container also helps you monitor the activity. Cover with cheesecloth to let in air and then let the mixture sit at room temperature for 24 hours. Nothing much will happen at this point.

TO REFRESH: After 24 hours, remove and discard 160 grams of the mixture (about 80% of it) and refresh it by mixing in 80 grams fresh flour and 80 grams fresh water. These refreshments provide the yeast and bacteria more to feed on so they can grow.

Every 24 hours (yes, every day), refresh the mixture by removing 160 grams of the mixture and mixing in 80 grams flour and 80 grams water. After a few days or several days, depending on the yeast and bacteria activity in your kitchen and your environment, you should notice signs of fermentation, such as small bubbles, a stronger sour aroma, and an increase in volume.

Refresh the starter until it becomes very active and bubbly and the aroma becomes more yeasty and sour. It could take 5 days, 10 days, or 14 days, depending on three main factors: the temperature of your kitchen, the biological activity of your environment, and the liveliness of your flour. If 4 days go by and the starter hasn't shown any signs of activity, throw it out and start over. If you're not sure whether it's ready, look at the starter and take a taste. When all goes right, it will have a sweet and slightly sour flavor with no aftertaste. The color will be tan from the whole grain flour. The texture will be soft, a bit wet, and not too sticky. If it's too weak, you will taste the wheat flour and not much sourness, and the consistency will be less airy. If it's too strong, it will smell pungent like rotting cheese and have a bitter taste and a gray tinge in the color. It will also be very sticky. To get it just right, adjust the ambient temperature. Making it colder will slow down the fermentation, and making it warmer will speed it up. A colder environment could be outside in cool weather, in a cooler, or in a refrigerator. A warmer environment could be outside in warm weather, on top of an oven, or on a heating radiator. Manipulate the temperature so the starter becomes active.

Before using it, refresh the starter and let it sit at room temperature until it's very active and bubbly and larger in volume, several hours or overnight. When 200 grams of this starter (the total in this recipe) is very active and bubbly, it should measure between 1 and 1½ cups in volume.

To keep your active starter going, you can store it the refrigerator so it grows slowly and requires fewer feedings. In the fridge (40°F/4°C), the starter will look more compact and stretchy, and you can feed it once or twice a week. At room temperature, it will look a bit more airy and larger in volume, and you'll need to feed it once or twice a day.

Unused, neglected, and unfed starter may look dormant, compact, gray in color, or have a sharp, sour aroma. You might also see a layer of light amber liquid on top of the starter. That's alcohol left behind by the yeast. Don't despair. Unless it smells truly putrid, you can revive a dormant starter. Stir the alcohol back into the starter and refresh it at room temperature twice a day. Within a few days, it should come back to life with activity, bubbles, and increased volume and be ready to bake with once again.

OPTIONS

This recipe makes just enough starter for the sourdough pizza dough recipes in this book. To have enough starter to bake with and keep it going, double the recipe.

BREAD FLOUR SOURDOUGH STARTER: To start, use 60 grams (7 tablespoons) King Arthur bread flour plus 40 grams (⅓ cup) whole grain flour (preferably fresh milled rye flour). To refresh, use only unbleached unbromated bread flour.

For every pizza dough recipe that calls for 500 grams (3⅔ cups) of bread flour, use 200 to 250 grams (1 to 1¾ cups) of active Bread Flour Sourdough Starter to replace the dry yeast called for in the recipe. To account for the flour and water already in the starter, reduce the flour and water in the dough by 100 to 125 grams each. If using Whole Grain Sourdough Starter at 100% Hydration, increase the amount of starter to 250 to 300 grams (1½ to 2¼ cups) starter for every 500 grams (3⅔ cups) flour.

WHOLE GRAIN SOURDOUGH PIZZA DOUGH AT 62% HYDRATION

MAKES 5 DOUGH BALLS,
EACH ABOUT
240 GRAMS/8.5 OUNCES

Why use sourdough instead of commercial yeast? It tastes better! This dough uses only wild yeast from a sourdough starter. It's mixed by hand and fermented with no refrigeration, sort of like the old-school Naples dough. At about 60% hydration, it's meant to be baked at 700°F (371°C) or higher. Starting with whole grain starter gives you about 17% total whole grain flour here. A little whole grain, the wild yeast, and the room temperature fermentation make this dough taste amazing. Start it first thing in the morning and you can have pizza tonight. Or stick the dough balls in the fridge if you want pizza the next day.

12 grams (2 teaspoons) fine sea salt

325 grams (1 cup plus 6 tablespoons) water at 55°F (13°C)

250 grams (about 2 cups) active Whole Grain Sourdough Starter at 100% Hydration (page 84)

600 grams (4⅓ cups) King Arthur bread flour

Remove any rings from your fingers. You'll be getting sticky!

TO MIX AND KNEAD: Dissolve the salt in the water in a large (about 6 quart) wooden mixing box or heavy ceramic bowl, swishing it around with your hands. You'll be kneading and folding in the box or bowl, and something heavy will stay put. After the salt dissolves, swish in the starter, stirring it around until it disperses. Gradually mix in the flour by hand until the little beads of water-coated flour begin to feel soft and dispersed throughout the mixture. Continue adding flour and mixing until there is no more loose flour in the box or bowl. As you continue to mix, knead the dough like a cat would, pressing your hands and fingers into it. It will be wet and sticky at first. Scrape the dough from your fingers with the opposite hand now and then. Observe the beauty of the dough as it comes together in a ragged mass. Yeast is a living thing, and you are giving it food (the flour) and helping it grow.

As the dough begins to firm up and take shape, periodically fold it over itself. Handle it gently. It is alive yet young, like a creature being born in your own hands. You will feel it start to spring back a bit as you knead it. With every knead and fold, you will create a stronger gluten network, and the

dough will become stretchier. The dough will also begin to feel less wet because the flour will continue to absorb the water. Knead and fold the dough for a total of 10 to 15 minutes. At that point, the dough will hold together in a lump and start to feel somewhat plump and resilient when poked. Scrape as much dough from your hands as possible, rubbing your palms together and patting the loose bits into the mass of dough in the box or bowl.

TO FERMENT: Cover the box or bowl tightly with wood (a large cutting board works well) or a clean kitchen towel and let the dough ferment at room temperature (about 70°F/21°C) for 6 hours.

TO BALL UP AND FERMENT AGAIN: After 6 hours, divide the dough into 5 pieces, each about 240 grams (8.5 oz). At this point, the dough will feel even more plump and resilient. Make a tight ball out of each piece using your dry hands and a dry work surface: pick up a piece of dough and make the smooth side of the dough the top, tucking the rough bottom side into itself to swell up the top. It's like stuffing a sock into itself (see the photos on page 63). When all the loose dough is tucked into the ball, firmly squeeze the ball near the bottom to get out any big air pockets. The top should swell up like a balloon and be smooth like a baby's bottom. Gently roll the bottom under your palm on a dry work surface, using a circular motion to close the bottom and smooth it out. Ideally, the dough ball will be tight and smooth all over.

Place the dough balls evenly on wooden or plastic trays, making sure they are separated and not touching. I don't dust them with flour. They get plenty of flour when you shape them. Cover tightly and let rest at room temperature for 3 hours. At that point, the pizza dough will be mature and ready to shape. Complete shaping and baking directions appear in each pizza recipe.

OPTIONS

Instead of mixing and kneading by hand, you can mix and knead the dough in a stand mixer on low speed for 15 minutes. The dough will be very similar, but the experience of making it will be different.

To freeze the dough balls, dust them lightly with flour, place each one in a quart-size zipper-lock bag, suck out the air, seal and freeze for up to 1 month. Thaw the dough in the refrigerator, and then let it warm up at room temperature for 1 to 3 hours before using.

To hold the dough longer and get a little more flavor, you can ferment it in the refrigerator instead of at room temperature. For instance, you can ferment the bulk dough in the fridge for up to 24 hours (instead of 6 hours at room temp) and then hold the dough balls in the fridge for 8 hours (instead of 3 hours at room temp). Adjust the time and temperature to suit your schedule.

WHOLE GRAIN SOURDOUGH PIZZA DOUGH AT 72% HYDRATION

MAKES 5 DOUGH BALLS,
EACH ABOUT
250 GRAMS/8.8 OUNCES

This sourdough has a little more water. At 72% hydration, it's best cooked at 500° to 600°F (260° to 316°C). The extra water also makes the dough feel pretty loose in your hands, so handle it gently. The payoff? Some whole grain flour and natural wild yeast give it incredible flavor.

12 grams (2 teaspoons) fine sea salt

400 grams (1⅔ cups) water at 55°F (13°C)

250 grams (about 2 cups) active Whole Grain Sourdough Starter at 100% Hydration (page 84)

600 grams (4⅓ cups) King Arthur bread flour

Remove any rings from your fingers. You'll be getting sticky!

TO MIX AND KNEAD: Dissolve the salt in the water in a large (about 6 quart) wooden mixing box or heavy ceramic bowl, swishing it around with your hands. You'll be kneading and folding in the box or bowl, and something heavy will stay put. After the salt dissolves, swish in the starter, stirring it around until it disperses. Gradually mix in the flour by hand until the little beads of water-coated flour begin to feel soft and dispersed throughout the mixture. Continue adding flour and mixing until there is no more loose flour in the box or bowl. As you continue to mix, knead the dough like a cat would, pressing your hands and fingers into it. It will be wet and sticky at first. Scrape the dough from your fingers with the opposite hand now and then. Observe the beauty of the dough as it comes together in a ragged mass. Yeast is a living thing, and you are giving it food (the flour) and helping it grow.

As the dough begins to firm up and take shape, periodically fold it over itself. Handle it gently. It is alive yet young, like a creature being born in your own hands. You will feel it start to spring back a bit as you knead it. With every knead and fold, you will create a stronger gluten network, and the dough will become stretchier. The dough will also begin to feel less wet because the flour will continue to absorb the water. Knead and fold the dough for a total of 10 to 15 minutes. At that point, the dough will hold together in a lump and start to feel somewhat plump and resilient when poked.

Scrape as much dough from your hands as possible, rubbing your palms together and patting the loose bits into the mass of dough in the box or bowl.

TO FERMENT: Cover the box or bowl tightly with wood (a large cutting board works well) or a clean kitchen towel and let the dough ferment at room temperature (about 70°F/21°C) for 6 hours.

TO BALL UP AND FERMENT AGAIN: After 6 hours, the dough will feel even more plump and resilient but a bit sticky from the 70% hydration here. Lightly flour your hands and a bench knife (the bigger the better). Resist the temptation to dust the dough or your work surface with more flour; that will just make the dough stiffer. You want to keep the dough soft. Use your hand to scrape and dump the dough onto a dry work surface. Use the bench knife to cut and divide the dough into 5 pieces, each about 250 grams (8.8 oz). Just cut and scrape away a 250-gram (8.8-oz) piece from the dough, transferring the piece to a scale to weigh it (at least weigh the first piece so you can eyeball the rest). The dough will be loose, wet, and sticky. Handle it with authority. Scoop it up with the bench knife and scrape it off with your fingers. Transfer the 250-gram piece to a 2-foot-square area on the dry work surface. Then scrape and shape the dough into a ball. To do that, position the knife at one edge of the dough and then push the dough in the opposite direction, scraping and pushing the dough at least a foot or two away from you. It will swell up and form an oval shape. Remove the knife (using your fingers if necessary), reposition the knife on the pointy end of the dough, and proceed to push the dough in a direction perpendicular to the first, tilting the knife down a bit and scraping the dough with some pressure, swelling up the dough again. Repeat this process of pushing, repositioning, and scraping the dough in opposite directions all around the 2-foot square, until the dough goes from a loose oval shape to a more organized round one. It's almost like shaping a water balloon, so it's a somewhat delicate operation. You want to gently squeeze all around the balloon to swell it up into a round ball, always increasing the surface tension. When the dough becomes a somewhat organized round ball, use the bench knife to quickly transfer the dough ball to a proofing box or a wide tray with a tight-fitting lid. It will flatten out quite a bit, so leave room for the other dough balls. Repeat the process with each lump of dough, transferring the dough balls to the container and leaving several inches between each—you don't want the balls reconnecting themselves. I don't dust them with flour. They get plenty of flour when you shape them. Cover tightly and let rest at room temperature for 3 hours. At that point, the pizza dough will be mature and ready to shape. Complete shaping and baking directions appear in each pizza recipe.

OPTIONS

Instead of mixing and kneading by hand, you can mix and knead the dough in a stand mixer on low speed for 15 minutes.

To hold the dough longer and get a little more flavor, you can ferment it in the refrigerator instead of at room temperature. For instance, you can ferment the bulk dough in the fridge for up to 24 hours (instead of 6 hours at room temp) and then hold the dough balls in the fridge for 8 hours (instead of 3 hours at room temp). Adjust the time and temperature to suit your schedule.

5

NAPLES DOUGH PIZZAS

"L'ALLEGRIA E UN INGREDIENT IMPORTANTE A NAPOLI . . . non si fanno piatti senza buon umore," the guy said. (Cheerfulness is an important ingredient in Naples . . . one doesn't make a dish without a good mood.) I had just told him I was a chef looking for L'antica Pizzeria da Michele and needed a place to park my car. If you've ever been to Naples, you know that the parking rules are as follows: every man for himself!

"Lascia la macchina qua—ci penso io," he continued. (Leave your car here—I'll watch it). *Chiudo io?* I asked. (Should I lock it?) *No, no, dammi le chiave!* (No, no, just leave the keys with me.) *Haha! Pensi che sono nato ieri? Trovo altro parcheggio . . . ciao!* (Haha! You think I was born yesterday? I'll find other parking . . . later dude!)

He gestured with his hand and said, *"Ma va!!!"* (Loosely translated . . . "Go fuck yourself!!!")

This was my introduction to Naples. It was a pretty good indication of what was to come as I traveled around this historic city. My first experience with pizza Napoletana was similar. Don't get me wrong . . . I have had some of the best pizza ever in Naples. 50 Kalò, Da Attilio, and Pizzaria La Notizia are fantastic. And in nearby Caiazzo, Pepe in Grani takes things to another level entirely—a rarefied expression of the art that's hard to comprehend unless you are deep in the pizza matrix. Even in the United States, chefs like Anthony Mangieri of Pizza Napoletana make incredible representations of true Naples-style pizza. Many traditionalists live and die by the VPN (Vera Pizza Napoletana) rules and certifications (see page 97 for details), and some of these pizzas are among the best I have ever eaten.

But my first experience definitely took a few years to get over. The truth is, traditional Naples-style pizza can be downright soupy. It's cooked in blazing-hot ovens that can leave the mozzarella barely melted and the sauce pooling around the cheese in the middle of the pizza. Sometimes, it's more like tomato soup with lukewarm bits of mozzarella held in a pizza shell with burnt edges. After tasting this kind of "true" Napoletana pizza, my first thought was, "No wonder they don't cut pizza here—the sauce would spill all over the place." As I stood outside and ate it, I was confused about all the fuss over pizza Napoletana.

Since that day, I have eaten many, many more pizzas in Naples and come to understand it in much more depth, including what it means to respect Italian traditions—in spite of almost losing my car! What we serve now at Pizzeria Vetri is mostly Naples-style pizza, but it's not VPN pizza. That isn't really what I like best, so I don't try to replicate it. VPN pizza is baked at 800° to 900°F (427° to 482°C). Our ovens are closer to 700°F (371°C) because I like the sauce to seep into the dough a little. VPN pizza also uses very fine tipo 00 flour, which makes the crust supersilky. We use bread flour. What can I say? I like a little more texture and chew in my pizza.

Other than that, my Naples dough is pretty traditional: just flour, water, salt, and yeast. I respect the simplicity of Naples-style pizza—and Italian cooking in general. Sure, I push the boundaries here and there, but the principles of Italian cooking are always rooted in two basic things: a minimal amount of the best-quality ingredients and a firm grasp of what goes with what.

I also know that Italians—and Americans—get very picky about all the fine points of pizza. Some want pizza baked in a wood oven or nothing else. Others—especially home bakers—have discovered the baking stone or the baking steel, and they won't make pizza any other way. Still others swear by pizza made on a Big Green Egg or kamado-style grill. Well, guess what? I give you recipes using *all* these cooking methods. I want everyone to enjoy a good Naples-style pizza no matter what kind of oven it's baked in.

I also want you play around with the shapes. If you're only making round pizzas, branch out! Pizza al metro (pizza cut by the meter) is a long, rectangular shape that supposedly got its start in the 1930s in Vico Equense, a little coastal town south of Naples. Now, pizza al metro is more common in Rome. Go figure! These superlong pizzas are loaded into deep wood ovens, but I show you how to make a similar rectangular shape directly on the hot grates of a big gas grill or on a big baking stone in a home oven.

One of the cool things about pizza al metro is that you can put different toppings on different sections of the rectangle. It's like getting a few different pizzas in one. Speaking of toppings, pick and choose your favorites for any of the Neapolitan pizzas in this chapter. The main recipes for "Pizza Style" show you how to shape and bake the dough using various cooking methods and ovens. The toppings themselves are interchangeable. That's why the toppings are in their own section. You could even use toppings from the chapter Roman Dough Pizzas (page 135). Top your pizza with whatever you like!

WOOD OVEN NEAPOLITAN PIZZA

**MAKES ONE 10- TO
12-INCH (25 TO 30 CM)
ROUND PIZZA**

A pizzeria used to be the only place you could get a pizza with a leopard spotted crust—a sure sign that it was baked in a very hot oven. Nowadays, they make home models of everything, and pizza ovens are no exception. If you have a wood-burning pizza oven in your home or backyard (or in your restaurant!), this is really the best way to get that type of crust. I like to keep the ambient temperature of my wood ovens at about 650° to 700°F (343° to 371°C). Any hotter, and my crust burns too fast. Any cooler, and it just browns without those beautiful charred spots. I've found that a dough hydration of 60% is perfect for baking in this temperature range.

1 dough ball, preferably
Naples Dough at 60%
Hydration (page 61), about
250 grams/8.8 ounces

Toppings of your choice
(pages 111 to 133)

Flour, for dusting

Light a wood fire on the oven floor directly where you will be cooking the pizza (for details on starting a fire, see page 15). Feed the fire until the ambient temperature in the oven is around 700°F (371°C), 1 to 2 hours. Quickly rake the fire to one side of the oven, containing it in a neat pile near the edge. Brush the cooking surface clean.

Let the dough warm up at room temperature for at least 1 hour or up to 4 hours. As it warms up, the dough will relax and become easier to shape.

Have your toppings ready to go.

TO SHAPE THE DOUGH: The goal is to stretch the dough to a 10- to 12-inch (25 to 30 cm) circle with an even thickness across the middle and a thicker rim around the edge. There are lots of ways. Here's how I usually do it. Lightly flour a work surface and a wooden pizza peel. Use a dough scraper to scrape the dough ball from the tray to the floured surface. Gently poke your fingers about ½ inch (1.3 cm) from the edge of the dough ball all around it to begin forming the rim. The center should look thicker like a hat. Leave the rim alone and press your fingers and palm gently into the center of the hat, moving your fingers and thumb outward to begin stretching the dough away from the center (see the photos on page 95). At this point, you should have a disk of dough about 5 inches (12 cm) in diameter. Slip one

hand under the disk and quickly flip it over. Repeat the poking and pressing process on the other side, poking your fingers around the edge first to make the rim, and then placing your palm on the center and gently stretching your fingers and thumb outward to stretch the dough from the center outward. As you work, gradually rotate the dough and keep your thumb against the rim to make the rim thick and round.

For stiffer dough like this, it's easiest to pick up the dough to stretch it. Transfer the dough from the work surface to the backs of your hands: just quickly grab the far edge of the rim and flip the dough onto the opposite hand and then slip your other hand under the dough. Keep both hands loosely closed as fists under the dough near the center. With the dough on the backs of your hands, essentially repeat the process of stretching the dough from the center outward: move your hands gently away from the center while rotating the dough around the backs of your fists. It helps to angle the dough downward slightly so it's not perfectly horizontal, which causes it to drape too quickly around the backs of your fists. Carefully and gently continue to stretch the dough until it is an evenly thin 10- to 12-inch (25 to 30 cm) circle with a rim about ½ inch (1.3 cm) thick.

CONTINUED

For the most even crust, I like to stretch both sides of the dough in my hands. To do that, flip the dough over on the backs of your hands by flipping it over much the same way you did when flipping it from the work surface to your hands. Of course, there are other ways to stretch the dough. Some people twirl it up in the air. Use whatever method works best for you to create an evenly stretched 10- to 12-inch (25 to 30 cm) circle with a nice thick rim. If the dough tears a hole, patch it by pulling a little dough from one side of the hole and pressing it over the hole with your thumb.

Lay the stretched dough onto the floured peel. The easiest way is to simply drape it over the peel and then remove your hands from beneath the dough. Reshape the dough round as necessary, keeping the rim thick. Give the peel a quick shake to make sure the dough can slide easily.

Add your toppings. Give the peel another quick shake to make sure the dough slides easily.

TO BAKE THE PIZZA: Throw another piece of wood on the fire to stoke it up and give the pizza an initial blast of heat. Slide and shake the pizza from the peel onto the clean cooking surface. Cook until the rim is puffed, the dough blisters and chars in spots, and the bottom is crisp, 2 to 3 minutes, depending on your oven's temperature. Use a metal pizza peel to rotate the dough as necessary for even cooking.

Remove the pizza from the oven to a wire rack to cool for a minute or so, just to keep the steam from making the crust soggy. Transfer the pizza to a pizza pan or cutting board, slice, and add any finishing ingredients. I like 6 slices for this size pizza.

HOME OVEN NEAPOLITAN PIZZA

**MAKES ONE 10- TO
12-INCH (25 TO 30 CM)
ROUND PIZZA**

You can make a damn good pizza in a home oven. This method is pretty common now. It uses a hot baking steel or baking stone and your oven's broiler to replicate the bottom heat and top heat of a wood-fired oven. A little more water in the dough helps the crust come out right when you're baking at 500° or 550°F (260° or 288°C).

1 dough ball, preferably
Naples Dough at 70%
Hydration (page 64), about
270 grams/9.5 ounces

Toppings of your choice
(pages 111 to 133)

Flour, for dusting

Let the dough warm up at room temperature for at least 1 hour or up to 4 hours. As it warms up, the dough will relax and become easier to shape.

Place a baking steel or stone on the upper rack of the oven 4 to 6 inches (10 to 15 cm) beneath the broiler for an electric oven or 6 to 8 inches (15 to 20 cm) beneath the broiler for a gas oven. Preheat the oven to its highest setting (usually 500° to 550°F/260° to 288°C) for 45 minutes.

Have your toppings ready to go.

When the oven is preheated and you are ready to bake pizza, open the oven door for 10 seconds if you have an electric oven. This step lets some heat escape to make sure the electric broiler will actually turn on even though the oven has reached its maximum temperature. Reset the oven to broil, and preheat the broiler for 5 to 10 minutes. The next steps of shaping and topping the pizza should take only 5 to 10 minutes if your toppings are ready to go.

TO SHAPE THE DOUGH: The goal is to stretch the dough to a 10- to 12-inch (25 to 30 cm) circle with an even thickness across the middle and a thicker rim around the edge. There are lots of ways. For 70% hydration dough, you'll need a bit more flour and a gentler hand, since the dough is softer. It's best to shape it completely on your work surface. The dough should be soft enough to stretch while it's flat. If you try to pick it up, it may tear a hole. Generously flour a work surface and a wooden pizza peel. Use a dough scraper to scrape the dough ball from the tray to the floured surface. Gently poke your fingers about ½ inch (1.3 cm) from the

edge of the dough ball all around it to begin forming the rim. The center should look thicker like a hat. Leave the rim alone and press your fingers and palm gently into the center of the hat, moving your fingers and thumb outward to begin stretching the dough away from the center (see the photos on page 95). At this point, you should have a disk of dough about 5 inches (12 cm) in diameter. Slip one hand under the disk and quickly flip it over. Repeat the poking and pressing process on the other side, poking your fingers around the edge first to make the rim, and then placing your palm on the center and gently stretching your fingers and thumb outward to stretch the dough from the center outward. As you work, gradually rotate the dough on the flour and keep your thumb against the rim to make the rim thick and round. The dough should be soft enough to continue this process until it is stretched to a 10- to 12-inch (25 to 30 cm) circle with an even thickness across the middle and a rim about ½ inch (1.3 cm) thick. If the dough tears a hole, patch it by pulling a little dough from one side of the hole and pressing it over the hole with your thumb.

Lay the stretched dough onto the floured peel. The easiest way is to simply drape it over the peel and then remove your hands from beneath the dough. Reshape the dough round as necessary, keeping the rim thick. Give the peel a quick shake to make sure the dough can slide easily.

Add your toppings. If using soft cheese, such as fresh mozzarella, you may need to add it halfway through the baking time to keep it from overcooking. Give the peel another quick shake to make sure the dough slides easily.

TO BAKE THE PIZZA: At this point, your oven should be on broil. Slide and shake the pizza from the peel onto the cooking surface. Cook until the rim is puffed, the dough blisters and chars in spots, and the bottom is crisp, 6 to 8 minutes. Use your hands or a long spatula to rotate the dough as necessary for even cooking.

Remove the pizza from the oven to a wire rack to cool for a minute or so, just to keep the steam from making the crust soggy. If you will be baking another pizza, reset the oven to its maximum temperature. Transfer the pizza to a pizza pan or cutting board, slice, and add any finishing ingredients. I like 6 slices for this size pizza.

What Is Pizza Napoletana?

Some people go to Naples, get a certificate showing that they've learned how to make "true" pizza Napoletana (which costs about $2,000), and then open up a pizza shop that says, "we serve true Neapolitan pizza." But a few days and a guidebook does not a master pizzaiolo make! It takes years to understand everything that goes into great pizza.

But I get it. Naples is the birthplace of pizza and when people throw together a gluten-free crust made from cauliflower, top it with sunflower seeds, and call it pizza, you have to draw the line. Back in 1984, the old guard pizzaiolos of Naples defined exactly what pizza Napoletana is and is not. Here's a summary, according to the Associazione Verace Pizza Napoletana (AVPN):

- Vera Pizza Napoletana (VPN, or true Neapolitan pizza) is limited to two types: marinara (tomato, oil, oregano, and garlic) and margherita (tomato, oil, mozzarella or fior di latte, grated cheese, and basil). But the association "reserves the right to accept variations of the product and recognize their authenticity if they are informed by the Neapolitan tradition of pizzas and are not in contrast with the rules of gastronomy."
- The finished pizza: should be soft, elastic, and easy to manipulate and fold.
- The dough: must use only finely milled white type 00 wheat flour, although up to 20% of slightly coarser type 0 flour is allowed. The hydration is 55 to 59%. The dough must also use sea salt and compressed fresh yeast (or natural yeast in sourdough). No dry yeast is allowed. No fat is permitted in the dough. The dough must be mixed by hand or in a low-speed mixer with fork or spiral beaters. No vertical or planetary mixers are allowed. The dough should ferment entirely at warm room temperature (77°F/25°C). The dough balls must be completely shaped by hand. No rolling pins or mechanical dough presses are allowed.
- The toppings: must be good quality, including DOP (*Denominazione di Origine Protetta* or protected designation of origin) fresh or canned San Marzano, Roma, or piennolo tomatoes; thinly sliced fresh garlic; DOP mozzarella, buffalo mozzarella, or fior di latte cheese; hard cheese such as Parmigiano-Reggiano, Grana Padano, or Pecorino Romano; extra-virgin olive oil; fresh basil; and sea salt.
- The oven: must be wood fired only. No coal, gas, electric, or other fuel may be used.
- Baking temperature: must be 800° to 900°F (427° to 482°C) on the dome and floor.
- Baking time: should not exceed 90 seconds.

CAST-IRON NEAPOLITAN PIZZA

MAKES ONE 10- TO
12-INCH (25 TO 30 CM)
ROUND PIZZA

Surprisingly, this method is one of the easiest and most effective for making a pizza at home. A cast-iron skillet gets rip-roaring hot, and when you run the pizza under the broiler, the effect is similar to the top and bottom heat of a wood-fired oven. The pizza cooks in just a couple minutes. All you need is a large cast-iron skillet (at least 12 inch/30 cm diameter) and a broiler. I like dough with 60% hydration here because it's a little firmer and easier to slide into the hot skillet.

1 dough ball, preferably
Naples Dough at 60%
Hydration (page 61), about
250 grams/8.8 ounces

Toppings of your choice
(pages 111 to 133)

Flour, for dusting

Let the dough warm up at room temperature for at least 1 hour or up to 4 hours. As it warms up, the dough will relax and become easier to shape.

Set an oven rack 4 to 6 inches (10 to 15 cm) beneath the broiler for an electric oven or 6 to 8 inches (15 to 20 cm) beneath the broiler for a gas oven. Preheat the oven to its highest setting (usually 500° to 550°F/260° to 288°C) for 45 minutes.

Have your toppings ready to go.

When the oven is preheated and you are ready to bake pizza, open the oven door for 10 seconds if you have an electric oven. This step lets some heat escape to make sure the electric broiler will actually turn on even though the oven has reached its maximum temperature. Reset the oven to broil, and preheat the broiler for 5 to 10 minutes. The next steps of shaping and topping the pizza should take only 5 to 10 minutes if your toppings are ready to go.

Heat a large cast-iron skillet (12 to 14 inches/30 to 35 cm) on the stovetop over medium-high heat until very hot, 3 to 5 minutes.

TO SHAPE THE DOUGH: The goal is to stretch the dough to a 10- to 12-inch (25 to 30 cm) circle with an even thickness across the middle and a thicker rim around the edge. There are lots of ways. Here's how I usually do it. Lightly flour a work surface and a wooden pizza peel. Use a dough scraper to scrape the dough ball from the tray to the floured surface. Gently poke your fingers about ½ inch (1.3 cm) from the edge of the dough ball all around it to begin forming the rim. The center should look thicker like a hat. Leave the rim alone and press your fingers and palm gently into the center of the hat, moving your fingers and thumb outward to begin stretching the dough away from the center (see the photos on page 95). At this point, you should have a disk of dough about 5 inches (12 cm) in diameter. Slip one hand under the disk and quickly flip it over. Repeat the poking and pressing process on the other side, poking your fingers around the edge first to make the rim and then placing your palm on the center and gently stretching your fingers and thumb outward to stretch the dough from the center outward. As you work, gradually rotate the dough and keep your thumb against the rim to make the rim thick and round.

For stiffer dough like this, it's easiest to pick up the dough to stretch it. Transfer the dough from the work surface to the backs of your hands: just quickly grab the far edge of the rim and flip the dough onto the opposite hand and then slip your other hand under the dough. Keep both hands loosely closed as fists under the dough near the center. With the dough on the backs of your hands, essentially repeat the process of stretching the dough from the center outward: move your hands gently away from the center while rotating the dough around the backs of your fists. It helps to angle the dough downward slightly so it's not perfectly horizontal, which causes it to drape too quickly around the backs of your fists. Carefully and gently continue to stretch the dough until it is an evenly thin 10- to 12-inch (25 to 30 cm) circle with a rim about ½ inch (1.3 cm) thick. For the most even crust, I like to stretch both sides of the dough in my hands. To do that, flip the dough over on the backs of your hands by flipping it over much the same way you did when flipping it from the work surface to your hands. Of course, there are other ways to stretch the dough. Some people twirl it up in the air. Use whatever method works best for you to create an evenly stretched 10- to 12-inch (25 to 30 cm) circle with a nice thick rim. If the dough tears a hole, patch it by pulling a little dough from one side of the hole and pressing it over the hole with your thumb.

Lay the stretched dough onto the floured peel. The easiest way is to simply drape it over the peel, and then remove your hands from beneath the dough. Reshape the dough round as necessary, keeping the rim thick. Give the peel a quick shake to make sure the dough can slide easily.

TO BAKE THE PIZZA: At this point, your oven should be on broil, and your cast-iron skillet should be smoking hot on the stovetop. Slide and shake the pizza from the peel into the hot skillet. Use a folded towel or oven mitt to quickly shake the pan and center the pizza inside the pan. Turn the heat to low and quickly add your toppings. Put the pan of pizza in the hot oven right under the broiler and cook until the rim puffs, browns, and chars in spots, 2 to 4 minutes. Rotate the pan as necessary for even cooking.

Transfer the pan to the stovetop and use a large spatula to transfer the pizza to a wire rack to cool for a minute or so, just to keep the steam from making the crust soggy. Transfer the pizza to a pizza pan or cutting board, slice, and add any finishing ingredients. I like 6 slices for this size pizza.

KAMADO-GRILLED NEAPOLITAN PIZZA

MAKES ONE 10- TO
12-INCH (25 TO 30 CM)
ROUND PIZZA

The Big Green Egg and other kamado-style grills get superhot, up to 800°F (427°C). They're typically made of ceramic, which is similar to the firebricks in a wood oven, so all in all, they make great pizza. Just be careful not to get them too hot or your crust will burn, especially on the bottom. With the high temperature and short bake time, Naples-style dough at 60% hydration works well, but I like the extra puff you get from a little more water in the dough, so I use Naples-style dough at 70% hydration.

1 dough ball, preferably
Naples Dough at 70%
Hydration (page 64), about
270 grams/9.5 ounces

Toppings of your choice
(pages 111 to 133)

Flour, for dusting

Let the dough warm up at room temperature for at least 1 hour or up to 4 hours. As it warms up, the dough will relax and become easier to shape.

Light the charcoal until it starts to glow red. Everyone has their favorite method. The fastest way is to use two chimney starters, each filled with 2½ pounds (1.1 kg) of charcoal. Place wadded-up newspaper in the bottom, charcoal in the top, and then light the paper and the perforated cans will feed the fire with oxygen so the charcoal lights quickly.

Dump the glowing coals onto the coal grate of the cooker. Place the heat diffuser over the coals, then place the grill grate and/or upper rack in the cooker and a baking stone on the upper rack. A baking stone is preferred here over a baking steel. Steel tends to burn the bottom of the pizza due to the grill's high heat and the steel's ability to transfer heat so quickly. Close the lid and preheat the grill with the top and bottom vents open for 50 to 60 minutes. The ambient temperature (on the grill's thermometer) should be 650° to 750°F (343° to 399°C). The cooking surface temperature should be about 600°F (316°C) when checked with an infrared thermometer through the top vent (to avoid opening the grill and losing heat).

Have your toppings ready to go.

TO SHAPE THE DOUGH: The goal is to stretch the dough to a 10- to 12-inch (25 to 30 cm) circle with an even thickness across the middle and a thicker rim around the edge. There are lots of ways. For 70% hydration dough, you'll need a bit more flour and a gentler hand, since the dough is softer. It's best to shape it completely on your work surface. The dough should be soft enough to stretch while it's flat. If you try to pick it up, it may tear a hole. Generously flour a work surface and a wooden pizza peel. Use a dough scraper to scrape the dough ball from the tray to the floured surface. Gently poke your fingers about ½ inch (1.3 cm) from the edge of the dough ball all around it to begin forming the rim. The center should look thicker like a hat. Leave the rim alone and press your fingers and palm gently into the center of the hat, moving your fingers and thumb outward to begin stretching the dough away from the center (see the photos on page 95). At this point, you should have a disk of dough about 5 inches (12 cm) in diameter. Slip one hand under the disk and quickly flip it over. Repeat the poking and pressing process on the other side, poking your fingers around the edge first to make the rim and then placing your palm on the center and gently stretching your fingers and thumb outward to stretch the dough from the center outward. As you work, gradually rotate the dough on the flour and keep your thumb against the rim to make the rim thick and round. The dough should be soft enough to continue

CONTINUED

*Kamado-Grilled Salsiccia
Neapolitan Pizza*

this process until it is stretched to a 10- to 12-inch (25 to 30 cm) circle with an even thickness across the middle and a rim about ½ inch (1.3 cm) thick. If the dough tears a hole, patch it by pulling a little dough from one side of the hole and pressing it over the hole with your thumb.

Lay the stretched dough onto the floured peel. The easiest way is to simply drape it over the peel and then remove your hands from beneath the dough. Reshape the dough round as necessary, keeping the rim thick. Give the peel a quick shake to make sure the dough can slide easily.

Add your toppings. Give the peel another quick shake to make sure the dough slides easily.

TO GRILL THE PIZZA: Open the grill and quickly brush or blow off any ash from the cooking surface. Quickly shake and load the pizza onto the cooking surface and close the lid. Close the top vents to trap heat and send it to the top of the pizza. Keep the bottom vents fully open to feed the fire oxygen and keep it burning hot. Cook until the rim is puffed, the dough blisters and chars in spots, and the bottom is crisp, 4 to 6 minutes. The pizza should cook evenly so there is no need to rotate it. Check the doneness by shining a light (a cell phone light works well) through the top vent to avoid opening the grill during cooking.

Remove the pizza from the grill to a wire rack to cool for a minute or so, just to keep the steam from making the crust soggy. If you will be baking another pizza, quickly close the lid, reopen the top vents, and let the cooking surface recover its heat for 15 to 20 minutes. Transfer the pizza to a pizza pan or cutting board, slice, and add any finishing ingredients. I like 6 slices for this size pizza.

GAS-GRILLED PIZZA AL METRO

MAKES 1 LARGE
RECTANGULAR PIZZA,
ABOUT 22 INCHES LONG
BY 10 INCHES WIDE
(56 BY 25 CM)

If you have a big grill, you're in luck. You can grill a big pizza. Put 2 dough balls end to end, press them into a long rectangle, and boom! You have pizza al metro. This recipe makes a rectangular pie that fits on most 3- or 4-burner gas grills. Or if you have a big charcoal grill, grill it there. Or, better yet, if you have a big pizza oven, make the same pizza without flipping it. Either way, you'll need twice the amount of toppings, since this pizza is essentially 2 smaller pies made into 1 big rectangular one.

2 dough balls, preferably
Naples Dough at 60%
Hydration (page 61), about
500 grams/17.6 ounces total

Toppings of your choice
(pages 111 to 133)

Flour, for dusting

Let the dough warm up at room temperature for at least 1 hour or up to 4 hours. As it warms up, the dough will relax and become easier to shape.

Preheat a 3- or 4-burner (or larger) gas grill to medium heat for 20 to 30 minutes. You'll need a grill space that's at least 22 inches long and 10 inches wide (56 by 25 cm).

Have your toppings ready to go.

TO SHAPE THE DOUGH: The goal is to stretch the dough to a large rectangle, about 22 inches long by 10 inches wide with an even thickness across the middle and a thicker rim around the edge. There are lots of ways. Here's how I usually do it for a pizza al metro. Lightly flour a large work surface and a large wooden pizza peel or cutting board (a board big enough to fit the stretched-out dough). Use a dough scraper to scrape the dough balls from the tray to the floured surface. Position the dough balls end to end and press the ends together, pinching them and reshaping the dough balls to make one larger piece of dough in a rough rectangular shape. Gently poke your fingers about ½ inch (1.3 cm) from the edge of the dough all around it to begin forming the rim. The center should look a bit thicker. Leave the rim alone and press your fingers and palms gently around the center portion to begin stretching the dough away from the center. Keep stretching to make a rectangle of dough about 12 inches long by 4 inches wide (30 by 10 cm). Slip one hand under the rectangle and quickly

flip it over. Repeat the poking and pressing process on the other side, poking your fingers around the edge first to make the rim, and then placing your palms on the center and gently stretching your fingers and thumb outward to stretch the dough from the center outward into a larger rectangle about 22 inches long by 10 inches wide. You may need to use both hands to stretch the dough. As you work, keep the rim thick. If the dough is difficult to stretch, let it relax for 5 minutes or so and then stretch it again. If the dough tears a hole, patch it by pulling a little dough from one side of the hole and pressing it over the hole with your thumb.

Lay the stretched dough onto the floured peel or cutting board. The easiest way is to slide it onto the peel or board, one end at a time, removing your hands from beneath the dough each time. Reshape the rectangle as necessary on the peel or board and then give the peel or board a quick shake to make sure the dough can slide easily.

TO GRILL THE PIZZA: Brush the grill grate clean and coat it with oil. An oily paper towel held with tongs works well. Shake and slide the pizza from the peel or board onto the grill. Close the lid and cook until the dough is nicely browned on the bottom and almost dry on top, 1 to 2 minutes total. After about a minute, use tongs and a large spatula to rotate the dough 45 degrees or so for even browning. Do not flip the dough.

When the dough is evenly browned on the bottom, use tongs to slide the dough back onto the peel or board. Close the grill lid. Flip the pizza on the peel or board. Add your toppings to the grilled side of the pizza off the heat.

Carefully slide the topped pizza back onto the grill and cover the grill. Cut the grill heat to medium low and cook until the bottom browns and the toppings cook, about 5 minutes, rotating the pizza 45 degrees once or twice for even browning.

Remove the pizza from the grill to a large cutting board. Slice and add any finishing ingredients. For this pizza, I like to make 12 rectangular slices by cutting the pizza in half lengthwise and then making 5 crosswise cuts.

OPTIONS

WOOD OVEN PIZZA AL METRO: Shape the dough the same way but add the toppings to the raw, pressed-out dough. Bake in a wood-fired oven at 700° to 800°F (371° to 427°C), rotating the pizza for even browning.

HOME OVEN PIZZA AL METRO: Use 1½ dough balls (about 400 grams/14 oz total), preferably Naples Dough at 70% Hydration (page 64). When shaping the dough, make the rectangle slightly smaller, about 21 inches long by 10 inches wide (53 by 25 cm). Preheat a large 22-inch (56 cm) baking stone or steel in the oven at 500° to 550°F (260° to 288°C), 4 to 6 inches (10 to 15 cm) beneath the broiler for 45 minutes. Bake on the hot stone or steel with the broiler on, the same way as for Home Oven Neapolitan Pizza (page 96). Don't throw away the remaining half dough ball! You can divide it and fry it up to make an appetizer of Parmesan Fried Dough (page 150) or a dessert of Fried Dough with Fennel Lemon Sugar (page 244).

CHARCOAL-GRILLED NEAPOLITAN PIZZA

MAKES ONE 10- TO
12-INCH (25 TO 30 CM)
ROUND PIZZA

"When life gives you lemons, make lemonade." And if all you have is a charcoal grill, you can still make good pizza! Just grill the dough right on the hot grate, flip it, top it, and grill the other side with the lid down to cook the toppings. The end result is more like flatbread, but it works. I like dough with about 60% hydration here because wetter dough can slump into the gaps between the grill grates.

1 dough ball, preferably
Naples Dough at 60%
Hydration (page 61), about
250 grams/8.8 ounces

Toppings of your choice
(pages 111 to 133)

Flour, for dusting

Let the dough warm up at room temperature for at least 1 hour or up to 4 hours. As it warms up, the dough will relax and become easier to shape.

Light the charcoal until it starts to glow red. Everyone has their favorite method. The fastest way is to use two chimney starters, each filled with 2½ pounds (1.1 kg) of charcoal. Place wadded-up newspaper in the bottom, charcoal in the top, and then light the paper and the perforated cans will feed the fire with oxygen so the charcoal lights quickly.

Dump the glowing coals onto the coal grate of the grill. Insert the grill rack, close the lid, and preheat the grill for 20 to 30 minutes.

Have your toppings ready to go.

TO SHAPE THE DOUGH: The goal is to stretch the dough to a 10- to 12-inch (25 to 30 cm) circle with an even thickness across the middle and a thicker rim around the edge. There are lots of ways. Here's how I usually do it. Lightly flour a work surface and a wooden pizza peel. Use a dough scraper to scrape the dough ball from the tray to the floured surface. Gently poke your fingers about ½ inch (1.3 cm) from the edge of the dough ball all around it to begin forming the rim. The center should look thicker like a hat. Leave the rim alone and press your fingers and palm gently into the center of the hat, moving your fingers and thumb outward to begin stretching the dough away from the center (see the photos on page 95). At this point, you should have a disk of dough about 5 inches (12 cm) in diameter. Slip one hand under the disk and quickly flip it over. Repeat the poking and pressing process on the other side, poking your fingers around the edge first to make the rim, and then placing your palm on the center and gently stretching your fingers and thumb outward to stretch the dough from the center outward. As you work, gradually rotate the dough and keep your thumb against the rim to make the rim thick and round.

For stiffer dough like this, it's easiest to pick up the dough to stretch it. Transfer the dough from the work surface to the backs of your hands: just quickly grab the far edge of the rim and flip the dough onto the opposite hand, and then slip your other hand under the dough. Keep both hands loosely closed as fists under the dough near the center. With the dough on the backs of your hands, essentially repeat the process of stretching the dough from the center outward: move your hands gently away from the center while rotating the dough around the backs of your fists. It helps to angle the dough downward slightly so it's not perfectly horizontal, which causes it to drape too quickly around the backs of your fists. Carefully and gently continue to stretch the dough until it is an evenly thin 10- to 12-inch (25 to 30 cm) circle with a rim about ½ inch (1.3 cm) thick. For the most even crust, I like to stretch both sides of the dough in my hands. To do that, flip the dough over on the backs of your hands by flipping it over much the same way you did when flipping it from the work surface to your hands. Of course, there are other ways to stretch the dough. Some people twirl it up in the air. Use whatever method works best for you to create an evenly stretched 10- to 12-inch (25 to 30 cm) circle with a nice thick rim. If the dough tears a hole, patch it by pulling a little dough from one side of the hole and pressing it over the hole with your thumb.

Lay the stretched dough onto the floured peel. The easiest way is to simply drape it over the peel and then remove your hands from beneath the dough. Reshape the dough round as necessary, keeping the rim thick. Give the peel a quick shake to make sure the dough can slide easily.

TO GRILL THE PIZZA: Adjust the top and bottom vents for medium heat in the grill. Brush the grill grate clean and coat it with oil. An oily paper towel held with tongs works well. Shake and slide the naked pizza from the peel onto the grill. Close the lid and cook until the dough is nicely browned on the bottom and almost dry on top, 1 to 2 minutes total. After about a minute, use tongs and a large spatula to rotate the dough about 45 degrees for even browning. Do not flip the dough.

When the dough is evenly browned on the bottom, use tongs to slide the dough back onto the peel. Close the grill lid and then close the grill vents on the top and bottom about 75% closed to lower the grill heat to medium low. Flip the pizza on the peel. Add your toppings to the grilled side of the pizza off the heat.

Carefully slide the topped pizza back onto the grill and cover the grill. Grill over medium-low heat until the bottom browns and the toppings cook, about 5 minutes, rotating the pizza 45 degrees once or twice for even browning.

Remove the pizza from the oven to a wire rack to cool for a minute or so, just to keep the steam from making the crust soggy. Transfer the pizza to a pizza pan or cutting board, slice, and add any finishing ingredients. I like 6 slices for this size pizza.

OPTION

You can add a pizza stone here to make your grill more like an oven. You won't really get grilled pizza that way. It'll be more like pizza baked on a grill. But some manufacturers such as KettlePizza make baking stones that have a cover assembly to trap heat and help cook the top of the pizza. Either way, preheat the stone and/or assembly directly on the grill over medium heat for at least 30 minutes. Then cook the pizza on the hot stone according to the manufacturer's directions, which usually means cooking the pizza as you would on any other baking stone, for 4 to 6 minutes without flipping it over.

PIZZA FRITTA

MAKES 1 ROUND 10- TO
11-INCH (25 TO 28 CM)
FRIED PIZZA

When I visited Pepe in Grani—Franco Pepe's hilltop shrine to Naples-style pizza—this is the first pizza he served. The dough was light, airy, crisp, and topped simply with paper-thin mortadella, buffalo ricotta, and lemon zest. It was perfect. The frying method couldn't be easier. Instead of baking the pressed-out dough in an oven, you fry it on the stovetop in a frying pan. If you prefer, you can use the Roman dough with this method. It just won't puff up quite as much. This pizza has its own special toppings because you add the toppings after the dough is completely cooked.

Vegetable oil, for frying

1 dough ball, preferably Naples Dough at 60% Hydration (page 61), about 250 grams/8.8 ounces

Toppings of your choice
(see "Options," page 110)

Flour, for dusting

Pour enough oil into a large frying pan or wok (at least 12-inch/30 cm diameter) so that the oil is at least 1 inch (2.5 cm) deep. Heat the oil to 350°F (177°C).

Let the dough warm up at room temperature for at least 1 hour or up to 4 hours. As it warms up, the dough will relax and become easier to shape.

Meanwhile, get your toppings prepped and ready to go (see "Options," page 110).

TO SHAPE THE DOUGH: The goal is to stretch the dough to a 10- to 11-inch (25 to 28 cm) circle with an even thickness across the entire surface. There are lots of ways. Here's how I usually do it. Lightly flour a work surface and a wooden pizza peel. Use a dough scraper to scrape the dough ball from the tray to the floured surface. Gently poke your fingers around the edge of the dough ball to begin forming a modest rim. The center should look thicker like a hat. Leave the rim alone and press your palm gently into the center of the hat, moving your fingers and thumb outward to begin stretching the dough away from the center (see the photos on page 95). At this point, you should have a disk of dough about 5 inches (12 cm) in diameter. Slip one hand under the disk and quickly flip it over. Repeat the poking and pressing process on the other side, poking your fingers around the edge first to make the rim and then stretching outward

with your fingers and thumb to stretch the dough from the center outward. As you work, keep your thumb against the rim.

The dough should stretch easily on the work surface. If you need to stretch it more, transfer the dough from the work surface to the backs of your hands: just quickly grab the far edge of the rim and flip the dough onto the opposite hand, and then flip it again on the back of the other hand. Keep both hands loosely closed as fists under the dough near the center. With the dough on the backs of your hands, essentially repeat the process of stretching the dough from the center outward: move your hands gently away from the center while rotating the dough around the backs of your fists. It helps to angle the dough downward slightly so it's not perfectly horizontal, which causes it to drape too quickly around the backs of your fists. Carefully and gently continue to stretch the dough until it is an evenly thin 10- to 11-inch (25 to 28 cm) circle with a modest rim. For the most even crust, I like to stretch both sides of the dough in my hands. To do that, flip the dough over on the backs of your hands by flipping it over much the same way you did when flipping it from the work surface to your hands. Of course, there are other ways to stretch the dough. Some people

CONTINUED

Caesar Pizza Fritta

twirl it up in the air. Use whatever method works best for you to create an evenly stretched circle with a modest rim. If the dough tears a hole, patch it by pulling a little dough from one side of the hole and pressing it over the hole with your thumb.

Lay the stretched dough onto the floured peel. The easiest way is to simply drape it over the peel and then remove your hands from beneath the dough. Reshape the dough round as necessary and then give the peel a quick shake to make sure the dough can slide easily.

TO FRY THE PIZZA: Slide and shake the pizza from the peel into the hot oil. Fry until golden brown on each side, 2 to 3 minutes per side, and turn with tongs. It will puff up. Use the tongs to lift the edges and make sure it cooks evenly. Adjust the heat to maintain a steady oil temperature of 350°F (177°C). When the dough is browned and firm, transfer the fried pizza shell to paper towels to drain briefly. Transfer again to a cutting board and cut into 6 pieces. Quickly divide the toppings among the pieces and serve.

OPTIONS

MORTADELLA RICOTTA: On each slice, place some thinly sliced mortadella (about 6 oz total), a dollop of ricotta, some finely grated lemon zest, chopped fresh parsley, freshly ground black pepper, and a drizzle of olive oil.

MELON AND SPECK: On each slice, layer on thinly sliced speck (about 6 oz total), finely chopped cantaloupe, shaved red onion, and olive oil.

CAPRESE: On each slice, layer on a few pieces of fresh hand-torn buffalo mozzarella (about 2 oz total), a slice of fresh tomato, a fresh basil leaf, sea salt, freshly ground black pepper, and a drizzle of olive oil.

CAESAR: Make a bagna cauda dressing by steeping 2 large garlic cloves and 5 oil-packed anchovy fillets in a small saucepan with ¾ cup extra-virgin olive oil, and ¾ cup grapeseed oil. Let it steep over medium-low heat until the garlic begins to brown lightly, about 15 minutes. Remove from the heat and let the mixture cool slightly. Discard 1 garlic clove and then pour the mixture into a blender and blend until smooth. With the blender running, gradually stream in ¾ cup whole milk. Then blend in 1 egg yolk until the mixture thickens slightly. Season with about 1½ teaspoons sherry vinegar, some sea salt, and freshly ground black pepper. Top each slice of fried pizza with julienned strips of fresh romaine lettuce, a drizzle of the bagna cauda dressing, an oil-packed anchovy fillet, a quarter of a soft-boiled egg, and some freshly grated Parmigiano-Reggiano. Delicious! You'll have some bagna cauda dressing left over. Use it as a warm dip for croutons or crudités. It keeps for several days in the fridge. Just warm it up a little before using.

PIZZA SAUCE

MAKES 1 QUART

Tomatoes, olive oil, basil and salt. What more do you need? You can blend up this sauce right in a tall 1-quart container.

1 can (28 oz) whole peeled plum tomatoes, such as La Valle, with liquid

3 tablespoons (44 ml) extra-virgin olive oil

¼ cup (21 g) packed fresh basil leaves

1 teaspoon (6 g) kosher salt

Pour everything into a blender jar or deep 1-quart container. Use a blender (stick blender or countertop) to blend everything just until a bit chunky. Short pulses are best because overblending can make this sauce thin. Use immediately or refrigerate for 4 to 5 days.

OPTIONS

For a more uniform texture without the seeds, pass the tomatoes through a food mill. In that case, chop the basil.

MUSSELS RAGU: Pour the blended sauce into a medium saucepan. Wash and debeard 1 pound (454 g) mussels (we use Prince Edward Island mussels, which are responsibly aquacultured on ropes). Toss any mussels that are already open or cracked. Add the mussels to the pizza sauce along with a pinch of salt and a generous amount of freshly ground black pepper. Cook over medium heat until the mussels open and release their juices into the sauce, 10 to 15 minutes. When the sauce smells nice and briny, de-shell the mussels, discarding the shells and reserving the mussels to top the pizza. A melon baller makes quick work of scooping a mussel from its shell. You'll have enough sauce for about six 10 to 12-inch (25 to 30 cm) pizzas. If you have leftover ragu after making pizza, toss it with cooked pasta. It keeps refrigerated for a day or two.

MARGHERITA

TOMATO, MOZZARELLA, AND BASIL

MAKES ENOUGH FOR
ONE 10- TO 12-INCH
(25 TO 30 CM) PIZZA

If you live in Naples, grabbing a margherita may be a daily activity like stopping at the coffee shop for an espresso and brioche. Elsewhere, making this pizza with its simple condiments of mozzarella and tomato, and doing it right, could be one of life's greatest endeavors.

⅓ cup (79 ml) Pizza Sauce
(page 111)

2 ounces (57 g) fresh
mozzarella cheese, torn
in bits

5 fresh basil leaves

Sea salt and freshly ground
black pepper

Extra-virgin olive oil

After shaping the pizza dough, spread the sauce on the dough in an even layer all the way to the rim. Scatter on the mozzarella and cook the pizza. After slicing, finish it with the basil leaves, a sprinkle of salt and pepper, and a drizzle of olive oil.

OPTION

CHERRY TOMATO MARGHERITA: As shown in the photo opposite, halve 6 cherry tomatoes and place them cut side up over the sauce. Bake the pizza without any cheese, and then after slicing, finish it with 2 ounces fresh buffalo mozzarella cheese, the basil leaves, salt, pepper, and oil.

Home Oven Cherry Tomato
Margherita Neapolitan Pizza

IL RE

HAND-CRUSHED TOMATO AND PARMIGIANO-REGGIANO

MAKES ENOUGH FOR ONE 10- TO 12-INCH (25 TO 30 CM) PIZZA

Marinara is my go-to pizza, but I like to add some grated Parmigiano-Reggiano before baking it. Everyone makes fun of me, saying it's not real marinara. So I came up with a name for it—The King (Il Re)—because Parmigiano-Reggiano is the king of cheeses. Sometimes, I'll even shave a little more Parm on top after the pizza comes out of the oven.

1 large clove garlic

2 tablespoons (30 ml) extra-virgin olive oil

½ cup (118 ml) Marinara Sauce (page 151)

¼ cup (25 g) freshly grated Parmigiano-Reggiano cheese

Shave the garlic paper thin on a mandoline—an inexpensive handheld one or even a truffle shaver works well. You can also use a sharp thin-bladed knife and a very steady hand. Place the shaved garlic slices in a small bowl or cup and pour in the olive oil, shaking the bowl to evenly coat the slices. Let sit at room temperature for at least 45 minutes (while the oven heats up), or up to 2 days.

After shaping the pizza dough, spread the sauce on the dough in an even layer all the way to the rim. Scatter on the garlic, and drizzle on a little of the garlic oil. Scatter on the cheese and cook the pizza.

OPTION

Instead of grating on the Parm before baking, just add a few basil leaves. When the pizza comes out of the oven, immediately shave the Parm over the top and let the cheese sweat and soften for a couple minutes. So good!

Wood Oven Il Re
Neapolitan Pizza

MAURIZIO

MOZZARELLA, PARMIGIANO-REGGIANO, ROSEMARY, AND SEA SALT

MAKES ENOUGH FOR
ONE 10- TO 12-INCH
(25 TO 30 CM) PIZZA

This pizza was originally called the Renato after Renato Riccio, the man who supplied us with the oven at our first Pizzeria Vetri. At the opening, he showed us this pizza, and we named it after him. Truth be told, he pissed me off so much on a few other jobs that we stopped using him. This pizza was my son Maurice's favorite, so I changed the name to the Maurizio. I still love ya, Renato. Thanks for the pizza!!

2 ounces (57 g) fresh mozzarella cheese, torn in bits

2 teaspoons (4 g) freshly grated Parmigiano-Reggiano cheese

Leaves from 2 sprigs rosemary

Extra-virgin olive oil, for drizzling

Sea salt and freshly ground black pepper

After shaping the pizza dough, scatter on the mozzarella, Parmigiano, and rosemary in an even layer all the way to the rim. Drizzle on some oil and cook the pizza. After slicing, finish it with salt and pepper.

Cast-Iron Maurizio
Neapolitan Pizza

COZZE

MUSSELS AND FENNEL SAUSAGE

MAKES ENOUGH FOR
ONE 10- TO 12-INCH
(25 TO 30 CM) PIZZA

Meat and seafood sometimes make perfect partners. A little sausage perks up the flavor of mild-tasting mussels. For a cool look, use this topping on the Black Naples Dough at 60% Hydration (page 62) to contrast the red sauce and orange mussels.

⅓ cup (79 ml) Mussels Ragu (page 111)

2 teaspoons (4 g) freshly grated Parmigiano-Reggiano cheese

⅓ cup (79 ml) cooked mussels from Mussels Ragu (page 111)

1½ ounces (42.5 g) loose, raw, Italian pork fennel sausage, torn in bits

Extra-virgin olive oil

Sea salt and freshly ground black pepper

1 teaspoon (1.25 g) chopped fresh Italian parsley

After shaping the pizza dough, spread the ragu on the dough in an even layer all the way to the rim. Scatter on the Parmigiano, mussels, and sausage. Cook the pizza until the sausage is no longer pink. After slicing, finish it with the oil, salt, pepper, and parsley.

POLPO

OCTOPUS, SMOKED MOZZARELLA, AND CHILI FLAKES

This pizza was on the original menu at Osteria and remains a best seller. Smoky mozzarella and crispy octopus make a killer combination.

12 ounces (340 g) baby octopus, cleaned

⅔ cup (158 ml) extra-virgin olive oil, plus some for drizzling

About ⅓ cup (79 ml) sparkling mineral water, such as San Pellegrino

1 small clove garlic, smashed

⅓ cup (79 ml) Pizza Sauce (page 111)

Pinch of red pepper flakes

2 ounces (57 g) smoked mozzarella cheese, torn in bits

Place the octopus in a small pot just big enough to hold it. Add the oil, water, and garlic, adding a little more water if necessary to cover the octopus. Bring the liquid to 180°F (82°C) over medium-high heat and then lower the heat to maintain a steady 180°F (82°C) temperature. Braise uncovered at 180°F (82°C) until the octopus is tender, about 1½ hours. Remove from the heat and let cool in the liquid. When cool, remove the octopus from the liquid and pat it dry.

Heat a heavy pan such as cast-iron over medium-high heat. When smoking hot, add the octopus and sear until both sides are darkly browned, about 1 minute per side. To get a really good sear, it helps to lay another heavy pan on top to weight down the octopus and press it into the pan. When seared, remove the octopus to a cutting board, let it cool a few minutes, and cut it into bite-size pieces.

After shaping the pizza dough, spread the sauce on the dough in an even layer all the way to the rim. Scatter on the pepper flakes and mozzarella and cook the pizza. After slicing, scatter the pieces of octopus evenly over the top and drizzle on a little oil.

OPTIONS

If your octo isn't cleaned, here's how to do it yourself: insert your fingers into the body and turn the octopus inside out. Scrape away and discard the ink sac and other innards and then rinse the body well. Turn the body right side out. Remove the eyes and black mouth, or beak, located at the center where the tentacles meet the body. Scrub the tentacles very well with rock salt, rinse, and repeat until you are sure the tentacles are clean. This process breaks down the muscle fibers a bit so the octopus becomes more tender. Set the cleaned octopus aside and discard the beak.

To make the octopus ahead of time, leave the octopus whole in the braising liquid and refrigerate it for up to 1 day. Remove the octopus from the liquid while preheating the oven and continue with the recipe.

CRUDO

PROSCIUTTO, BUFFALO MOZZARELLA, AND PARMIGIANO-REGGIANO

MAKES ENOUGH FOR
ONE 10- TO 12-INCH
(25 TO 30 CM) PIZZA

When you lay paper-thin slices of prosciutto over a hot, cheesy pizza, the meat warms up, and the fat almost melts into the crust. I love that. For something even richer, try another crudo (cured uncooked meat) instead of prosciutto, such as thin slices of lardo.

2 ounces (57 g) fresh mozzarella cheese, torn in bits

1 tablespoon (6.25 g) freshly grated Parmigiano-Reggiano cheese

Extra-virgin olive oil, for drizzling

2 ounces (57 g) buffalo mozzarella cheese, torn in bits

3 ounces (85 g) paper-thin slices Prosciutto di Parma

Flake salt, such as Maldon

Freshly ground black pepper

After shaping the pizza dough, scatter the fresh mozzarella and Parmigiano evenly over the top. Drizzle with some oil and cook the pizza. As soon as it comes out of the oven, scatter on the buffalo mozzarella. If you're starting with cold bufala, put the pizza back in the oven to take the chill off it.

Or use room-temperature bufala and it should soften from the heat of the pizza. After slicing, drape the prosciutto artfully over the softening bufala. Finish it with salt, pepper, and another drizzle of oil.

Wood Oven Crudo
Neapolitan Pizza

PEPPERONI

PEPPERONI AND TOMATO SAUCE

**MAKES ENOUGH FOR
ONE 10- TO 12-INCH
(25 TO 30 CM) PIZZA**

At the pizzeria, we use Hormel Rosa Grande pepperoni. It's not a great eating pepperoni when raw, but when cooked, it crisps up and tastes amazing!

⅓ cup (79 ml) Pizza Sauce (page 111)

2 ounces (57 g) fresh mozzarella cheese, torn in bits

2 ounces (57 g) thinly sliced pepperoni

Leaves from a few sprigs oregano

Sea salt and freshly ground black pepper

Extra-virgin olive oil, for drizzling

After shaping the pizza dough, spread the sauce on the dough in an even layer all the way to the rim. Scatter on the mozzarella and then the pepperoni and cook the pizza. After slicing, finish it with the oregano, salt, pepper, and oil.

*Wood Oven Pepperoni
Pizza al Metro*

SALSICCIA

FENNEL SAUSAGE, ROASTED FENNEL, AND TOMATO SAUCE

MAKES ENOUGH FOR
ONE 10- TO 12-INCH
(25 TO 30 CM) PIZZA

I love adding a little roasted fennel to sausage pizza. It gives you the taste of fennel two different ways. For a third way, sprinkle on some fennel pollen, a citrus- and licorice-scented "dust" collected from wild fennel. It's available online and in gourmet stores.

⅓ cup (79 ml) Pizza Sauce (page 111)

⅓ cup Roasted Fennel (below)

2 ounces (57 g) fresh mozzarella cheese, torn in bits

2 ounces (57 g) loose, raw, Italian pork fennel sausage, torn in bits

1 teaspoon (2 g) freshly grated Parmigiano-Reggiano cheese

Sea salt and freshly ground black pepper

Small fennel fronds, for garnish (optional)

After shaping the pizza dough, spread the sauce on the dough in an even layer all the way to the rim. Scatter on the fennel, mozzarella, sausage, and Parmigiano. Cook the pizza until the sausage is no longer pink. After slicing, finish it with salt and pepper and garnish with a few small fennel fronds.

ROASTED FENNEL

MAKES ABOUT 2 CUPS

1½ pounds (680 g) fennel bulbs

½ lemon

¼ cup (59 ml) extra-virgin olive oil

1 teaspoon (1.25 g) fresh thyme or oregano leaves

½ teaspoon (3 g) fine sea salt

⅛ teaspoon (0.25 g) freshly ground black pepper

⅛ teaspoon (0.25 g) red pepper flakes

Heat the oven to 500°F (260°C). Cut the fennel bulbs into quarters lengthwise, then cut out the cores from each piece. With the cores gone, cut each piece of fennel lengthwise into slices about ⅛ inch (0.3 cm) thick. You'll end up with a bunch of short fennel strips. Reserve the fennel fronds to top the pizza.

Move the fennel into a medium bowl and squeeze in the juice from the lemon (through your other hand to catch the seeds). Cut the lemon rind into 4 pieces and drop them in the bowl. Add the oil, thyme, salt, pepper, and pepper flakes.

Mix well to coat everything. Taste a piece of fennel and add any seasoning if you think it needs it.

Lay the seasoned fennel on a sheet pan in a single layer. Place in the oven and cook until the fennel is tender and lightly browned at the tips, 25 to 30 minutes, stirring now and then to prevent burning. When done, let the fennel cool on the pan. Use immediately or refrigerate in an air-tight container for up to 4 days. Reheat any leftover fennel as a vegetable side dish or mix it into pasta.

Kamado-Grilled Salsiccia
Neapolitan Pizza

ZUCCHINE

SHAVED ZUCCHINI, STRACCIATELLA, AND MINT

MAKES ENOUGH FOR ONE 10- TO 12-INCH (25 TO 30 CM) PIZZA

This pizza is all about the details. The zucchini must be shaved right before baking so it doesn't lose water and get limp. And the fresh mint leaves take this pizza from zero to sixty in a millisecond! All in all, the taste is like a fresh spring garden.

1 small zucchini, finely grated (about ¾ cup)

½ cup (50 g) freshly grated Parmigiano-Reggiano cheese, plus some for sprinkling

1 tablespoon (15 ml) extra-virgin olive oil, plus some for finishing

Sea salt and freshly ground black pepper

2 ounces (57 g) stracciatella or burrata cheese

5 or 6 fresh mint leaves

Just before baking the pizza, grate the zucchini and mix it with the Parmigiano and oil in a small bowl. Season with salt and pepper until it tastes good to you. Quickly shape your pizza dough so that water doesn't leak out of the zucchini and make the pizza soggy.

After shaping the pizza dough, quickly spread the zucchini mixture over the pizza in an even layer all the way to the rim. Sprinkle with a little more Parmigiano. Cook the pizza until it is slightly darker than usual to help drive some of the water out of the zucchini. After slicing, finish it with dollops of the stracciatella. Scatter on the mint leaves and drizzle on a little oil.

Wood Oven Zucchine
Neapolitan Pizza

GRANCHIO

FRESH CRAB AND ROASTED PEPPERS

MAKES ENOUGH FOR
ONE 10- TO 12-INCH
(25 TO 30 CM) PIZZA

When we opened a pizzeria in Washington, DC, we wanted a signature pizza that used local ingredients. The Chesapeake Bay came to mind right away. Boom! The Granchio pizza was born.

2 ounces (57 g) jumbo lump crabmeat

½ cup (170 g) finely chopped mixed roasted bell peppers (red, yellow, and green)

¼ teaspoon (0.75 g) seeded and minced Serrano chile pepper

1 tablespoon (7 g) capers (minced if large)

4 oil-packed anchovy fillets, minced

½ teaspoon (0.6 g) each minced fresh dill, tarragon, parsley, chives, and chervil

2½ tablespoons (37 ml) extra-virgin olive oil, plus some for drizzling

Juice and zest of ½ lemon

Sea salt and freshly ground black pepper

2 ounces (57 g) fresh mozzarella cheese, torn in bits

In a small bowl, mix together the crabmeat, roasted peppers, Serrano pepper, capers, anchovies, herbs, 2½ tablespoons oil, and the lemon juice and zest. Season with salt and pepper until it tastes good to you.

After shaping the pizza dough, scatter on the mozzarella. Drizzle with a little oil and cook the pizza. When the pizza comes out of the oven, let it rest for a minute before slicing. Slice and then top with the crab mixture.

OPTION

To roast whole bell peppers yourself, just put a few peppers of various colors in a pan under the heat of a wood oven or under a broiler, turning them so the skins blacken all over. When the peppers are black all over and start to slump, put them in a bowl, cover tightly, and let them steam for 15 minutes. When cool enough to handle, peel off and discard the skins, then pull out and discard the cores and seeds.

Gas-Grilled Granchio Pizza
al Metro

CACIO E PEPE

PECORINO CHEESE AND BLACK PEPPER

MAKES ENOUGH FOR ONE 10-INCH (25 CM) PIZZA

This is a very special pizza. Thanks to Roman chef Stefano Callegari for showing me the ice technique (read more about Stefano on page 9). The whole concept of using starchy water to make a sauce on pizza—just as you would with pasta—epitomizes the perfect marriage of tradition and innovation.

½ cup (70 g) coarsely crushed ice

About ¾ cup (75 g) grated Pecorino Romano cheese

Freshly ground black pepper

Extra-virgin olive oil, for drizzling

This pizza is best made with Naples Dough at 60% Hydration (page 61) because it holds a nice thick rim, which helps keep the water in the cooked pizza shell. Follow me here. Shape your pizza dough into a 10-inch (25 cm) circle with a thick rim at least ½ inch (1.3 cm) high. Shape the dough completely on your work surface because picking it up could make the dough too thin. You want the dough a little thicker across the middle than you would for a typical Naples-style pizza; hence, the smaller diameter. Spread the ice evenly across the dough and cook the pizza until it is fully baked, rotating it for even cooking. The ice will melt, leaving a shallow pool of water on the fully cooked pizza shell.

When the pizza comes out of the oven, scatter on ½ cup Pecorino Romano and shake the pizza to mix the cheese into the hot water. Some of the cheese will melt and create a creamy sauce. After slicing, finish with a little more Pecorino Romano, a generous amount of pepper, and a generous drizzle of oil.

Wood Oven Cacio e Pepe Neapolitan Pizza

CARBONARA

EGGS, PECORINO CHEESE, AND GUANCIALE

MAKES ENOUGH FOR ONE
10-INCH (25 CM) PIZZA

If this book had come out a year later, I would have tried every traditional Roman pasta dish on a pizza! This technique and topping is essentially the same as the Cacio e Pepe (page 130) but made like pasta carbonara.

2 small eggs (or 1 large egg plus 1 large egg yolk)

¼ cup (25 g) grated Pecorino Romano cheese

¼ cup (25 g) freshly grated Parmigiano-Reggiano cheese, plus some for garnish

Sea salt and freshly ground black pepper

½ cup (70 g) coarsely crushed ice

2 ounces (57 g) thinly chopped guanciale, pancetta, or other cured bacon

Extra-virgin olive oil, for drizzling

In a small bowl, use a fork to beat together the eggs, Pecorino, and Parmigiano and then season with salt and pepper. Beat well and set aside.

This pizza is best made with Naples Dough at 60% Hydration (page 61) because it holds a nice thick rim, which helps keep the water in the cooked pizza shell. Follow me here. Shape your pizza dough into a 10-inch (25 cm) circle with a thick rim at least ½ inch (1.3 cm) high. Shape the dough completely on your work surface because picking it up could make the dough too thin. You want the dough a little thicker across the middle than you would for a typical Naples-style pizza; hence, the smaller diameter. Spread the ice evenly across the dough and cook the pizza until it is fully baked, rotating it for even cooking. The ice will melt, leaving a shallow pool of water on the fully cooked pizza shell.

When the pizza comes out of the oven, pour the egg mixture into the pizza shell, and then quickly mix the egg into the hot water with a fork until creamy. Scatter on the guanciale and return the pizza to the oven. In a wood oven, keep the pizza at the mouth of the oven where the temperature is a bit lower to avoid overcooking the eggs. In a home oven, watch it carefully. Bake gently until the guanciale is cooked through and the eggs are custardy, about 2 minutes more, rotating and shaking the pizza every 30 seconds to make sure the eggs cook slowly and get custardy rather than forming firm curds in any one spot. When the eggs are custardy and barely set, remove the pizza to a cutting board. After slicing, finish with some more Parmigiano, a little salt and pepper, and a little drizzle of oil.

*Home Oven Carbonara
Neapolitan Pizza*

6

ROMAN DOUGH PIZZAS

THE LAST TIME I VISITED ROME, I HAD A FLASHBACK. I was eating pizza marinara at a little trattoria in Monteverde called Trattoria Da Cesare. The crust was so perfectly thin and crisp, it sent me right back to Los Angeles in 1991. That's where I first learned how to make pizza at Wolfgang Puck's Granita. I didn't know it then, but we were definitely making Roman-style dough. We mixed it up one night with no starter, and it was ready the next day. Sometimes we threw in a little leftover dough from the day before, and always, right at the end, we mixed in some olive oil. That's what makes Roman dough different from Naples-style dough. A little oil makes the dough softer, richer, and easier to stretch superthin. Pizza Romana tends to have almost no rim, either—very unlike the big, puffy rim on pizza Napoletana. When it bakes, that thin crust and the oil inside it make pizza Romana rich and crunchy.

Cesare's crispy marinara gave me visions of those very first pizzas I had made decades ago. As I continued eating my way around Rome, I came to fully appreciate all the different Roman pizzas in all their glory. Not every Roman pizza is round. At old-school places like Antico Forno Roscioli and Forno Campo de' Fiori, they also make superlong rectangular pizzas and load them into deep deck ovens. You buy these pizzas *al metro* (by the meter), and they cut them into smaller rectangles or squares. Sometimes they fold the rectangle of pizza in half like a book (*pizza libretto*) so you can walk down the street with it.

At home, I make a similar kind of pizza by rolling a single Roman dough ball with a rolling pin. It flattens out so easily into a nice, long oval—and you can bake it in your home oven. Personal pizza al metro!

Pizza al taglio (by the cut) is another popular pizza shape in Rome. These pizzas are baked in sheet pans and then cut to order with scissors and reheated in the oven. The toppings tend to be more adventurous, and the dough is a little thicker and puffier. When I first tasted pizza al taglio at Gabriele Bonci's Pizzarium in Rome, I fell so hard for that light, airy dough. It's crisp on the bottom yet soft and full of bubbles. I love that pizza so much I ended up devoting an entire chapter here to Pizza al Taglio (see page 165).

But, honestly, Roman dough with a little oil in it is still the kind I make most often at home. It's so easy to mix up and shape. It comes together overnight, and you can shape it by hand or roll it with a pin. You can put a couple dough balls together and bake them, split them, and fill them to make stuffed pizza. Or you can fry up little bits of Roman dough and toss them in seasoned Parmigiano-Reggiano. It's so versatile. Or maybe it's all just nostalgia for me at this point? Try the different pizzas here and decide for yourself.

WOOD OVEN PIZZA ROMANA

**MAKES ONE 12-INCH
(30 CM) ROUND PIZZA**

Making this pizza reminds me of slinging pies in the wood oven for Los Angeles celebrities at Granita. This kind of dough—with a little oil in it—gets supercrunchy in the oven. Just be careful stretching it. You want it thin but not so thin that you get a hole. I like to mix a little less water into this dough—about 57% hydration—so the pizza crust stays thin and gets really crisp.

1 dough ball, preferably
Roman Dough at 57%
Hydration (page 76), about
230 grams/8.1 ounces

Flour, for dusting

Toppings of your choice
(pages 151 to 162)

Light a wood fire on the oven floor directly where you will be cooking the pizza (for details on starting a fire, see page 15). Feed the fire until the ambient temperature in the oven is around 700°F (371°C), 1 to 2 hours. Quickly rake the fire to one side of the oven, containing it in a neat pile near the edge. Brush the cooking surface clean.

Let the dough warm up at room temperature for at least 1 hour or up to 4 hours. As it warms up, the dough will relax and become easier to shape.

Have your toppings ready to go.

TO SHAPE THE DOUGH: The goal is to stretch the dough to a 12-inch (30 cm) circle that is very thin and even across the middle with little to no rim around the edge. There are lots of ways. Here's how I usually do it. Lightly flour a work surface and a wooden pizza peel. Use a dough scraper to scrape the dough ball from the tray to the floured surface. Gently poke your fingers about ¼ inch (0.6 cm) from the edge of the dough ball all around it. The center should look thicker like a hat. Press your fingers and palm gently into the center of the hat, moving your fingers and thumb outward to begin stretching the dough away from the center

(see the photos on page 95). At this point, you should have a disk of dough about 5 inches (12 cm) in diameter. Slip one hand under the disk and quickly flip it over. Repeat the poking and pressing process on the other side, poking your fingers around the edge first, and then placing your palm on the center and gently stretching your fingers and thumb outward to stretch the dough from the center outward. As you work, gradually rotate the dough to keep it round.

For slightly stiffer dough like this, it's easiest to pick up the dough to fully stretch it. Transfer the dough from the work surface to the backs of your hands: just quickly grab the far edge of the rim and flip the dough onto the opposite hand and then slip your other hand under the dough. Keep both hands loosely closed as fists under the dough near the center. With the dough on the backs of your hands, essentially repeat the process of stretching the dough from the center outward: move your hands gently away from the center while rotating the dough around the backs of your fists. It helps to angle the dough downward slightly so it's not perfectly horizontal, which causes it to drape too quickly around the backs of your fists. Carefully and gently continue to stretch the dough until it is an evenly thin 12-inch (30 cm) circle with little to no rim. For the most even crust, I like to stretch both sides of the dough in my hands. To do that, flip the dough over on the backs of your hands by flipping it over much the same way you did when flipping it from the work surface to your hands. Of course, there are other ways to stretch the dough. You could use a rolling pin. Use whatever method works best for you to create a 12-inch (30 cm) circle that is evenly stretched as thin as possible with almost no rim. If the dough tears a hole, patch it by pulling a little dough from one side of the hole and pressing it over the hole with your thumb.

Lay the stretched dough onto the floured peel. The easiest way is to simply drape it over the peel and then remove your hands from beneath the dough. Reshape the dough round as necessary. Give the peel a quick shake to make sure the dough can slide easily.

Add your toppings. Give the peel another quick shake to make sure the dough slides easily.

TO BAKE THE PIZZA: Slide and shake the pizza from the peel onto the cooking surface. Cook until the rim is slightly puffed, the dough blisters and chars in spots, and the bottom is very crisp, 2 to 3 minutes, depending on your oven's temperature. Use a metal pizza peel to rotate the dough as necessary for even cooking.

Remove the pizza from the oven to a wire rack to cool for a minute or so, just to keep the steam from making the crust soggy. Transfer the pizza to a pizza pan or cutting board, slice, and add any finishing ingredients. I like 6 slices for this size pizza.

HOME OVEN PIZZA ROMANA

MAKES ONE 12-INCH (30 CM) ROUND PIZZA

Roman dough remains my go-to mix for pizza at home. A little oil makes it so easy to shape. It's fermented for less time so it doesn't taste quite as complex as Naples dough, but if you like thin-crust pizza, you can't go wrong. It bakes at a slightly lower temperature in a home oven, so I add a bit more water to the dough to keep it from getting too dry.

1 dough ball, preferably Roman Dough at 67% Hydration (page 78), about 250 grams/8.8 ounces

Flour, for dusting

Toppings of your choice (pages 151 to 162)

Let the dough warm up at room temperature for at least 1 hour or up to 4 hours. As it warms up, the dough will relax and become easier to shape.

Place a baking steel or stone on the upper rack of the oven 4 to 6 inches (10 to 15 cm) beneath the broiler for an electric oven or 6 to 8 inches (15 to 20 cm) beneath the broiler for a gas oven. Preheat the oven to its highest setting (usually 500° to 550°F/260° to 288°C) for 45 minutes.

Have your toppings ready to go.

When the oven is preheated and you are ready to bake pizza, open the oven door for 10 seconds if you have an electric oven. This step lets some heat escape to make sure the electric broiler will actually turn on even though the oven has reached its maximum temperature. Reset the oven to broil and preheat the broiler for 5 to 10 minutes. The next steps of shaping and topping the pizza should take only 5 to 10 minutes if your toppings are ready to go.

TO SHAPE THE DOUGH: The goal is to stretch the dough to a 12-inch (30 cm) circle that is very thin and even across the middle with little to no rim around the edge. There are lots of ways. For 67% hydration dough, you'll need a bit more flour and a gentler hand, since the dough is softer. It's best to shape it completely on your work surface. If you try to pick it up, it may tear a hole. Generously flour a work surface and a wooden pizza peel. Use a dough scraper to scrape the dough ball from the tray to the floured surface. Gently poke your fingers about ¼ inch (0.6 cm) from the edge of the dough ball all around it. The center should look thicker like a hat. Press your fingers and palm gently into the center of the hat, moving your fingers and thumb outward to begin stretching the dough away from the center (see the photos on page 95). At this point, you should have a disk of dough about 5 inches (12 cm) in diameter. Slip one hand under the disk and quickly flip it over. Repeat the poking and pressing process on the other side, poking your fingers around the edge first and then placing your palm on the center and gently stretching your fingers and thumb outward to stretch the dough from the center outward. As you work, gradually rotate the dough on the flour to keep it round. The dough should be soft enough to continue this process until it is stretched to a 12-inch (30 cm) circle that is very thin and even across the middle with almost no rim. If the dough tears a hole, patch it by pulling a little dough from one side of the hole and pressing it over the hole with your thumb.

Lay the stretched dough onto the floured peel. The easiest way is to simply drape it over the peel and then remove your hands from beneath the dough. Reshape the dough round as necessary. Give the peel a quick shake to make sure the dough can slide easily.

Add your toppings. If using soft cheese, such as fresh mozzarella, you may need to add it halfway through the baking time to keep it from overcooking and separating. Give the peel another quick shake to make sure the dough slides easily.

TO BAKE THE PIZZA: At this point, your oven should be on broil. Slide and shake the pizza from the peel onto the cooking surface. Cook until the rim is puffed, the dough blisters and chars in spots, and the bottom is crisp, 6 to 8 minutes. Use your hands or a long spatula to rotate the dough as necessary for even cooking.

Remove the pizza from the oven to a wire rack to cool for a minute or so, just to keep the steam from making the crust soggy. If you will be baking another pizza, reset the oven to its maximum temperature. Transfer the pizza to a pizza pan or cutting board, slice, and add any finishing ingredients. I like 6 slices for this size pizza.

HOME OVEN PERSONAL PIZZA AL METRO

MAKES 1 LONG OVAL
PIZZA, ABOUT 14 BY
6 INCHES (35 BY 15 CM)

Not into shaping dough rounds by hand? No problem. Just roll out the dough with a rolling pin. It looks different but tastes the same! With a baking steel or a cast-iron griddle underneath and your oven's broiler on top, the pizza comes out nice and crispy. Any of the toppings for a 12-inch (30 cm) round pizza will fit on this shape. Or use half the amount of 2 different toppings on each half of the oval—2 toppings in 1 pizza.

1 dough ball, preferably
Roman Dough at 67%
Hydration (page 78), about
250 grams/8.8 ounces

Flour, for dusting

Toppings of your choice
(pages 151 to 162)

Let the dough warm up at room temperature for at least 1 hour or up to 4 hours. As it warms up, the dough will relax and become easier to shape.

Place a large cast-iron griddle, baking steel or stone (at least 16 inches long and 8 inches wide/40 cm long and 20 cm wide) on the upper rack of the oven 4 to 6 inches (10 to 15 cm) beneath the broiler for an electric oven or 6 to 8 inches (15 to 20 cm) beneath the broiler for a gas oven. Preheat the oven to its highest setting (usually 500° to 550°F/260° to 288°C) for 45 minutes.

Have your toppings ready to go.

When the oven is preheated and you are ready to bake pizza, open the oven door for 10 seconds if you have an electric oven. This step lets some heat escape to make sure the electric broiler will actually turn on even though the oven has reached its maximum temperature. Reset the oven to broil and preheat the broiler for 5 to 10 minutes. The next steps of shaping and topping the pizza should take only 5 to 10 minutes if your toppings are ready to go.

TO SHAPE THE DOUGH: The goal is to stretch the dough to an oval about 14 inches long and 6 inches wide (35 cm long and 15 cm wide) and make it very thin and even across the middle with little to no rim around the edge. There are lots of ways. For 67% hydration dough, you'll need a bit more flour and a gentler hand, since the dough is softer. It's best to shape it completely on your work surface. If you try to pick it up, it may tear a hole. Generously flour a work surface and a large wooden pizza peel or cutting board that is at least 16 inches (40 cm) long. Use a dough scraper to scrape the dough ball from the tray to the floured surface. Use a rolling pin or your hands to stretch the dough. For a pin, lightly flour the pin and gently roll from the center outward and then again from the center outward in the opposite direction. It should roll pretty easily. To use your hands, lightly flour them and then flatten the dough under your palm. Place both palms on the dough and stretch in opposite directions. Change direction and widen the dough. The dough should be soft enough to stretch on the work surface. You can also grab the rim on opposite ends and stretch the dough that way. If it's a little stiff, pick it up, gently draping it over the backs of your closed fists, and gradually stretch your fists away from each other to form the oval. With the pin or your hands, continue stretching the dough to an oval 14 inches long and 6 inches wide (35 cm long and 15 cm wide) with an even thickness of about ¼ inch (0.6 cm). If the dough tears a hole, patch it by pulling a little dough from one side of the hole and pressing it over the hole with your thumb.

Lay the stretched dough onto the floured peel or board. The easiest way is to simply drape it over the peel or board and then remove your hands from beneath the dough. Reshape the dough into an oval as necessary. Give the peel or board a quick shake to make sure the dough can slide easily.

Add your toppings. If using soft cheese, such as fresh mozzarella, you may need to add it halfway through the baking

time to keep it from overcooking and separating. Give the peel another quick shake to make sure the dough slides easily.

TO BAKE THE PIZZA: At this point, your oven should be on broil. Slide and shake the pizza from the peel onto the cooking surface. Cook until the rim is slightly puffed, the dough blisters and chars in spots, and the bottom is crisp, 6 to 8 minutes. Use your hands or a long spatula to slightly rotate the dough as necessary for even cooking.

Remove the pizza from the oven to a wire rack to cool for a minute or so, just to keep the steam from making the crust soggy. If you will be baking another pizza, reset the oven to its maximum temperature. Transfer the pizza to a pizza pan or cutting board, slice, and add any finishing ingredients. For this pizza, I like to make 8 trapezoid slices by cutting the pizza in half lengthwise and then making 3 crosswise cuts on an angle (see photo on page 159).

OPTION

PINSA PIZZA: This classic Roman pizza has a similar oval shape but a lighter, airier texture and crisper crust from the long fermentation and mix of flours in Pinsa Dough (page 81). To make a single oval-shaped Pinsa Pizza, use 230 grams (8.1 oz) of Pinsa Dough (page 81), and shape it into an oval using your hands. Instead of stretching the dough flat on a work surface, you want to dimple it directly on a wooden pizza peel. Cut a piece of parchment at least 12 inches long and 8 inches wide (30 cm long and 20 cm wide). Place it on a wooden peel or cutting board that's at least that big or bigger. Flour the parchment. Flour your hands, and dig the dough from the bowl to the floured parchment with your hands or a dough scraper, tilting the bowl to ease out the dough. The dough will be very soft and bubbly, and you want it to stay that way. Use your fingers to gently press and dimple the dough into an oval about 12 inches long and 8 inches wide (30 cm long and 20 cm wide). This shaping technique is more pressing and dimpling than it is pulling and stretching the dough. The oval-shaped dough should look deeply dimpled all over. Heat your oven to its highest setting as directed, but put the baking steel or stone on the center rack (you won't be using the broiler). Use the parchment to slide the naked pizza from the peel or cutting board directly onto the cooking surface, keeping the parchment underneath. Cook until the pizza is puffed and very lightly browned, 5 to 7 minutes. Add your toppings then bake without the parchment for a few minutes longer to crisp the crust and to melt any cheese. This pizza is baked naked at first much like the Home Oven Pizza al Taglio (page 172). For that reason, the al Taglio toppings beginning on page 151 work best for pinsa pizza. Since pinsa pizza is a smaller personal size, use about half of the amounts called for in those toppings.

Pizza Toppings

My friend Chris Bianco is one of the people I admire the most in the world. I always leave conversations with him a little happier and with a little more hope and enthusiasm for the future. A few years ago, we were talking about one of the questions chefs get asked all the time, "What is your favorite _____?" Just fill in the blank . . . thing to cook, thing to eat, thing on the menu, place to eat other than your own restaurant, your favorite meal, knife, pan, fruit, meat, dessert. . . . people want to know it all! And now I have an answer for them:

"The best of anything is anything you like the best."

Thanks for the quote, Chris! For instance, I like marinara pizza. In general, I like minimal toppings more than a ton of them. To me, simple is beautiful and sexy and one of the hardest things to

achieve. But that's just me. The great thing about eating pizza is . . . there are no rules. There is no best. Maybe you don't like tomato. Or maybe you have to have cheese on pizza, and you will never like marinara pizza. Sure, for me, it's perfection. Does that make you an idiot because you don't agree? Of course not. What it does, however, is bring me to my second favorite Bianco quote:

"You can't argue with another man's passion."

Amen. When it comes to pizza toppings, just pick the ones that you love the most. The toppings in this book are the ones that I love the most and have played with a lot over the years. Try them, experiment with them, and most importantly, change them! Make them your own. No one can decide what you like best better than you.

Just please, no matter what you choose, choose good quality. Whether it's tomatoes, cheese, or meat, if it doesn't taste good on its own, it won't taste any better on pizza. For canned tomatoes, look for the best-quality plum tomatoes you can find. Yes, San Marzano tomatoes taste pretty good, but they're not necessarily the best. San Marzano is both a type of tomato and a region in Italy, so there are a lot of crappy tomatoes out there masquerading as San Marzano. People will tell you to always buy DOP (*Denominazione di Origine Protetta*, or protected designation of origin) San Marzanos, but again, there's no guarantee that DOP San Marzanos will taste great. Just find a brand of tomatoes you like and stick with it. At Pizzeria Vetri, we tend to use La Valle. The most important thing is that you buy *whole* canned plum tomatoes, not crushed or pureed. The best-quality tomatoes are canned whole. The seconds are what get crushed and pureed. And if you're looking for a really good variety of fresh cherry tomatoes for your pizza, try piennolos. These tomatoes are small and pointy with a great balance of acidity, minerality, and sweetness.

Whatever toppings you choose, just keep them simple. The hardest thing to teach in a kitchen is restraint. Cooks love to load everything up with more ingredients—especially in the United States, where more is more. Well, I'm here to tell you that less is more. Or as Bianco says, "Sometimes less is already too much." When cooks give me new dishes to try, the one thing I do more than any other is take out ingredients. With confidence comes restraint. And that's so important with pizza toppings. Try this: let a single flavor take center stage. You know why marinara is my go-to pizza? Because it's just tomatoes. If you can do marinara pizza correctly, I'm impressed. That's also why zucchini pizza is one of my new favorites. It's just shaved zucchini mixed with Parmigiano and olive oil. That's it. I finish it with fresh mint and bits of stracciatella cheese but nothing else. It's like eating a fresh spring garden. The mint and stracciatella are only there to enhance the main ingredient, zucchini.

Always ask yourself, "Is there too much on this pizza?" If you can't pick up a slice without the toppings falling off, the answer is yes!

One last point about toppings: make them ahead whenever you can. Have your sauce made, your cheese grated, and your vegetables cut or cooked. Set up a little station or work area with all your prepped toppings before you shape your pizza dough. If you forgot something, wait to add any toppings until right before you bake the pizza. It's better to shape the dough and let it sit naked than to let it sit there with toppings on it. Why? Because the toppings are usually wet. They can

make the pizza stick to the peel, and that makes it a pain to load the pizza into the oven. And let me tell you, if your raw pizza folds up into a jumbled mess in the oven, it will be a sad day indeed. Shape it, top it, and bake it. Do these three steps one right after the other. It's the little things!

HOME OVEN STUFFED PIZZA

MAKES ONE
12-INCH (30 CM) ROUND
STUFFED PIZZA

When I was cooking at New York City's Bella Blu in 1997, we used to give these bites away to VIPs. It's like a creamy sandwich—a great way to start a meal. You just press 2 dough balls together, shape them into a round, bake it, and then split it in half through the side so it's like two pieces of round sandwich bread. For fillings, the possibilities are endless. At Bella Blu, we filled them with creamy robiola cheese and truffle oil. Sometimes I stuff them with fontina cheese, prosciutto, and dressed arugula leaves. That combo reminds me of the sandwiches I get at the Autogrill in Italy when traveling the A4 motorway from Milan's Malpensa airport to Bergamo. Memories!

2 dough balls, preferably Roman Dough at 67% Hydration (page 78), about 500 grams/17.6 ounces total

Flour, for dusting

Fillings of your choice (see "Options," page 148)

Let the dough warm up at room temperature for at least 1 hour or up to 4 hours. As it warms up, the dough will relax and become easier to shape.

Place a baking steel or stone on the upper rack of the oven 4 to 6 inches (10 to 15 cm) beneath the broiler for an electric oven or 6 to 8 inches (15 to 20 cm) beneath the broiler for a gas oven. Preheat the oven to its highest setting (usually 500° to 550°F/260° to 288°C) for 45 minutes.

Have your fillings ready to go.

When the oven is preheated and you are ready to bake pizza, open the oven door for 10 seconds if you have an electric oven. This step lets some heat escape to make sure the electric broiler will actually turn on even though the oven has reached its maximum temperature. Reset the oven to broil and preheat the broiler for 5 to 10 minutes. The next steps of shaping and topping the pizza should take only 5 to 10 minutes if your fillings are ready to go.

TO SHAPE THE DOUGH: The goal is to combine the dough balls and stretch the dough to a 12-inch (30 cm) circle that is even across the middle with little to no rim around the edge. There are lots of ways. For 67% hydration dough, you'll need a bit more flour and a gentler hand, since the dough is softer. It's best to shape it completely on your work surface. If you try to pick it up, it may tear a hole.

Generously flour a work surface and a wooden pizza peel. Use a dough scraper to scrape the dough balls from the tray to the floured surface. Stack 1 dough ball on top of the other and press them together into 1 bigger disk of dough. Gently poke your fingers about ¼ inch (0.6 cm) from the edge of the dough ball all around it. The center should look thicker like a hat. Press your fingers and palm gently into the center of the hat, moving your fingers and thumb outward to begin stretching the dough away from the center (see the photos on page 95). At this point, you should have a disk of dough 4 to 5 inches (10 to 12 cm) in diameter. Slip one hand under the disk and quickly flip it over. Repeat the poking and pressing process on the other side, poking your fingers around the edge first and then placing your palm on the center and gently stretching your fingers and thumb outward to stretch the dough from the center outward. As you work, gradually rotate the dough on the flour to keep it round. The dough should be soft enough to continue this process until it is stretched to a 12-inch (30 cm) circle that is even across the middle with almost no rim. It should be about ½ inch (1.3 cm) thick. If the dough tears a hole, patch it by pulling a little dough from one side of the hole and pressing it over the hole with your thumb.

CONTINUED

Home Oven Prosciutto and Arugula Stuffed Pizza

Lay the stretched dough onto the floured peel. The easiest way is to simply drape it over the peel and then remove your hands from beneath the dough. Reshape the dough round as necessary. Dock the dough by poking holes all over it with a fork or a dough docker, which helps prevent it from puffing up too much in the oven. Give the peel a quick shake to make sure the dough can slide easily.

TO BAKE THE PIZZA: At this point, your oven should be on broil. Slide and shake the pizza from the peel onto the cooking surface. Cook until the dough is slightly puffed and golden brown on top, 3 to 4 minutes total. Check the dough during cooking and as it begins to puff up, use a long metal spatula or half-sheet pan to press down on the dough to keep any one bubble from puffing up and browning too much. Ideally, you want an evenly puffy and browned disk of dough. Use your hands or a long spatula to rotate the dough as necessary for even cooking.

Remove the pizza from the oven to a wire rack to cool for a minute or so, just to keep the steam from making the crust soggy. Transfer the pizza to a cutting board and use a long serrated knife to cut the cooked dough in half through the side to make two thinner dough rounds. Cut all the way around the outside edge first, gradually working the knife toward the middle until the dough is cleaved in two. Keep the knife perfectly flat at all times to avoid cutting a hole in the top or bottom crust.

Separate the two halves and open them like a book. Use a spoon or your fingers to scrape away any soft, undercooked dough from both halves. You want to scrape away and discard most of the undercooked dough. Spread or layer your cheese evenly across the bottom half of the dough (see "Options" below). Return the cheese-topped bottom half of the dough to the oven and bake just until the cheese melts, 2 to 3 minutes.

Remove the pizza to a cutting board and layer on the remaining filling ingredients. Cover with the top half of the dough and compress the sandwich very gently. Cut into 6 wedges, and add any finishing ingredients. If you will be baking another pizza, reset the oven to its maximum temperature.

OPTIONS

TRUFFLE AND ROBIOLA STUFFED PIZZA: Scatter 6 to 8 ounces sliced robiola cheese on the bottom half of the dough and sprinkle with sea salt, freshly ground black pepper, and a drizzle of the highest-quality white truffle oil. After baking, cover the melted cheese with the top half of the dough. Slice and finish it with another drizzle of truffle oil. Be sure to use real white truffle oil. There's a lot of crap out there made with some kind of truffle fragrance and no actual truffle! If you can't find real truffle oil, spread some white truffle pâté on the bottom crust instead.

PROSCIUTTO AND ARUGULA STUFFED PIZZA: Scatter 4 to 6 ounces (1 to 1½ cups) shredded fontina cheese on the bottom half of the dough. After baking, drape about 3 ounces paper-thin prosciutto slices over the melted cheese. Top with about 1½ ounces (⅓ cup) baby arugula leaves, a drizzle of high-quality aged balsamic vinegar, a drizzle of extra-virgin olive oil, and some flake salt, such as Maldon. Cover with the top half of the dough, slice, and finish it with another drizzle of olive oil.

PARMESAN FRIED DOUGH

MAKES 9 PIECES

I like fried anything. You could fry shoe leather, and it would taste good! Here's the perfect snack: just fried bits of Roman-style dough seasoned with Parmesan cheese. It perfectly captures the essence of Roman street food. If you're hanging around at a table, serve it with warm Marinara Sauce (page 151) for dipping.

1 dough ball, preferably Roman Dough at 57% Hydration (page 76), about 230 grams/8.1 ounces

Vegetable oil, for frying

1 cup (100 g) freshly grated Parmigiano-Reggiano

1½ tablespoons (4.5 g) dried oregano

½ teaspoon (1 g) red pepper flakes

¼ teaspoon (0.5 g) freshly ground black pepper

¼ teaspoon (0.7 g) garlic powder

Flour, for dusting

Let the dough sit out at room temperature for 1 hour to take the chill off.

Heat the oil in a deep fryer to 400°F (204°C). At least 2 inches (5 cm) of oil is a good depth, and a large deep pan like a wok will let you fry a bunch of these at once.

In a large bowl, mix together the Parmigiano, oregano, red pepper flakes, black pepper, and garlic powder.

When you're ready to fry, lightly flour a work surface. Use a dough scraper to scrape the dough ball from the tray to the floured surface. Lightly flour the top of the dough and then shape and pat the dough ball into a nice, thick, 8-inch (20 cm) square. Use a bench knife to cut the square like a tic-tac-toe board into 9 square pieces.

Fry the dough squares in batches. Don't crowd the fryer, or the dough will get greasy. Adjust the heat to keep the oil at a constant temperature of 400°F (204°C). Fry until the pieces are golden brown, about 2 minutes, turning with tongs as necessary. Remove from the oil with tongs or a spider strainer, let drip dry, and immediately toss the pieces with the Parmigiano mixture, coating every nook and cranny. Serve hot.

MARINARA SAUCE

MAKES ABOUT
3 CUPS (710 ML)

When I want to taste tomato on my pizza, this is my favorite sauce. Just crush up some canned plum tomatoes with oil and salt.

1 can (28 oz) whole peeled plum tomatoes, such as La Valle, drained

3 tablespoons (44 ml) extra-virgin olive oil

1 teaspoon (3 g) kosher salt

Pour everything into a large deep bowl. You'll be using your hands to crush the tomatoes into small chunks, and sometimes they squirt! A large bowl minimizes the mess. Squeeze all the tomatoes by hand until the sauce is chunky with no big tomato pieces left behind. Or, for a smoother sauce, pass the tomatoes through a food mill instead to catch the seeds. Mix everything together and use immediately or refrigerate for 4 to 5 days.

MARINARA

TOMATO SAUCE

MAKES ENOUGH FOR
ONE 10- TO 12-INCH
(25 TO 30 CM) PIZZA

This pizza is for the purist who still likes a little zest in life. It's basically a round pizza rossa (crust and tomato) plus dried oregano and sliced garlic. To be honest, this is my benchmark for great pizza. If you can nail this pizza, you can make them all.

1 large clove garlic

2 tablespoons (30 ml) extra-virgin olive oil, plus some for drizzling

½ cup (118 ml) Marinara Sauce (page 151)

⅛ teaspoon (0.125 g) dried oregano

Flake salt, such as Maldon

Freshly ground black pepper

Shave the garlic paper-thin on a mandoline—an inexpensive handheld one or even a truffle shaver works well. You can also use a sharp thin-bladed knife and a very steady hand. Place the shaved garlic slices in a small bowl or cup and pour in the oil, shaking the bowl to evenly coat the slices. Let sit at room temperature for at least 45 minutes (while the oven heats up), or up to 2 days.

After shaping the pizza dough, spread the sauce on the dough in an even layer all the way to the rim. Scatter on the oregano and garlic slices and drizzle on a little of the garlic oil. Cook the pizza. After slicing, finish it with salt, pepper, and another drizzle of garlic oil.

Wood Oven Marinara
Pizza Romana

QUATTRO FORMAGGI

FOUR CHEESE

MAKES ENOUGH FOR
ONE 10- TO 12-INCH
(25 TO 30 CM) PIZZA

The idea here is incredibly versatile. Just cheese, no sauce. One strong cheese, one melty, one grated, and one wildcard is a great formula to follow. Or, add two wild cards and make it cinque formaggi!

1 ounce (28 g) fresh mozzarella cheese, torn in bits

1 ounce (28 g) gorgonzola cheese, crumbled

1 ounce (28 g) smoked scamorza cheese, shredded

1 ounce (28 g) fontina cheese, shredded

½ ounce (14 g) freshly grated Parmigiano-Reggiano cheese (optional)

1 teaspoon (5 ml) extra-virgin olive oil

Flake salt, such as Maldon

Freshly ground black pepper

After shaping the pizza dough, scatter the mozzarella, gorgonzola, scamorza, fontina, and Parmigiano (if using) evenly over the pizza all the way to the rim. Drizzle with the olive oil and cook the pizza as directed. After slicing, finish it with salt and pepper.

*Wood Oven Quattro
Formaggi Pizza Romana*

MELANZANA

EGGPLANT AND STRACCIATELLA

MAKES ENOUGH FOR ONE 10- TO 12-INCH (25 TO 30 CM) PIZZA

Eggplant is the world's most underrated vegetable. I use it in so many ways, and it goes with some things that you would never think of . . . like chocolate! Don't worry, this isn't a dessert pizza. It's just roasted eggplant, stracciatella cheese, and fresh oregano. Super-satisfying.

½ medium eggplant (about 8 oz/227 g)

Extra-virgin olive oil, for coating pan and drizzling

Sea salt and freshly ground black pepper

⅓ cup (79 ml) Marinara Sauce (page 151)

1½ ounces (42.5 g) stracciatella cheese

Leaves from 2 sprigs fresh oregano

Preheat the oven to 500°F (260°C). Thinly slice the eggplant, with skin, into rounds about ⅛ inch (0.3 cm) thick. A mandoline is the easiest tool to use—even an inexpensive handheld one—but you could also use a sharp, thin-bladed knife and a steady hand.

Coat a sheet pan with oil and then add the eggplant slices in a single layer. Flip the slices over so they are evenly coated with oil and still in a single layer. Season the slices with salt and pepper and roast in the oven until tender but not browned, 5 to 8 minutes. Keep in mind that the eggplant will cook again on top of the pizza.

After shaping the pizza dough, spread the sauce on the dough in an even layer all the way to the rim. Arrange the eggplant slices over the top and cook the pizza. Immediately place dollops of the stracciatella evenly over the sauce in between the eggplant pieces. If it doesn't melt, give it a little top heat in your oven. After slicing, finish it with another drizzle of oil and the oregano.

PERA

FRESH PEARS AND GUANCIALE

MAKES ENOUGH FOR
ONE 10- TO 12-INCH
(25 TO 30 CM) PIZZA

Putting fruit on savory pizza adds such an unexpected flavor. Here, sliced ripe pears balance out the rich, salty taste of cured meat and savory melted provolone. I love that juxtaposition.

2 ounces (57 g) shredded
provolone cheese

½ ripe pear, such as Bosc
or Bartlett, thinly sliced
lengthwise

2 ounces (55 g) finely
chopped guanciale,
pancetta, or other cured
bacon

Extra-virgin olive oil,
for drizzling

Leaves from 2 sprigs
fresh thyme

After shaping the pizza dough, scatter on the provolone all the way to the rim. Arrange the pears over the top and scatter on the guanciale. Cook the pizza. After slicing, finish it with a little olive oil and thyme.

PATATA PESTO

POTATO AND BASIL PESTO

MAKES ENOUGH FOR
ONE 10- TO 12-INCH
(25 TO 30 CM) PIZZA

This one is like pasta Genovese on pizza. I love making it into an oval shape. For a more rustic texture, just crumble the roasted fingerlings by hand over the pizza instead of slicing them.

4 fingerling potatoes
with skins, about 4 ounces
(113 g) total

½ cup (118 ml) extra-virgin
olive oil, plus some for
potatoes and drizzling

6 tablespoons (57 g)
pine nuts

1 small clove garlic

5 cups (425 g) loosely
packed fresh basil leaves

Sea salt and freshly ground
black pepper

2 ounces (57 g) fresh
mozzarella cheese, torn
in bits

½ ounce (14 g) freshly grated
Parmigiano-Reggiano
cheese

Heat the oven to 500°F (260°C). Toss the fingerlings with a little oil on a sheet pan and roast in the oven until tender, 15 to 20 minutes. Let the potatoes cool a bit and then slice them lengthwise about ¼ inch (0.6 cm) thick. Set aside. You could even refrigerate them for a couple days. Just return them to room temperature before using.

For the pesto, put the ½ cup oil, nuts, and garlic in a small food processor and process until mostly smooth, about 1 minute. Add the basil and process to a coarse paste, about a minute more. Taste the pesto, adding salt and pepper until it tastes good to you. You should have about 1 cup pesto. Refrigerate any leftover for up to 3 days or freeze it for up to a month.

After shaping the pizza dough, spread about ¼ cup of the pesto on the dough in an even layer all the way to the rim. Scatter on the mozzarella, Parmigiano, and potatoes. Season with salt and pepper and cook the pizza. After slicing, finish it with a little more olive oil.

Home Oven Patata Pesto
Personal Pizza al Metro

LOMBARDA

FENNEL SAUSAGE, BITTO CHEESE, AND SUNNYSIDE-UP EGG

MAKES ENOUGH FOR ONE 10- TO 12-INCH (25 TO 30 CM) PIZZA

If you're ever in Bergamo, get ready to eat lots of sausage, eggs, and cheese. It's what they do. Why not put it all on pizza? This pie was on the opening menu at Osteria and is still the most requested one we make there.

⅓ cup (79 ml) Pizza Sauce (page 111)

2 ounces (57 g) shredded Bitto cheese

2¼ ounces (64 g) fresh mozzarella cheese, torn in bits

3 ounces (85 g) cotechino or loose, raw, Italian pork fennel sausage

1 egg

½ teaspoon (0.6 g) chopped fresh herbs (such as thyme, oregano, rosemary and/or parsley)

After shaping the pizza dough, spread the sauce on the dough in an even layer all the way to the rim. Scatter on the cheeses and sausage evenly over the top, leaving a little well right in the center of the pizza. Crack an egg into the center and cook the pizza. The sausage should be cooked until it is no longer pink, and the egg should be cooked until the yolk is still a little runny in the center. If you are cooking the pizza in a wood oven, you can add the egg along with the other toppings. In a home oven or other oven at 500° to 600°F (260° to 316°C), cook the pizza for a few minutes without the egg and then crack the egg into the center to avoid over-cooking the egg, since the lower oven temperature requires a longer cooking time for the pizza as a whole. After slicing, top with the herbs.

Home Oven Lombarda
Pizza Romana

PARMA

PROSCIUTTO, FONTINA, AND ARUGULA

MAKES ENOUGH FOR
ONE 10- TO 12-INCH
(25 TO 30 CM) PIZZA

Warm, fatty prosciutto and melty mozzarella and fontina cheeses need only one thing to perk them up: a lightly dressed arugula salad. It makes a fantastic combination of flavors.

2 cups (about 2 oz/57 g) packed small arugula leaves

1 tablespoon (15 ml) extra-virgin olive oil

1 teaspoon (5 ml) sherry vinegar

Sea salt and freshly ground black pepper

½ cup (66 g) fresh mozzarella cheese, torn in bits

½ cup (57 g) shredded fontina cheese

2½ ounces (71 g) paper-thin slices Prosciutto di Parma

Toss the arugula, oil, and vinegar in a small bowl. Season with salt and pepper until it tastes good to you.

After shaping the pizza dough, scatter the mozzarella and fontina over the top all the way to the rim. Cook the pizza. After slicing, finish it with the prosciutto and arugula salad.

TONNO

SICILIAN TUNA WITH SHAVED VIDALIA ONION

MAKES ENOUGH FOR
ONE 10- TO 12-INCH
(25 TO 30 CM) PIZZA

This pizza reminds me of the open-face tuna melt sandwiches I used to eat when I was a kid. Only ten times better!

⅓ cup (79 ml) Pizza Sauce (page 111)

2 ounces (57 g) fresh mozzarella cheese, torn in bits

2 ounces (57 g) Sicilian tuna packed in olive oil, drained and flaked

¼ cup (35 g) very thinly sliced Vidalia or other sweet onion

1 teaspoon (1 g) dried oregano

¼ teaspoon (0.5 g) red pepper flakes

Sea salt and freshly ground black pepper

Extra-virgin olive oil, for drizzling

After shaping the pizza dough, spread the sauce on the dough in an even layer all the way to the rim. Scatter on the mozzarella, tuna, onions, oregano, and pepper flakes. Cook the pizza. After slicing, finish it with salt and pepper and drizzle on a little oil.

7

PIZZA AL TAGLIO

IF WE'RE BEING HONEST, THEN I HAVE TO GIVE FULL DISCLOSURE.
My first love of square pie started at a very young age. But it wasn't called square pie, or pizza al taglio, and it didn't have big, airy fermentation pockets. It was called Ellio's pizza. Yup. I'm not afraid to say that it was frozen, out-of-the-box, and into-the-toaster-oven Ellio's. I would char the hell out of it. I loved it supercrispy on the edges, almost burnt. I probably downed a couple boxes a week as after-school snacks. I lived on that square pizza. Even later, when I saw round pizzas at the local pizzeria, I would always opt for a thick slice of square tomato pie. It was thicker and chewier than Ellio's, but it was all the same to me.

Yes, my tastes have become more refined as I've gotten older. I've come to appreciate all kinds of different pizzas. But I'll always have a soft spot for square pie. There's something about that thick, airy crust that moves me. And a trip to Rome a few years ago with my wife resurrected that childhood obsession. Before opening our Philadelphia trattoria Amis, we ate our way, once again, through Rome and stopped at Gabriele Bonci's Pizzarium for a slice.

Ellio's is one thing, but Pizzarium is an entirely different experience. At first glance, you see the most colorful display window you've ever seen in a restaurant. Just one look in the case tells you whether it is spring, summer, fall, or winter. The season's bounty is on full display with innovative flavor combinations like persimmons, 'nduja (spreadable salami), and ricotta in the fall; potatoes, eggs, and almonds in the spring; and green tomatoes, mango, baccala (salt cod), and bitter greens in the summer. You order whatever you want by the cut (*al taglio*), and pay for it by weight.

The beauty of the toppings draws you in, but it's the dough that keeps you coming back! Gabriele Bonci ferments his dough at a low temperature for a long time, so it develops incredible flavor. He also incorporates fresh-milled whole grain flour into the dough, adding another layer of flavor. I can't stress enough how important these two factors are in pizza dough. Yes, slow fermentation takes longer. And fresh milling does take a little extra effort. But the flavor benefits are soooo worth it.

Even if you use store-bought bread flour, you'll love al taglio dough. You just mix it with a spoon and a bowl—no stand mixer needed—and then fold it over itself a few times. No kneading! It's so simple. It's also saturated with water—about 80% hydration. All that water makes the dough puff up with nice big holes, and when it bakes, al taglio pizza comes out superlight and airy. The dough is satisfying and chewy, yet light at the same time.

Not many people talk about having a relationship with their dough. But when you mix and fold this kind of pizza dough only with your hands—instead of in a machine—that is precisely what happens. You get a feel for it. You start to know what it needs. You feel when it's a little cold and wants to be put in a warmer spot. You feel when it's too loose and needs another fold to firm it up a bit. I can tell you with 100% certainty that when you make something with only your hands, over time, you develop a relationship with it. You begin to understand the dough, and it begins to tell you things.

Quick story. When I first started making hand-mixed al taglio dough, I had trouble figuring out when to put the salt in. I tried so many different ways, and I got different results every time. The salt always affected the yeast in a different way. Finally, I did it the old-school Neapolitan way. I dissolved the salt in some water, but then I added the salt water later on. It turns out that adding the salt in the second round of folding the dough was the perfect timing. The dough told me that this was the right way. When I made the third fold, I could feel how happy the dough was. The yeast was bubbly and alive, and the gluten in the flour was starting to firm up and tighten the whole thing.

If this is your first time making pizza from scratch, I highly recommend making al taglio dough. It will give you a feel for dough in general, and it's almost impossible to screw up. The pizza itself couldn't be simpler. Just shape it and bake it on a sheet pan in your oven. Like the other pizzas in this book, choose whatever toppings you want. The toppings here make enough for 1 half-sheet pan pizza (18 by 13 inches/ 45 by 33 cm). And if you want to use one of these al taglio toppings on a 10- or 12-inch (25 or 30 cm) round pie, just use half the amount. For that matter, if you want to use any of the round pie toppings (pages 111 to 133 and 151 to 162) on an al taglio pie, just double the amounts.

HOME OVEN PIZZA ROSSA

**MAKES 1 RECTANGULAR
PIZZA, ABOUT 20 BY
12 INCHES (50 BY 30 CM)**

B.B. King is one of the greatest blues guitarists of all time, yet his solos are often one note on one string. Why is he so important to the history of the blues? For the same reason that pizza rossa is important to the history of pizza. Rossa is just pureed raw tomatoes, salt, and olive oil. It is one note—tomato—and the essence of pizza. Simplicity done right can be the highest form of sophistication, and pizza rossa done right is the B.B. King of pizza.

920 grams (2 pounds)
Al Taglio Dough at 80%
Hydration (page 80)

1 cup (237 ml) Marinara
Sauce (page 151)

Flour, for dusting

Let the dough warm up at room temperature for at least 1 hour or up to 3 hours. As it warms up, the dough will relax and become easier to shape.

Preheat the oven to 500°F (260°C) and set a large baking steel or stone (at least 22 by 13 inches/56 by 33 cm) on the middle rack with no racks above it so you have easy access to the middle rack. Preheat for at least 45 minutes.

Have the sauce ready to go.

TO SHAPE THE DOUGH: The goal is to stretch the dough into a rectangle about 20 inches long by 12 inches wide (50 by 30 cm) with an even thickness across the entire surface. There are lots of ways. Here's how I usually do it. Generously flour a large rectangular wooden pizza peel or cutting board that's at least 22 inches long by 13 inches wide (56 by 33 cm). If you're nervous about transferring the dough to the oven, cut a piece of parchment with slightly larger dimensions than the pizza peel or cutting board and place the parchment on the peel or board. Flour the parchment. Use a dough scraper to scrape the dough from the bowl and transfer it to the floured surface. Lightly flour your hands and then gently flatten the dough under your palms, dimpling, pressing, and stretching it in opposite directions. The dough should be soft enough to easily stretch on the work surface. You can also grab the edge on opposite ends

and stretch the dough that way. Continue stretching the dough to a rectangle about 20 inches long by 12 inches wide (50 by 30 cm) with an even thickness of about ¼ inch (0.6 cm). If it's difficult to stretch, let it rest a few minutes and stretch it again. When fully stretched, give the peel or board a quick shake to make sure the dough can still slide on it.

TO BAKE THE PIZZA: Spread the sauce on the dough, leaving about a ¼-inch (0.6 cm) border of dough all around the edge. Slide and shake the pizza from the peel or board onto the steel or stone with the parchment still in place, if using. Bake until the sauce seeps into the dough a bit and the dough is golden brown and puffed on the edges, 10 to 12 minutes. Some darker spots on the dough are okay but you don't want burnt and blistered dough in this pizza. Slightly rotate the dough as necessary for even cooking. If using parchment, remove the parchment halfway through baking to prevent the parchment from scorching.

Remove the pizza from the oven to a cutting board and slice. I like to cut the entire pizza in half lengthwise, then make 6 or 7 crosswise cuts to make rectangles.

CONTINUED

*Home Oven Pizza Rossa
baked in a sheet pan*

OPTIONS

The long rectangular shape of this pizza is similar to what you find in Rome, where pizza rossa is baked in deep deck ovens. If you don't have a large baking steel or stone for your home oven, shape the dough on an oiled half-sheet pan (18 by 13 inches/45 by 33 cm) instead and then bake it right in the pan as shown on page 168. The pizza will be slightly thicker but still delicious.

PIZZA BIANCA: Instead of using marinara sauce, just drizzle the pressed-out dough with olive oil and flake salt, such as Maldon.

STUFFED PIZZA BIANCA: Make a Pizza Bianca and cut it into rectangles. Then cut each rectangle through the side to open it up like a book. Layer mortadella, prosciutto cotto, fresh mozzarella, or your favorite fillings on the bottom half and then put on the top half. For a twist on this idea using focaccia dough, see Focaccina (page 220).

Home Oven Pizza Bianca

The Great Cheese Debate

What is the best cheese for pizza? If you like marinara pizza—none!—because it doesn't have any cheese. Forget about "the best" pizza cheese. Sure, you can make fresh cow's milk mozzarella (*fior di latte*) yourself, but my recommendation is to try a bunch of different fresh mozzarellas and find the maker or brand that you like the most. You see, some guys make their mozzarella wetter than others. Maybe you like it that way. Personally, I like it a little drier, so the pizza doesn't get too soupy. For the Naples-style pizzas at Pizzeria Vetri, we actually let our mozzarella chill for a bit to keep the cheese from leaking out too much moisture when it cooks. We also found out when testing Naples-style pizzas in home ovens that fresh mozzarella sometimes overcooks and separates from the long cooking time under the broiler. With that method, depending on your cheese and the heat of your oven, you may want to add your fresh mozzarella halfway through the bake time to make sure the crust puffs up nice and big, but the cheese doesn't overcook.

So many variables come into play. Some of my pizzas don't even use fresh mozzarella. Sometimes, I use shredded whole-milk mozzarella, which is chilled even longer so it's even drier and easier to shred. Does that make this cheese any worse than fresh mozzarella? No! It's just drier. I mostly use shredded mozzarella on pizza *al taglio*. These sheet pan pizzas are bigger and thicker, and when you slice them with scissors, the drier mozzarella just cuts better. Yes, we also use traditional Italian mozzarella di bufala. Made from the milk of water buffalos, bufala is even softer and wetter than cow's milk mozzarella. It also tastes tangier. Bufala is more expensive, so we save it for special pies. It's so wet that we usually add it after the pizza comes out of the oven.

For hard cheese, Parmigiano-Reggiano is the king. I don't think anyone will dispute you on that. It's my go-to grating cheese, but we use it so much at Pizzeria Vetri that it does get pricey. Sometimes we'll finish pizzas or calzones with a sprinkle of Grana Padano instead. Grana tastes *slightly* less complex than Parm, but it's still an excellent grating and finishing cheese. When we want a little more oomph, we'll use Pecorino Romano, which is made with sharper-tasting sheep's milk. Sometimes we mix Parmigiano and Pecorino for both richness and sharpness. Do what makes you happy!

HOME OVEN PIZZA AL TAGLIO

MAKES 1 HALF-SHEET
PAN PIZZA
(18 BY 13 INCHES/
45 BY 33 CM)

If you're new to making pizza, give this one a shot. It's baked in a pan, so you don't have to handle the dough much, and it bakes in a 500°F (260°C) oven, about the same temperature used for pizza al taglio in Rome. It's pretty foolproof, and the dough puffs up like focaccia with a light, airy crumb. The truth is, I've fallen in love with this dough and this pizza because it's so easy and delicious.

920 grams (2 pounds)
Al Taglio Dough at 80%
Hydration (page 80)

Olive oil, for the pan

Flour, for dusting

Pizza Al Taglio Toppings
(pages 174 to 190)

Let the dough warm up at room temperature for at least 1 hour or up to 3 hours. As it warms up, the dough will relax and become easier to shape.

Set a baking steel or stone on the center rack of the oven and heat the oven to 500°F (260°C) for 45 minutes. Oil a half-sheet pan (18 by 13 inches/45 by 33 cm).

TO SHAPE THE DOUGH: Generously flour a work surface and your hands. Dig the dough from the bowl to the floured surface with your hands or a dough scraper, inverting the bowl to ease out the dough. The dough will be very soft and bubbly, and you want it to stay that way. Use your fingers to gently press the dough from the outside edge toward the center, going all the way around the edge first, working your way toward the center. The final dough shape will be rectangle, so press the dough into that shape. This shaping technique is more pressing and dimpling than it is pulling and stretching the dough. Keep pressing and dimpling the dough from the outside edge toward the center until the dough is completely dimpled out to a rectangle roughly the size of the half-sheet pan. Add more flour to your hands as necessary. The dough is soft and pliable, so the whole process takes only 5 minutes or so.

Carefully slip your hands beneath the dough, separating them to opposite ends of the dough, and then quickly lift and move the dough onto the oiled pan. Press and dimple the dough to fit into the pan all the way to the edges. Then pat it gently or stretch it here and there to eliminate most of the dimples and make an even layer of dough.

Add your toppings and get them to within ¼ inch (0.6 cm) of the outside edges. You don't really want much of a rim in this style of pizza.

TO BAKE THE PIZZA: Bake for 10 minutes. Add any other toppings you may need to add and then rotate the pan and bake until the pizza is puffed and golden brown on the edges, about 10 minutes more.

Remove the pizza from the oven and add any finishing ingredients. Then cut the pizza into pieces with scissors, the traditional Roman way. Cutting on the pan with a pizza wheel or knife would scar the pan and dull your blade. You could slide the whole pizza onto a large cutting board and wheel-cut it there. Either way, out of a half-sheet pan, I like to get 12 rectangular pieces. To do that, cut the entire pizza in half lengthwise and then make 6 crosswise cuts.

OPTION

Pizza is always best served fresh and hot, but you can parbake this pizza up to 8 hours ahead of time. Just bake it without any toppings for the first 10 minutes. Let it cool, then cover and chill the pizza for up to 8 hours. When ready to finish baking it, say, for a pizza party that night, just set out your toppings so everyone can make their own pizza. Cut rectangular sections of the parbaked dough with scissors and let the pizza sit at room temperature for 30 to 45 minutes. Have each person top a section of the parbaked pizza and then finish baking the pieces of pizza in the pan for the final 10 minutes or so.

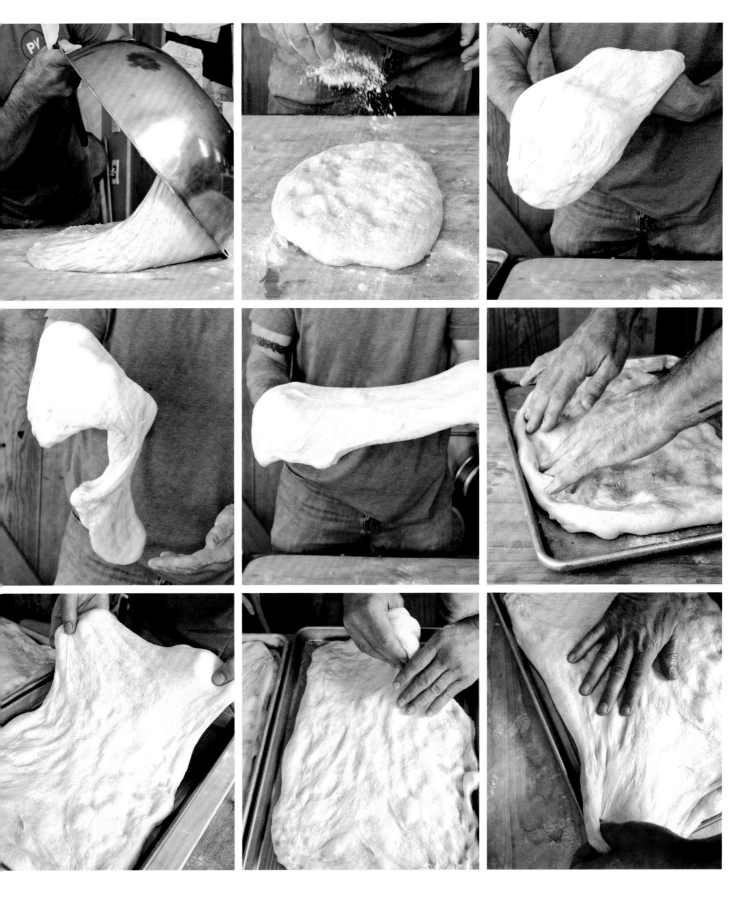

MARGHERITA AL TAGLIO

TOMATO, MOZZARELLA, AND BASIL

MAKES ENOUGH FOR
1 HALF-SHEET PAN PIZZA
(18 BY 13 INCHES/
45 BY 33 CM)

What can I say? Tomato, mozzarella, and basil work well on any pizza. Margherita is like the diamond stud earring of pizzas: timeless, classic, and universally loved. Fresh tomatoes and mozzarella di bufala make it even more special. Just be sure to put the bufala on the pizza after it comes out of the oven. With great ingredients and great technique, you just can't go wrong.

1½ pounds (680 g) fresh tomatoes, cored and sliced ¼ inch (0.6 cm) thick

¼ cup (21 g) packed fresh basil leaves

12 ounces (340 g) buffalo mozzarella cheese, torn in bits

Extra-virgin olive oil, for drizzling

Flake salt, such as Maldon

Freshly ground black pepper

Arrange the tomatoes over the dough, overlapping them slightly. Bake for 10 minutes and then rotate the pan and bake until puffed and golden brown on the edges, about 10 minutes more.

Remove the pizza from the oven and immediately scatter on the basil and mozzarella. Let the pizza sit in the pan until the cheese melts, about 5 minutes. Drizzle on some olive oil and season with salt and pepper. Cut with scissors.

CACIO E PEPE AL TAGLIO

PECORINO CHEESE AND BLACK PEPPER

MAKES ENOUGH FOR
1 HALF-SHEET PAN PIZZA
(18 BY 13 INCHES/
45 BY 33 CM)

Traditional Roman cacio e pepe is just Pecorino cheese and black pepper. This version takes some liberties by adding Parmesan and mozzarella into the mix. If you really want to go nuts, serve it with Marinara Sauce (page 151) on the side for dipping.

2¾ cups (284 g) grated Pecorino Romano cheese

10 ounces (284 g) shredded whole-milk mozzarella cheese

¾ cup (71 g) freshly grated Parmigiano-Reggiano cheese

1 tablespoon (7 g) freshly ground black pepper

Mix all the cheeses together and scatter half of the mixture over the dough in an even layer. Bake for 10 minutes and then scatter on the remaining half of the cheese mixture. Return to the oven and bake until puffed and golden brown on the edges, about 10 minutes more. Remove the pizza from the oven and grind some pepper over the top. Cut with scissors.

ZOLA AL TAGLIO

SPECK WITH RADICCHIO, APPLES, AND GORGONZOLA

MAKES ENOUGH FOR
1 HALF-SHEET PAN PIZZA
(18 BY 13 INCHES/
45 BY 33 CM)

Speck is cold-smoked prosciutto from Italy's northern Alto Adige region. It has a strong juniper aroma, but you could use prosciutto di Parma if you want. It just won't taste like smoke and juniper. Try pairing this pizza with a Negroni in the fall.

12 ounces (340 g) radicchio or Belgian endive

4 teaspoons (20 ml) honey

2 tablespoons (30 ml) white balsamic vinegar

⅓ cup (79 ml) extra-virgin olive oil, plus some for drizzling

Sea salt and freshly ground black pepper

1½ cups (170 g) cored and thinly sliced apples, with peel

9½ ounces (269 g) crumbled gorgonzola

¼ cup (15 g) packed small fresh parsley leaves

5 ounces (142 g) thinly sliced speck

Slice the radicchio very thin, about ⅛ to ¼ inch (0.3 to 0.6 cm) thick. Whisk together the honey, 1½ tablespoons of the vinegar, and ¼ cup of the oil in a small bowl. Add the radicchio and toss to coat. Season with salt and pepper until it tastes good to you.

Arrange the radicchio over the dough in an even layer. Bake for 10 minutes and then rotate pan and bake until puffed and golden brown on the edges, about 10 minutes more.

Meanwhile, toss the apples with the gorgonzola, parsley, remaining 1⅓ tablespoons olive oil, and remaining ½ tablespoon vinegar. Season with salt and pepper until it tastes good to you.

Remove the pizza from the oven and top with the apple-gorgonzola mixture and speck. Drizzle with a little oil and then cut with scissors.

Home Oven Zola Pizza al Taglio

PANNOCCHIA AL TAGLIO

SWEET CORN, SHISHITO PEPPERS, AND BUFFALO MOZZARELLA

**MAKES ENOUGH FOR
1 HALF-SHEET PAN PIZZA
(18 BY 13 INCHES/
45 BY 33 CM)**

When sweet corn is in season, I love it on pizza. But that is the key. The corn must be superfresh. With roasted whole green shishito peppers, this pizza is a looker, too. Creamy mozzarella di bufala takes it over the top.

4 large ears fresh corn on the cob

12 ounces (340 g) shishito peppers, stems removed

3 tablespoons (44 ml) extra-virgin olive oil, plus some for drizzling

Sea salt and freshly ground black pepper

¾ cup (71 g) freshly grated Parmigiano-Reggiano cheese

9½ oz (269 g) buffalo mozzarella cheese, torn in bits

7 tablespoons (21 g) chopped fresh chives

Preheat the oven to 550°F (288°C) or 500°F (260°C) with convection on if you have it.

Shuck the corn and place the cobs on a large baking sheet. Place the whole peppers on another baking sheet. Drizzle the oil over everything and then rub the oil into the corn and peppers until they are completely coated. Season the corn and peppers all over with salt and pepper, making sure the peppers are in a single layer.

Roast the corn and peppers on the baking sheets until lightly charred in spots, turning a few times for even cooking. The peppers will be done first, 6 to 8 minutes total, and the corn next, about 10 to 15 minutes total. Leave the peppers whole. Remove the roasted corn to a cutting board and let cool. When cool enough to handle, cut the kernels from the cobs with a sharp knife.

Scatter the corn kernels and peppers evenly over the dough and then scatter on the Parmigiano. Bake for 10 minutes and then rotate the pan and bake until puffed and golden brown on the edges, about 10 minutes more.

Remove the pizza from the oven and immediately top with the mozzarella and chives. Let stand until the mozzarella melts a bit. Cut with scissors.

SALSICCIA AL TAGLIO

FENNEL SAUSAGE AND ROASTED PEPPERS

MAKES ENOUGH FOR
1 HALF-SHEET PAN PIZZA
(18 BY 13 INCHES/
45 BY 33 CM)

Savory sausage and sweet roasted peppers were made for each other. A little ground fennel seed and fresh rosemary make those two ingredients even happier together.

3 bell peppers (red, yellow, and green), about 1½ pounds (680 g) total

3 tablespoons (44 ml) extra-virgin olive oil, plus some for drizzling

Sea salt and freshly ground black pepper

2½ cups (591 ml) Marinara Sauce (page 151)

8 ounces (227 g) loose, raw, Italian pork fennel sausage, torn in bits

9½ ounces (269 g) shredded whole-milk mozzarella cheese

Leaves from 2 large sprigs fresh rosemary

½ teaspoon (1.5 g) ground fennel seed

Preheat the broiler and position a rack 4 to 6 inches (10 to 15 cm) below it.

Rub the bell peppers with oil on a rimmed baking sheet and then broil the peppers on the baking sheet until the skins are bubbly and charred in spots, 10 to 15 minutes, turning a few times.

Transfer the peppers to a bowl, cover tightly with plastic wrap, and let steam until they are cool enough to handle, 10 to 15 minutes. Peel off the skins with your fingers and drain off any liquid. Pull out and remove the cores and seeds and then cut the peppers lengthwise into long ½-inch (1.3 cm)-wide strips. Season the strips with salt and pepper. You'll have 2½ to 3 cups roasted peppers.

Spread the sauce evenly over the dough. Top with small bits of sausage and the roasted peppers in an even layer. Drizzle some oil over the top and grind on some more pepper.

Bake for 10 minutes and then remove the pan from the oven and scatter on the mozzarella. Return to the oven and bake until puffed and golden brown on the edges, about 10 minutes more.

Remove the pizza from the oven and scatter on the rosemary and fennel seed. Cut with scissors.

PROSCIUTTO AND ARUGULA AL TAGLIO

PROSCIUTTO AND ARUGULA

MAKES ENOUGH FOR
1 HALF-SHEET PAN PIZZA
(18 BY 13 INCHES/
45 BY 33 CM)

For this pizza, I like to warm up the prosciutto and arugula for a minute in the oven. It crisps up the prosciutto and wilts the arugula, giving the pizza a really interesting texture. Try this one alongside the Naples Crudo (page 121) and compare notes.

2 ¼ cups (532 ml) Marinara Sauce (page 151)

8 ounces (227 g) shredded whole-milk mozzarella cheese

2 ⅓ cups (71 g) packed arugula leaves

5 ounces (142 g) thinly sliced prosciutto

2 tablespoons (30 ml) extra-virgin olive oil

Spread the sauce evenly over the dough. Bake for 10 minutes and then rotate the pan and bake until puffed and lightly browned on the edges, another 8 to 9 minutes.

Remove the pizza from the oven and scatter on the mozzarella, arugula, prosciutto, and oil. Return to the oven just until the arugula wilts and the prosciutto begins to crisp up, 1 to 2 minutes. Remove from the oven and cut with scissors.

Home Oven Prosciutto and Arugula Pizza al Taglio

ANCHOVY PECORINO AL TAGLIO
ANCHOVIES AND PECORINO CHEESE

MAKES ENOUGH FOR
1 HALF-SHEET PAN PIZZA
(18 BY 13 INCHES/
45 BY 33 CM)

I love the simplicity of Roman flavors. Anchovies and pecorino—boom! You don't need anything else except maybe a little olive oil and parsley to top it off. For an interesting look, use a mix of anchovy fillets . . . white and dark, oil-packed and salted.

About ⅓ cup (79 ml)
extra-virgin olive oil

One 12-ounce (340 g) chunk
Pecorino Romano cheese

12 ounces (340 g)
anchovy fillets

Freshly ground black pepper

2 tablespoons (8 g)
chopped fresh parsley

Drizzle about ¼ cup oil all over the dough. Use a hand-held mandoline or vegetable peeler to shave thin pieces of Pecorino over the dough until it is completely covered, except for about ¼ inch (0.6 cm) all around the edge. Use about half of the total amount of Pecorino.

Bake for 10 minutes and then rotate the pan and bake until puffed and golden brown on the edges, about 10 minutes more.

Remove the pizza from the oven and immediately grate the remaining Pecorino over the top. Cut with scissors and then arrange the anchovies on each piece. Finish with another drizzle of olive oil, pepper, and parsley.

OPTION

If you use whole salted anchovies, fillet them by rinsing off the salt under cold running water. Pull off the dorsal fin and reach a fingertip into the seam under the removed fin to split the fish in two. Grab the tail and use it to lift the backbone away from the body. Run your fingers along the inside of each fillet to remove any more tiny bones, rinsing the fillets under the water. Pat dry before using.

Home Oven Anchovy
Pecorino Pizza al Taglio

ZUCCA AL TAGLIO

BUTTERNUT SQUASH WITH CRISPY SAGE AND TALEGGIO

MAKES ENOUGH FOR
1 HALF-SHEET PAN PIZZA
(18 BY 13 INCHES/
45 BY 33 CM)

There are so many ways to use squash. When you put raw slices of butternut squash on raw dough with some butter, sage, and Parmigiano, the squash bakes right into the pizza. A little Taleggio cheese melted over the top sends it home. If you don't have butternut squash, use sweet potato instead.

15 ounces (425 g) peeled and very thinly sliced butternut squash (about ¼ of a medium-size squash)

3 tablespoons (43 g) butter

¼ cup (21 g) small fresh sage leaves (or chopped if large)

⅔ cup (67 g) freshly grated Parmigiano-Reggiano

8 ounces (227 g) sliced Taleggio cheese

Freshly ground black pepper

It's easiest to cut off a chunk of squash, peel it with a sharp Y-shaped vegetable peeler, then slice the squash into super-thin rounds on a mandoline. You could also use a knife, but each slice should be no more than ⅛ inch (0.3 cm) thick.

Spread the squash evenly over the dough, overlapping the slices to fit. Top with bits of butter, sage, and Parmigiano in an even layer. Bake for 10 minutes and then rotate the pan and bake until puffed and golden brown on the edges, about 10 minutes more.

Remove the pizza from the oven and immediately top with the Taleggio and several grindings of pepper. Let stand until the Taleggio melts a bit. Cut with scissors.

Home Oven Zucca Pizza al Taglio

PEPPERONI AL TAGLIO
PEPPERONI AND TOMATO SAUCE

MAKES ENOUGH FOR
1 HALF-SHEET PAN PIZZA
(18 BY 13 INCHES/
45 BY 33 CM)

This pizza reminds me of a big old-school Sicilian pepperoni pie—only better! It's a little different from the Naples-style pepperoni topping because we use hand-crushed marinara sauce and shredded mozzarella instead of blended pizza sauce and fresh mozzarella.

2¼ cups (532 ml) Marinara Sauce (page 151)

13 ounces (369 g) shredded whole-milk mozzarella cheese

8 ounces (227 g) thinly sliced pepperoni

1 tablespoon (15 ml) extra-virgin olive oil

Spread the sauce evenly over the dough. Scatter on the mozzarella and then the pepperoni. Bake for 10 minutes and then rotate the pan and bake until the pepperoni starts to crisp up and the pizza is puffed and golden brown on the edges, about 10 minutes more.

Remove the pizza from the oven and drizzle with a little oil. Cut with scissors.

DELICATA GUANCIALE AL TAGLIO
DELICATA SQUASH WITH GUANCIALE

MAKES ENOUGH FOR
1 HALF-SHEET PAN PIZZA
(18 BY 13 INCHES/
45 BY 33 CM)

Shaped like zucchini, delicata squash are available in the fall, and they taste like candy! You could also use spaghetti squash or sweet dumpling, a more squat shape. Either way, you can eat these squash skins and all. I like them sautéed with cinnamon, nutmeg, ginger, and honey until they are practically charred.

3 delicata squash (about 3½ lbs/1.6 kg)

3 tablespoons (28 g) unsalted butter

3 tablespoons (44 ml) extra-virgin olive oil, plus some for drizzling

Sea salt and freshly ground black pepper

⅛ teaspoon (0.3 g) ground cinnamon

⅛ teaspoon (0.3 g) ground nutmeg

⅛ teaspoon (0.3 g) ground ginger

2 tablespoons (30 ml) honey

13 ounces (369 g) shredded whole-milk mozzarella cheese

6 ounces (170 g) chopped guanciale, pancetta, or other cured bacon

Leaves from 5 sprigs fresh oregano

Cut each squash in half lengthwise and then scrape out and discard the seeds. Slice the squash crosswise into half-moons about ¼ inch (0.6 cm) thick, leaving on the skin.

Melt the butter and oil in two large sauté pans over medium-high heat (you want both butter and olive oil in each pan). When hot and bubbly, divide the squash between the pans, toss to coat, and cook for 1 to 2 minutes, tossing occasionally. Season with salt and pepper and then add the cinnamon, nutmeg, and ginger. Add the honey, tossing to coat the squash, and cook until the squash begins to caramelize, a minute or so, trying to keep the squash in a single layer. Add a splash of water if necessary to loosen the squash from the pan and continue cooking until the squash is tender and nicely caramelized, adding a little more water as needed, 1 to 2 minutes. Remove from the heat and set aside.

Scatter the cheese and guanciale evenly over the dough. Bake for 10 minutes and then rotate the pan and bake until puffed and golden brown on the edges, about 10 minutes more.

Remove the pizza from the oven and top with the squash in an even layer. Scatter on the oregano and drizzle with olive oil. Cut with scissors.

PATATA MOZZARELLA AL TAGLIO
POTATO AND MOZZARELLA

MAKES ENOUGH FOR
1 HALF-SHEET PAN PIZZA
(18 BY 13 INCHES/
45 BY 33 CM)

You could use fingerlings here, but I prefer russet potatoes. They crisp up better in the oven. Just make sure you put olive oil all over the potatoes so they get nice and brown. You'll be happy you did!

2 russet potatoes with skins (about 1½ lbs/680 g)

¼ cup (59 ml) extra-virgin olive oil, plus some for drizzling

2 tablespoons (5.5 g) coarsely chopped fresh rosemary

Sea salt and freshly ground black pepper

13 ounces (369 g) shredded whole-milk mozzarella cheese

Put the potatoes in a medium saucepan and cover with 1 inch (2.5 cm) of water. Cover the pan, bring to a boil over high heat, and then boil until a knife slides in and out of the potatoes easily, 25 to 30 minutes. Remove the potatoes from the water and let cool. When cool enough to handle, peel off and discard the skins.

Put the potatoes in a bowl and break them up into bite-size chunks with your hands. Stir in the oil and rosemary and season generously with salt and pepper.

Scatter the mozzarella evenly over the dough. Scatter the potato chunks over the cheese and drizzle on a little more oil to make sure they will crisp up nicely. Bake for 10 minutes and then rotate the pan and bake until puffed and golden brown on the edges, about 10 minutes more.

Remove the pizza from the oven and finish with a little more oil, salt, and pepper. Cut with scissors.

Home Oven Patata Mozzarella Pizza al Taglio

CALVOFIORE AL TAGLIO

CAULIFLOWER AND CACIOCAVALLO CHEESE

MAKES ENOUGH FOR
1 HALF-SHEET PAN PIZZA
(18 BY 13 INCHES/
45 BY 33 CM)

If you like roasted cauliflower, you'll love this pizza. It's topped with a lightly dressed endive salad for fresh crunch. For something a little different, you can make a kale salad instead. Pistachios and raisins in that version add some amazing texture (see the Option and the photo).

1 pound (454 g) small cauliflower florets

¼ cup (59 ml) extra-virgin olive oil, plus some for escarole

Sea salt and freshly ground black pepper

½ head escarole or curly endive, rinsed

½ teaspoon (2.5 ml) red wine vinegar

11 ounces (312 g) grated caciocavallo cheese

¾ cup (71 g) freshly grated Parmigiano-Reggiano cheese

1¾ teaspoons (3.5 g) red pepper flakes

½ cup (14 g) fresh Italian parsley, chopped

Preheat the oven to 500°F (260°C). If you have a whole head of cauliflower, turn it upside down and trim the florets from the core, going all around the core. Repeat with any large florets so you're left with 1 pound of small florets.

Rub the cauliflower all over with olive oil and then season with the salt and pepper. Roast on a baking sheet until tender, 10 to 12 minutes.

Meanwhile, cut the escarole lengthwise into strips. Toss with a little olive oil and the vinegar. Mix together the caciocavallo and Parmigiano.

Scatter the roasted cauliflower and cheese mixture over the dough and then season with black pepper. Bake for 10 minutes and then rotate the pan and bake until puffed and golden brown on the edges, about 10 minutes more.

Remove the pizza from the oven and scatter on the pepper flakes and parsley. Cut with scissors and top with the escarole.

OPTION

SHAVED CAULIFLOWER AL TAGLIO: Shave the cauliflower paper thin on a mandoline—even an inexpensive handheld one. Lay three-fourths of the shaved cauliflower evenly on the dough and drizzle with oil, salt, and pepper. Then scatter on the cheeses. Bake the pizza and skip the escarole. Instead, while the pizza bakes, toss 4 cups (120 g) baby kale leaves with the remaining one-fourth of the shaved cauliflower, ½ cup (75 g) chopped pistachios, ⅓ cup (50 g) golden raisins, 3 tablespoons (44 ml) olive oil, 2 teaspoons (10 ml) sherry vinegar, salt, and pepper. When the pizza is finished baking, cut it with scissors and scatter on the kale mixture.

Home Oven Calvofiore
Pizza al Taglio

8

CALZONES AND ROTOLOS

EVERYONE KNOWS THE CALZONE. You take a dough round and make a kind of folded pizza with less sauce and more cheese. But rotolo is something completely different. It takes pizza dough in an entirely new direction.

Like a lot of the best dishes, the rotolo was kind of an accident. We were getting ready to open Pizzeria Vetri in 2013, and we were thinking that we needed to have something original, something a little esoteric that you wouldn't find at any other pizzeria. We had traveled around Italy that year and had seen lots of interesting shapes and sizes and "mini" this and that but nothing completely out of the ordinary.

When we got back to Philadelphia, we let our minds think on it for a bit. It was June, and we had to focus on the Great Chefs Event. This event has become such an important part of our lives. We invite forty amazing chefs from across the country to cook food and help raise money for two local nonprofits that benefit kids: Alex's Lemonade Stand, which raises awareness about pediatric cancer, and Vetri Community Partnership, which provides healthy school lunches and nutrition education to kids in Philly. We're so humbled to say that the event raises more than half a million dollars every year, and it's been going for more than twelve years now. It's just incredible!

We have a pretty kick-ass after party, too. A few years back, we somehow got the idea to make a giant mortadella (large, smooth sausage) for the party. And I mean giant! The mortadella-making process itself has taken on a life of its own. We started with a fifty-pound mortadella and cooked it in a big tub with sous vide circulators. Over the years, we got the mortadella up to more than three hundred pounds. Eventually, we had to cook it in an unused fermentation tank at Victory Brewing Company.

Anyway, it was June, the Great Chefs Event had just ended, and we had an abundance of mortadella left over. We were at Amis, our Philadelphia trattoria, tweaking the menu for Pizzeria Vetri and playing around with some Naples dough. Brad Spence, the chef at Amis, said, "I'm gonna make something." He thought for a second and then said, "What if we did a cinnabun but rolled it up with mortadella and ricotta instead of cinnamon and sweet stuff?" My face lit up! He grabbed a couple dough balls and went at it. Boom! The mortadella rotolo was born—a sort of pizza roll stuffed with mortadella, ricotta, and pistachio pesto.

Since that day, different rotolos and variations have popped up here and there, but the original mortadella and ricotta with pistachio pesto is still near and dear to my heart. Like Cacio e Pepe pizza, it's the perfect marriage of tradition and innovation . . . a classic flavor combination thrown into a whole new light. It's the kind of thing that really inspires me.

The next time you're staring at a ball of raw pizza dough, think to yourself, what else can I make with this? How can I shape this differently? Look at it like Play-Doh. Let your imagination run wild. Mold it like clay and invent something new!

WOOD OVEN CALZONE

MAKES ONE 10- TO 12-INCH (25 TO 30 CM) HALF-MOON CALZONE

Wood ovens can get blazing hot. They're great for leopard spotting on pizza Napoletana. For calzones, they're a little trickier. You don't want to bake up a blackened football! The solution? Let the fire burn down so it's a little cooler. It also helps to pull the calzone to the coolest spot of the oven—right at the mouth—for the last couple minutes. That gives the filling a little time to get hot and melty inside.

1 dough ball, preferably Naples Dough at 60% Hydration (page 67 or 72), about 250 grams/8.8 ounces

Calzone fillings of your choice (page 204 to 208)

Flour, for dusting

Light a wood fire on the oven floor directly where you will be cooking the calzone (for details on starting a fire, see page 15). Feed the fire until the ambient temperature in the oven is around 600°F (316°C), 1 to 2 hours. You want a slightly cooler fire for calzones so the filling cooks through before the dough burns on the outside. Quickly rake the fire to one side of the oven, containing it in a neat pile near the edge. Brush the cooking surface clean.

Let the dough warm up at room temperature for at least 1 hour or up to 4 hours. As it warms up, the dough will relax and become easier to shape.

Have your fillings ready to go.

TO SHAPE THE DOUGH: The goal is to stretch the dough to a 10- to 12-inch (25 to 30 cm) circle with an even thickness across the middle and no rim at the edge. There are lots of ways. Here's how I usually do it. Lightly flour a work surface and a wooden pizza peel. Use a dough scraper to scrape the dough ball from the tray and transfer it to the floured surface. Gently poke your fingers around the edge of the dough ball. The center should look thicker like a hat. Press your fingers and palm gently into the center of the hat, moving your fingers and thumb outward to begin stretching the dough away from the center (see the photos on page 95). At this point, you should have a disk of dough about 5 inches (12 cm) in diameter. Slip one hand under the disk and quickly flip it over. Repeat the poking and pressing process on the other side, poking your fingers around

the edge first and then placing your palm on the center and gently stretching your fingers and thumb outward to stretch the dough from the center outward. As you work, make sure you keep the edge round.

For stiffer dough like this, it's easiest to pick up the dough to stretch it. Transfer the dough from the work surface to the backs of your hands: just quickly grab the far edge of the rim and flip the dough onto the opposite hand and then slip your other hand under the dough. Keep both hands loosely closed as fists under the dough near the center. With the dough on the backs of your hands, essentially repeat the process of stretching the dough from the center outward: move your hands gently away from the center while rotating the dough around the backs of your fists. It helps to angle the dough downward slightly so it's not perfectly horizontal, which causes it to drape too quickly around the backs of your fists. Carefully and gently continue to stretch the dough until it is an evenly thin 10- to 12-inch (25 to 30 cm) circle with no rim. For the most even crust, I like to stretch both sides of the dough in my hands. To do that, flip the dough over on the backs of your hands by flipping it over much the same way you did when flipping it from the work surface to your hands. Of course, there are other ways to stretch the dough. Some people twirl it up in the air. Use whatever method works best for you to create an evenly stretched 10- to 12-inch (25 to 30 cm) circle with no rim. If the dough tears a hole, patch it by pulling a little dough from one side of the hole and pressing it over the hole with your thumb.

Lay the stretched dough onto the floured peel. The easiest way is to simply drape it over the peel and then remove your hands from beneath the dough. Reshape the dough round as necessary. Give the peel a quick shake to make sure the dough can slide easily.

Add your fillings to half the dough, leaving a 1-inch (2.5 cm) border at the edge (see the photos above). Fold the dough over the filling and pinch the edges tightly to seal. Stretch the points of the half-moon toward each other so the points are almost touching. Give the peel another quick shake to make sure the dough slides easily.

TO BAKE THE CALZONE: Slide and shake the calzone from the peel onto the cooking surface a little closer to the mouth of the oven where it is cooler. Cook until the crust is deep golden brown and starts to blister in spots and the bottom crust is crisp, 6 to 8 minutes. Rotate the calzone often for even cooking and during the last minute or two, keep the calzone very close to the mouth of the oven, at its coolest spot, to give the filling a little time to fully cook.

Remove the calzone from the oven to a wire rack to cool for a minute or so, just to keep the steam from making the crust soggy. Add any finishing ingredients, transfer to a cutting board, and cut in half or thirds crosswise.

HOME OVEN CALZONE

MAKES ONE 10- TO 12-INCH (25 TO 30 CM) HALF-MOON CALZONE

I love the broiler method for cooking the top of pizza in a home oven. But it doesn't work as well for calzones. Just set your oven to its highest temperature and bake the calzone on a baking stone or baking steel. The bake time is a little longer, so I like a little more water in the dough to keep the crust from drying out too much.

1 dough ball, preferably Naples Dough at 70% Hydration (page 64), about 270 grams/9.5 ounces

Calzone fillings of your choice (page 204 to 208)

Flour, for dusting

Let the dough warm up at room temperature for at least 1 hour or up to 4 hours. As it warms up, the dough will relax and become easier to shape.

Place a baking steel or stone on the center rack of the oven and preheat the oven to its highest setting (500° to 550°F/260° to 288°C) for 45 minutes.

Have your fillings ready to go.

TO SHAPE THE DOUGH: The goal is to stretch the dough to a 10- to 12-inch (25 to 30 cm) circle with an even thickness across the middle and no rim at the edge. There are lots of ways. For 70% hydration dough, you'll need a bit more flour and a gentler hand, since the dough is softer. It's best to shape it completely on your work surface. If you try to pick it up, it may tear a hole. Generously flour a work surface and a wooden pizza peel. Use a dough scraper to scrape the dough ball from the tray and transfer it to the floured surface. Gently poke your fingers around the edge of the dough ball. The center should look thicker like a hat. Press your fingers and palm gently into the center of the hat, moving your fingers and thumb outward to begin stretching the dough away from the center (see the photos on page 95). At this point, you should have a disk of dough about 4 inches (10 cm) in diameter. Slip one hand under the disk and quickly flip it over. Repeat the poking and pressing process on the other side, poking your fingers around the edge first and then placing your palm on the center and stretching outward with your fingers and thumb to stretch the dough from the center outward. As you work,

gradually rotate the dough on the flour to keep it round. The dough should be soft enough to continue this process until it is stretched to a 12-inch (30 cm) circle with almost no rim. If the dough tears a hole, patch it by pulling a little dough from one side of the hole and pressing it over the hole with your thumb.

Lay the stretched dough onto the floured peel. The easiest way is to simply drape it over the peel and then remove your hands from beneath the dough. Reshape the dough round as necessary. Give the peel a quick shake to make sure the dough can slide easily.

Add your fillings to half the dough, leaving a 1-inch (2.5 cm) border at the edge (see the photos on page 197). Fold the dough over the filling to make a half-moon shape and pinch the edges tightly to seal. Stretch the points of the half-moon toward each other so the points are almost touching. Give the peel another quick shake to make sure the dough slides easily.

TO BAKE THE CALZONE: Slide and shake the calzone from the peel onto the cooking surface. Cook until the crust is deep golden brown and starts to blister in spots and the bottom crust is crisp, 8 to 10 minutes. Rotate the calzone as necessary for even cooking.

Remove the calzone from the oven to a wire rack to cool for a minute or so, just to keep the steam from making the crust soggy. Add any finishing ingredients, transfer to a cutting board, and cut in half or thirds crosswise.

FRIED MINI-CALZONES

MAKES 4 SMALL 5- TO
6-INCH (12 TO 15 CM)
HALF-MOON CALZONES

Any calzone you can make big, you can make small. And any dough you can bake, you can fry. These little snacks, sometimes called panzerotto, are a surefire hit. Fry up these babies with whatever fillings you like. Just don't make them too saucy, or you'll burn your mouth. To take them with you, let them cool a minute or two, wrap them loosely in parchment, and they're good to go.

1 dough ball, preferably
Naples Dough at 60%
Hydration (page 72), about
250 grams/8.8 ounces

Calzone fillings of your
choice (page 204 to 208)

Flour, for dusting

Let the dough warm up at room temperature for at least 1 hour or up to 4 hours. As it warms up, the dough will relax and become easier to shape.

Have your fillings ready to go.

Heat a deep fryer to 350°F (177°C). At home, a large wok works well so you can fry a few mini-calzones at once without overcrowding them.

TO SHAPE THE DOUGH: Lightly flour a work surface and a large wooden pizza peel or cutting board. Use a dough scraper to scrape the dough ball from the tray to the floured surface. Cut the dough into 4 pieces with a bench knife and then reshape each piece into a ball. To shape each piece, gently poke your fingers around the edge of the ball to begin stretching it. Then poke your fingers in the center, moving your fingers outward to stretch the dough away from the center. At this point, you should have a disk of dough about 3 inches (7 cm) in diameter. Slip one hand under the disk and quickly flip it over. Repeat the poking and stretching process on the other side to stretch the dough outward. If the dough is stiff, you can also pick it up and gently stretch it while draped over your balled-up fists.

Continue stretching the dough to a circle 5 to 6 inches (12 to 15 cm) in diameter with an even thickness and no rim. As you work, make sure you keep the edge round. Repeat with each dough ball. If the dough tears a hole, patch it by pulling a little dough from one side of the hole and pressing it over the hole with your thumb.

Lay the stretched circles of dough onto the floured peel or board. Divide the filling among the pressed-out circles of dough, arranging the filling on one half of each circle and leaving a ½-inch (1.3 cm) border all around the edge of the circle. Fold the dough over the filling and pinch the edges tightly to seal.

TO FRY THE CALZONES: Use a bench scraper to transfer the mini-calzones to the hot oil. Fry them in batches until they are golden brown all over, 2 to 3 minutes, turning with tongs.

Remove the mini-calzones to a cutting board and let cool for a minute. Add any finishing ingredients and then cut each circle in half.

WOOD OVEN ROTOLO

MAKES TWELVE 3- TO 4-INCH (7 TO 10 CM) ROTOLOS

Like calzones, rotolos are best baked in a cooler wood oven. When you roll the dough around itself, it actually gets thicker, and it takes more time for the dough to cook through to the center. A lower baking temperature helps. If your wood oven is really hot (more than 600°F/316°C), let it cool down a bit or bake the rotolos at the mouth of the oven where it's cooler and move the pan around a lot to make sure they cook evenly. A little attention goes a long way here.

Olive oil, for the pan

3 dough balls, preferably Naples Dough at 60% Hydration (page 61), about 750 grams/26.5 ounces total

Rotolo fillings of your choice (page 209 to 215)

Flour, for dusting

Light a wood fire on the oven floor directly where you will be cooking the rotolo (for details on starting a fire, see page 15). Feed the fire until the ambient temperature in the oven is about 450°F (232°C), 1 to 2 hours. You want a slightly cooler fire for rotolo so the filling cooks through before burning on the outside. Quickly rake the fire to one side of the oven, containing it in a neat pile near the edge. Brush the cooking surface clean.

Let the dough warm up at room temperature for at least 1 hour or up to 4 hours. As it warms up, the dough will relax and become easier to shape.

Have your fillings ready to go.

TO SHAPE THE DOUGH: The goal is to stretch the dough into a rectangle about 18 inches long by 13 inches wide (45 by 33 cm) with an even thickness across the middle and no rim at the edge. Flour a work surface and lay the dough balls end to end in a horizontal line in front of you. Gently flatten and pinch the ends of the dough together to make one bigger piece of dough. Dust the top with flour and then press the dough with your palms and fingers, stretching outward to shape the dough into a large rectangle that roughly matches the dimensions of a half-sheet pan, about 18 by 13 inches (45 by 33 cm). If the dough is stiff, you can also pick up the edges of the dough to stretch it outward, or use a rolling pin. As you work, loosen the dough from the work surface with a bench knife and reflour the work surface as necessary. You don't want the dough to stick. When the dough is an even thickness of about ½ inch (1.3 cm), square up the edges with your hands to make a nice rectangle.

Add your fillings, spreading them in an even layer all the way to the edges of the dough. Fold the short sides of the dough rectangle over the filling, about ½ inch (1.3 cm). Then starting at the long side (nearest you), begin rolling the dough over the filling into a tight roll, enclosing the filling in a spiral. The sides will want to spread as you roll. Try to keep the roll tight. When fully rolled, compress gently around the roll with your palms to make it nice and compact. Cut the roll crosswise into 12 pieces, each 1½ to 2 inches (3 to 5 cm) wide.

Oil a half-sheet pan (18 by 13 inches/45 by 33 cm). Place the rotolos, cut sides up, on the baking sheet, reshaping them as necessary so each is a nice, stable spiral. Cover and let stand at room temperature until puffy and almost doubled in size, about 1 hour.

TO BAKE THE ROTOLOS: Bake the rotolo near the mouth of the oven where it is slightly cooler until the rotolos are puffed and golden brown, 15 to 20 minutes. Watch carefully and rotate the pan often for even cooking. Remove the entire pan from the oven, let cool for a minute, and then use a metal spatula to transfer the rotolos to a platter or plates.

To make these ahead of time, proof the filled and cut rotolo in the fridge instead of at room temperature. Cover and let them ferment in the fridge for 2 to 6 hours.

MINI-ROTOLOS: These are great for parties. After rolling out the dough, cut the rectangle of dough in half lengthwise to make 2 smaller rectangles. Top, roll, cut, proof, and bake as directed. Each rotolo will come out a little smaller.

For two different fillings in a single batch of rotolos, prepare half the amount of each filling. Roll the dough into an 18 by 13-inch (45 by 33 cm) rectangle and, with the longest side horizontal in front of you, cut the dough in half vertically. When cut, the dough should look like 2 halves of an open book. Place the toppings on each half and roll away from you as directed.

HOME OVEN ROTOLO

MAKES TWELVE 3- TO
4-INCH (7 TO 10 CM)
ROTOLOS

Truth be told, a home oven is more foolproof than a wood oven for rotolos. The even heat helps them cook through without burning on the outside. Just leave a couple inches between each rotolo. I've also baked them in oiled muffin tins for perfect roundness. I like the dough a little drier here. Any wetter, and it would be a mess to roll and cut the rotolo after filling them.

Olive oil, for the pan

3 dough balls, preferably Naples Dough at 60% Hydration (page 61), about 750 grams/26.5 ounces total

Rotolo fillings of your choice (page 209 to 215)

Flour, for dusting

Let the dough warm up at room temperature for at least 1 hour or up to 4 hours. As it warms up, the dough will relax and become easier to shape.

Have your fillings ready to go.

TO SHAPE THE DOUGH: The goal is to stretch the dough into a rectangle about 18 inches long by 13 inches wide (45 by 33 cm) with an even thickness across the middle and no rim at the edge. Flour a work surface and lay the dough balls end to end in a horizontal line in front of you. Gently flatten and pinch the ends of the dough together to make one bigger piece of dough. Dust the top with flour and then press the dough with your palms and fingers, stretching outward to shape the dough into a large rectangle that roughly matches the dimensions of a half-sheet pan (18 by 13 inches/45 by 33 cm). If the dough is stiff, you can also pick up the edges of the dough to stretch it outward, or use a rolling pin. As you work, loosen the dough from the work surface with a bench knife and reflour the work surface as necessary. You don't want the dough to stick. When the dough is an even thickness of about ½ inch (1.3 cm), square up the edges with your hands to make a nice rectangle.

Add your fillings, spreading them in an even layer all the way to the edges of the dough. Fold the short sides of the dough rectangle over the filling, about ½ inch (1.3 cm). Then starting at the long side (nearest you), begin rolling the dough over the filling into a tight roll, enclosing the filling in a spiral. The sides will want to spread as you roll. Try to keep the roll tight. When fully rolled, compress gently around the roll with your palms to make it nice and compact. Cut the roll crosswise into 12 pieces, each 1½ to 2 inches (3 to 5 cm) wide.

Oil a half-sheet pan (18 by 13 inches/45 by 33 cm) or a 12-cup jumbo muffin tin. Place the rotolos, cut sides up, on the baking sheet or in the tin, reshaping them as necessary so each is a nice, stable spiral. Cover and let stand at room temperature until puffy and almost doubled in size, about 1 hour.

Preheat the oven to 450°F (232°C) and place a baking stone or steel on the middle rack. Let the oven preheat for at least 45 minutes.

TO BAKE THE ROTOLOS: Bake the rotolos until puffed and golden brown, 15 to 20 minutes, rotating the pan once or twice for even cooking. Remove the entire pan from the oven, let cool for a minute, and then use a metal spatula to transfer the rotolos to a platter or plates.

OPTIONS

To make these ahead of time, proof the filled and cut rotolos in the fridge instead of at room temperature. Cover and let them ferment in the fridge for 2 to 6 hours.

MINI-ROTOLOS: These are great for parties. After rolling out the dough, cut the rectangle of dough in half lengthwise to make 2 smaller rectangles. Top, roll, cut, proof, and bake as directed. Each rotolo will come out a little smaller.

For two different fillings in a single batch of rotolos, prepare half the amount of each filling. Roll the dough into an 18 by 13-inch (45 by 33 cm) rectangle and, with the longest side horizontal in front of you, cut the dough in half vertically. When cut, the dough should look like 2 halves of an open book. Place the toppings on each half and roll away from you as directed.

SALSICCIA CALZONE

FENNEL SAUSAGE, MOZZARELLA, AND TOMATO SAUCE

**MAKES ENOUGH FOR
1 LARGE CALZONE OR
4 FRIED MINI-CALZONES**

It's a good idea to cook raw sausage for a couple minutes before putting it inside a calzone. Fillings take a little while to heat up in there, and you want the sausage fully cooked!

2 ounces (57 g) loose, raw, Italian pork fennel sausage, torn in bits

2 tablespoons (30 ml) Pizza Sauce (page 111)

2 ounces (57 g) fresh mozzarella cheese, torn in bits

Pinch of fennel seeds

½ ounce (14 g) chopped escarole, optional

Extra-virgin olive oil, for drizzling

Sea salt

1 teaspoon (2 g) freshly grated Parmigiano-Reggiano cheese

Preheat the oven to 500°F (260°C). Put the bits of sausage on a baking sheet and bake until cooked through, 3 to 5 minutes.

After shaping the pizza dough, spread the sauce on half the dough. Layer on the mozzarella, cooked sausage, fennel seeds, and escarole, if using. Fold the dough over the filling and pinch the edges to seal it. Bake the calzone.

After the calzone comes out of the oven, finish it with some oil, salt, and the Parmigiano.

FINOCCHIO CALZONE

SHAVED FENNEL, OLIVES, AND ANCHOVIES

MAKES ENOUGH FOR
1 LARGE CALZONE OR
4 FRIED MINI-CALZONES

If you've only ever had fennel roasted or sautéed until it's really soft, try it shaved. It will be a revelation. When fennel still has some crunch, you can really taste the licorice flavor. It has better texture, too. For the cherry tomatoes here, try piennolos if you can find them. Their flavor is incredible with a nice balance of minerals, sharpness, and natural sugar.

½ small fennel bulb, white part only

2 tablespoons (30 ml) extra-virgin olive oil, plus some for drizzling

Juice of ¼ lemon

Pinch of sea salt

Pinch of red pepper flakes

4 ounces (113 g) fresh mozzarella cheese, torn in bits

2 tablespoons (30 g) pitted Gaeta olives, chopped

6 oil-packed anchovy fillets, torn in pieces

4 cherry tomatoes (preferably piennolo), thinly sliced

1 teaspoon (2 g) freshly grated Parmigiano-Reggiano cheese

Use a mandoline—even an inexpensive handheld one—to shave the fennel paper thin. You could also use a thin, sharp knife and a steady hand. Toss the shaved fennel in a bowl with the oil, lemon juice, salt, and red pepper flakes. Let marinate at room temperature for 20 minutes.

After shaping the pizza dough, layer the mozzarella and fennel mixture on half the dough. Add the olives, anchovies, and tomatoes, overlapping the tomato slices for fit. Fold the dough over the filling and pinch the edges to seal it. Bake the calzone.

After the calzone comes out of the oven, finish it with some oil, salt, and the Parmigiano.

PROSCIUTTO COTTO CALZONE

COOKED HAM, RICOTTA, AND MOZZARELLA

MAKES ENOUGH FOR
1 LARGE CALZONE OR
4 FRIED MINI-CALZONES

This is like the best ham and cheese sandwich you've ever had. I like a tiny amount of tomato sauce in there, too, but you could easily leave it out.

2 tablespoons (30 ml) Pizza Sauce (page 111)

2 ounces (57 g) fresh mozzarella cheese, hand-torn in bits

2 ounces (57 g) prosciutto cotto, or other cooked ham

2 ounces (57 g) ricotta cheese

Sea salt and freshly ground black pepper

Extra-virgin olive oil, for drizzling

1 teaspoon (2 g) freshly grated Parmigiano-Reggiano cheese

After shaping the pizza dough, spread the sauce on half of the dough. Layer on the mozzarella and prosciutto. Add small dollops of the ricotta and season the ricotta with salt and pepper. Fold the dough over the filling and pinch the edges to seal it. Bake the calzone.

After the calzone comes out of the oven, finish it with some oil, salt, and the Parmigiano.

Wood Oven Prosciutto Cotto Calzone

VERDURA CALZONE

GREENS, MOZZARELLA, AND PARMIGIANO-REGGIANO

MAKES ENOUGH FOR
1 LARGE CALZONE OR
4 FRIED MINI-CALZONES

Wilted greens and a little cheese make a beautiful calzone filling. Just make sure the greens are superfresh—and preferably local. You could put almost any greens in there and get a great result.

1 ounce (28 g) chopped or torn greens, such as kale, escarole, and/or arugula

1 tablespoon (15 ml) extra-virgin olive oil, plus some for finishing

1 teaspoon (5 ml) red wine vinegar

1 tablespoon (6.25 g) freshly grated Parmigiano-Reggiano cheese

Sea salt and freshly ground black pepper

2 ounces (57 g) fresh mozzarella cheese, torn in bits

In a medium bowl, toss the greens with the oil, vinegar, and 2 teaspoons of the Parmigiano. Season with salt and pepper until it tastes good to you.

After shaping the pizza dough, layer the mozzarella on half of the dough. Add the dressed greens, fold the dough over the filling, and pinch the edges to seal it. Bake the calzone.

After the calzone comes out of the oven, finish it with some oil, salt, and the remaining Parmigiano.

CAVOLO ROTOLO

KALE, MOZZARELLA, AND RICOTTA

MAKES ENOUGH FOR TWELVE 3- TO 4-INCH (7 TO 10 CM) ROTOLO

This one opens up so many possibilities. You mix raw kale into ricotta and shredded mozzarella along with some roasted onions. Try other braising greens like escarole or chard.

2 cups (284 g) sliced white onions

4 cloves garlic, crushed

¼ cup (59 ml) extra-virgin olive oil

Sea salt and freshly ground black pepper

12 ounces (340 g) kale leaves, large stems removed

1 pound (454 g) shredded whole-milk mozzarella cheese

8 ounces (227 g) ricotta cheese

Preheat the oven to 500°F (260°C). Toss the onions and garlic with 2 tablespoons of the oil on a baking sheet until everything is coated. Spread in a single layer and season with salt and pepper. Roast until the onions are soft and just starting to brown at the tips, 5 to 8 minutes.

Put the kale in a food processor. Scrape the roasted onion mixture over the kale and pour in the remaining 2 tablespoons of oil. Process to a coarse and chunky paste like pesto. Briefly pulse in the mozzarella and ricotta and then season the mixture with salt and pepper until it tastes good to you. Use it immediately or refrigerate it for up to 8 hours.

After shaping the pizza dough, spread the kale mixture all over the dough. Roll up the rotolo, cut it, and proof it on the baking sheet. Bake the rotolo. Serve warm.

MORTADELLA AND PISTACHIO ROTOLO

MORTADELLA, PISTACHIO, AND RICOTTA CHEESE

MAKES ENOUGH FOR TWELVE 3- TO 4-INCH (7 TO 10 CM) ROTOLOS

This is the rotolo that started the phenomenon! It is the perfect combination, and a drizzle of pistachio pesto brings it to the next level. Try this one first and then move on to the others.

¾ cup (113 g) deshelled pistachios, preferably Sicilian

¾ cup (177 ml) extra-virgin olive oil

1 small clove garlic, finely minced

Sea salt and freshly ground black pepper

12 ounces (340 g) sliced mortadella

18 ounces (510 g) ricotta cheese

Place the pistachios, oil, and garlic in a food processor or blender and process or blend until chunky, not smooth. Add salt and pepper until it tastes good to you. You could also chop the pistachios by hand and then mix in everything else. Either way, you can use the mixture immediately or store it in an airtight container at room temperature for up to 8 hours or refrigerate it for up to 3 days. Return it to room temperature before using.

After shaping the pizza dough, arrange the mortadella all over the dough so that each slice lies flat, overlapping the slices as necessary. Spread on the ricotta and season it with salt and pepper. Roll up the rotolo, cut it, and proof it on the baking sheet. Bake the rotolo.

After transferring the rotolo to a platter or plates, spoon the pistachio mixture over the top. Serve warm.

Home Oven Mortadella and Pistachio Rotolo

CALABRESE ROTOLO

PEPPERONI, TOMATO SAUCE, AND MOZZARELLA

MAKES ENOUGH FOR
TWELVE 3- TO 4-INCH
(7 TO 10 CM) ROTOLO

Nothing like spicing it up a little. I like making these as mini-rotolo (see page 203), so you can pop a whole one in your mouth!

1¼ cups (296 ml) Pizza Sauce (page 111)

2 to 3 tablespoons (30 to 45 g) oil-packed Calabrian chiles or pickled red peperoncini

10 ounces (284 g) thinly sliced pepperoni

1 pound (454 g) shredded whole-milk mozzarella cheese

Freshly ground black pepper

Place the sauce and chiles in a blender or food processor and process until smooth. Pour the sauce into a medium bowl.

Julienne the sliced pepperoni by cutting it into narrow strips about ⅛ inch (0.3 cm) wide. You can stack several at a time like poker chips to speed the process. Add the pepperoni strips to the bowl of tomato sauce along with the mozzarella. Stir everything together and then season with pepper until it tastes good to you. Use the mixture immediately or refrigerate it for up to 8 hours.

After shaping the pizza dough, spread the pepperoni mixture all over the dough. Roll up the rotolo, cut it, and proof it on the baking sheet. Bake the rotolo. Serve warm.

Wood Oven
Calabrese Rotolo

FUNGHI ROTOLO

MUSHROOMS, ROSEMARY, AND FONTINA CHEESE

MAKES ENOUGH FOR
TWELVE 3- TO 4-INCH
(7 TO 10 CM) ROTOLO

We call for cremini mushrooms here but try switching up the shrooms with the seasons. Do porcinis in the fall, morels in the spring, and chanterelles in the summer.

1¾ pounds (794 g) cremini mushrooms, sliced about ⅛ inch (0.3 cm) thick

Leaves from 4 sprigs fresh rosemary

2 large cloves garlic, smashed

¼ cup (59 ml) extra-virgin olive oil, plus some for drizzling

Sea salt and freshly ground black pepper

8 ounces (227 g) shredded fontina cheese

8 ounces (227 g) shredded whole-milk mozzarella cheese

Preheat the oven to 500°F (260°C). Toss the mushrooms, rosemary, garlic, and oil on a large rimmed baking sheet until thoroughly mixed. Season with salt and pepper until it tastes good to you, and then spread the mushrooms in a single layer. Roast the mushrooms in the oven until they give up most of their liquid, 6 to 8 minutes, stirring once or twice. Remove from the oven and let cool in the pan. When cool, discard the garlic and drain away any excess liquid.

After shaping the pizza dough, scatter the mushroom mixture all over the dough. Scatter on the fontina and mozzarella and season with a little more salt, pepper, and olive oil. Roll up the rotolo, cut it, and proof it on the baking sheet. Bake the rotolo. Serve warm.

9

FOCACCIA

MANY PEOPLE THINK THAT FOCACCIA IS BASICALLY NAKED PIZZA AL taglio, a loose dough baked in a sheet pan. And they're right, except for a few small details. Those details make all the difference. It's about technique and what you're trying to achieve. Pizza al taglio can have some pretty elaborate toppings. And the dough is usually shaped to be flat on top to accommodate the toppings. The truth is, pizza al taglio is more like a small meal. But focaccia is more like bread. It's simpler. And it's often not completely flat on top but dimpled really deep, so olive oil pools in the hollows and makes the crust nice and crunchy. It's often cut in half through the side, too, so you can use the focaccia like sandwich bread.

The simplicity of focaccia puts the focus not on the top-pings but on the dough itself. That's what we're exploring in this chapter. Different flours—from superfine tipo 00 flour to whole grain heritage wheat flours—give you different effects in the dough. Durum flour makes a chewy focaccia. Buckwheat makes it more earthy. More water in the dough loosens it, puffs it up in the oven, and makes the focaccia big and airy when baked. Less water makes the focaccia slightly firmer and denser. Playing with the flour and water alone will give you completely different flavors and textures in focaccia. If you use natural wild yeast (sourdough) instead of commercial yeast, you'll add yet another layer of flavor.

The recipes here are intended to bring you into a closer relationship with dough, to help you understand it, and to show you the various ways that it can be hydrated, mixed, fermented, and flavored. Instead of topping the focaccia like pizza, I like to stuff it or fold various ingredients into the dough. That's the idea behind Turmeric Sourdough Focac-cia (page 230), which has caramelized onions, turmeric, and poppy seeds mixed right into the dough. Focusing on the dough itself lays the foundation for you to experiment with different flours and add-ins to achieve the kind of focaccia you like best. Play around with the recipes here. The more you experiment, the more you'll know what the outcome will be before you even heat up the oven . . . and that's a beautiful thing!

00 FLOUR FOCACCIA

MAKES 1 HALF-SHEET PAN
(18 BY 13 INCHES/
45 BY 33 CM)

At 86% hydration, this focaccia comes out superlight and fluffy with lots of air holes. The tipo 00 flour, which is milled fine like talcum powder, also makes it very soft and silky. It's the perfect focaccia for making sandwiches. It takes 8 to 10 hours to ferment, so if you start it first thing in the morning, you can have focaccia tonight.

STARTER

200 grams (1⅓ cups) tipo 00 flour for pizza and bread

177 grams (¾ cup) water at 70°F (21°C)

2 grams (⅔ teaspoon) active dry yeast

DOUGH

435 grams (1¾ cups plus 1½ tablespoons) water at 70°F (21°C)

4 grams (1¼ teaspoons) active dry yeast

510 grams (3⅓ cups) tipo 00 flour, plus some for dusting

17 grams (2¾ teaspoons) fine sea salt

Extra-virgin olive oil, for the pan and drizzling

For the starter, mix everything together in the bowl of an electric mixer with a spoon. Mix for a few minutes to make sure all the flour is wet and the starter is wet and sticky. Cover tightly with plastic wrap and let rest in a warm place (about 85°F/29°C) for 4 hours.

TO MIX AND KNEAD: For the dough, pour the water over the starter and then sprinkle on the yeast. Add the flour and then the salt. Attach the dough hook and mix on low speed for 10 minutes. Scrape the bottom of the bowl once or twice to make sure all the flour is incorporated. The dough will be loose and wet.

TO FERMENT: Cover tightly and let the dough ferment in a warm place until doubled in size, 2 to 4 hours.

TO SHAPE: Lightly oil a half-sheet pan (18 by 13 inches/45 by 33 cm) up the sides as well. Scrape the dough onto the oiled pan. This dough is very wet and will almost pour into the pan. Use your fingers to gently press and stretch the dough to fit the pan all the way to the edges. Cover with another half-sheet pan turned upside down and let rest at room temperature for 1 hour. The dough is too wet to cover it with plastic wrap because the plastic will stick. An inverted sheet pan works well.

Place a pizza stone on the middle rack of your oven and preheat the oven to 450°F (232°C) for at least 45 minutes.

TO BAKE: Drizzle the dough with oil, tilting the pan so it pools all over the dough. Bake until light golden brown, 18 to 20 minutes. Let cool slightly and then cut into 3-inch (7 cm) squares. This focaccia is very pillowy in texture, and scissors work well for cutting it.

OPTIONS

If you don't have 00 flour, you can use all-purpose flour. The focaccia won't come out quite as light and tender, but it will still be delicious. The two flours measure differently by volume, so to get the same weight if you are measuring by volume, use 1⅔ cups all-purpose flour in the starter and then 4 cups plus 1¼ tablespoons all-purpose flour in the dough.

FOCACCINA: Split the cooked focaccia in half through the side to make thinner pieces of sandwich bread. Fill with whatever you want, especially while the focaccia is still warm. Use whatever sandwich spreads and fillings you like, from pesto, provolone, and fresh mozzarella to prosciutto, roasted peppers, arugula, and fresh tomatoes.

HERITAGE WHEAT ROSEMARY FOCACCIA

MAKES 1 HALF-SHEET PAN
(18 BY 13 INCHES/
45 BY 33 CM)

I like to play around with different wheat varieties. If you think of wheat like wine grapes, it helps you understand that wheat gets its flavor from the soil, and different varieties of wheat grown in different areas will bring different flavors to your dough. Use this recipe as a template to experiment with different wheat varieties like spelt, Redeemer (a popular bread wheat in the northeastern United States), and emmer. I think you'll be blown away with the results.

258 grams (2 cups) whole grain spelt or other heritage wheat bread flour, preferably fresh milled

258 grams (2 cups) King Arthur bread flour

307 grams (1⅓ cups) water at 55°F (13°C)

7 grams (2¼ teaspoons) active dry yeast or 14 grams (1½ tablespoons) fresh yeast

9 grams (1½ teaspoons) fine sea salt

13 grams (1 tablespoon) extra-virgin olive oil, plus some for the pan and for drizzling

Leaves from 2 sprigs fresh rosemary

Flake salt, such as Maldon

TO MIX AND KNEAD: Put the wheat flour, bread flour, and water in the bowl of a stand mixer, fitted with the dough hook. Add the yeast and mix on low speed for 2 to 3 minutes. Switch to medium speed, add the salt, and then stream in the oil. Mix until the dough is smooth and silky, about 10 minutes.

TO FERMENT: Transfer the dough to an oiled bowl, cover, and let rise in a warm place until doubled in size, about 1 hour.

Lightly oil a half-sheet pan (18 by 13 inches/45 by 33 cm) and then punch down the dough and turn it out onto the oiled pan. Fold the dough over itself in thirds, cover tightly, and let rise in a warm spot for 30 minutes more. After 30 minutes, punch down the dough, fold it over itself again in thirds, cover tightly, and let rise in a warm spot for another 30 minutes.

TO SHAPE AND FERMENT AGAIN: Press the dough into the baking sheet, all the way to the edges of the pan, so the dough is about ½ inch (1.3 cm) thick. Dimple the surface all over with your fingertips. Cover and let rise in a warm spot for a final 30 minutes. The multiple risings help create lots of bubbles and flavor in the dough.

TO BAKE: Preheat the oven to 500°F (260°C). Drizzle the top of the focaccia with oil and tilt the pan to get oil into most of the hollows. Or press the oil right into the holes with your fingertips. Scatter on the rosemary and some salt. Bake until golden brown, 20 to 25 minutes. Cool in the pan on a wire rack and then cut into 3-inch (7 cm) squares. Serve warm or at room temperature.

BUCKWHEAT STECCA

Buckwheat has a pretty intense taste—sort of like dark roasted coffee and cinnamon. It adds great flavor to focaccia. We had some fun with this dough and shaped it into sticks (stecche) instead of squares. But you could just as easily press the dough into a big square or oval on the baking sheet. Another fun thing to try: use chestnut flour instead of buckwheat for a richer, nuttier taste.

188 grams (1⅓ cups) King Arthur bread flour, plus some for dusting

188 grams (1½ cups) buckwheat flour

5 grams (1⅔ teaspoons) fresh yeast or 2.1 grams (⅔ teaspoon) active dry yeast

233 grams (1 cup) water at 70°F (21°C)

33 grams (2½ tablespoons) olive oil, plus some for the pan and for drizzling

13 grams (1¾ teaspoons) honey

12 grams (2 teaspoons) fine sea salt

Flake salt, such as Maldon, and freshly ground black pepper

TO MIX AND KNEAD: Put everything but the sea salt in the bowl of a stand mixer, fitted with the dough hook, and mix on medium speed for 8 minutes. Add the sea salt and mix for another 2 minutes. The dough should look smoother and feel somewhat resilient when poked.

TO FERMENT: Cover tightly with plastic wrap and let the dough ferment at room temperature (about 70°F/21°C) until doubled in size, 1 to 1½ hours.

TO SHAPE AND FERMENT AGAIN: Line a half-sheet pan (18 by 13 inches/45 by 33 cm) with parchment paper. Use a dough scraper to scrape the dough out onto a lightly floured surface. Dust the top with flour and divide the dough in half with a bench knife. Gently pull and stretch each piece to shape it into a long oval stick about 12 to 15 inches long by 2 to 3 inches wide (30 to 38 by 5 to 7 cm). Transfer the sticks to the parchment, evenly spaced apart. Cover with plastic wrap and let ferment again at room temperature until doubled in size again, 1 to 1½ hours.

TO BAKE: Preheat the oven to 450°F (232°C). Rub some oil all over the sticks, re-shaping them into nice, plump sticks if necessary, and season them with flake salt and pepper. Bake until firm and light brown, about 20 minutes. Remove to a rack to cool.

OPTIONS

If you have more time, you can ferment the shaped stecche in the refrigerator for 6 to 8 hours instead of at room temperature for 1½ hours.

To top the stecche, poke deep dimples in the dough before baking it. Press your fingers almost all the way to the bottom of the dough so that your toppings (as shown in photo opposite) will not fall off when baked and the dough puffs up. Tomatoes and garlic scapes make a nice, minimal topping. Just cut 6 to 8 cherry tomatoes in half and cut 1 garlic scape (or 1 scallion) into ½-inch to 1-inch (1.3 to 2.5 cm) pieces. Press the tomatoes and garlic scapes deep into the dimples in the dough. Drizzle with the oil and sprinkle with flake salt and pepper before baking. You could also top these with sliced pan-roasted leeks (or almost any species of *Allium*), Gaeta olives, fresh halved grapes, and whatever fresh herbs you like.

DURUM FOCACCIA

MAKES 1 HALF-SHEET PAN
(18 BY 13 INCHES/
45 BY 33 CM)

At Vetri, we serve this focaccia with all of our pasta courses. It has a lot of water in it, which puffs up the dough in the oven and makes the focaccia nice and airy. Yet, the hard durum flour gives it great chew. It's like the most delicious sponge you could ever imagine!

STARTER

140 grams (1⅛ cups) durum flour

160 grams (⅔ cup) water at 55°F (13°C)

2 grams (heaping ½ teaspoon) fresh yeast or 0.8 grams (heaping ⅛ teaspoon) active dry yeast

DOUGH

550 grams (2⅓ cups) water at 55°F (13°C)

22 grams (2 tablespoons plus 1 teaspoon) fresh yeast or 8.2 grams (heaping 2½ teaspoons) active dry yeast

680 grams (5½ cups) durum flour

22 grams (3⅔ teaspoons) fine sea salt

6 tablespoons (89 ml) olive oil, plus some for the bowl and the pan

Flake salt, such as Maldon

DAY 1: For the starter, put everything together in the bowl of an electric mixer, crumbling in the yeast if it's fresh or sprinkling the dry yeast over the water. Mix just long enough to make sure all the flour is wet. The starter will be wet and sticky. Cover tightly with plastic wrap and let the starter rest at room temperature (about 70°F/21°C) for 24 hours.

DAY 2: By this time, the starter should be very lively, bubbly, and smell like sex. For the dough, pour the water into a small bowl, crumble in the yeast, and whisk together until no lumps remain or, if using dry yeast, just sprinkle the yeast over the starter.

TO MIX AND KNEAD: Add the water (or water/yeast mixture) to the starter and then add the flour and the sea salt. Attach the dough hook and mix on low speed for 6 minutes. Switch to medium-low speed and mix for another 4 minutes. The dough will be loose but should feel resilient when poked.

TO FERMENT: Transfer the dough to an oiled bowl, cover, and let rise in a warm place until doubled in size, 1 to 1½ hours.

TO SHAPE AND FERMENT AGAIN: Lightly oil a half-sheet pan (18 by 13 inches/45 by 33 cm) and turn the dough out onto the pan. Press the dough into the pan all the way to the edges, so the dough is about ½ inch (1.3 cm) thick. Cover and let rise in a warm spot for 30 minutes.

Dimple the surface of the dough all over with your fingertips. Cover and let rise in a warm spot for a final 30 minutes. The multiple risings help create lots of bubbles and flavors in the dough.

TO BAKE: Preheat the oven to 475°F (246°C). Spoon the oil over the top of the focaccia, letting some pool in the dimples. Scatter on some flake salt and bake for 20 minutes. Lower the oven temperature to 350°F (177°C) and bake until the focaccia is lightly browned on top, about 10 minutes more. Transfer to a wire rack and cool in the pan until warm. Cut into 3-inch (7 cm) squares.

OPTION

For a more free-form focaccia shape, you can shape the dough on a piece of parchment on the back of a baking sheet. Just form it into an oval on the parchment and then proceed with the rest of the recipe. If you want to make a larger, thicker focaccia (as shown in photo opposite), use 1½ times the recipe and fold the dough in thirds on a work table for the second fermentation instead of pressing and fermenting the dough in the baking sheet.

STUFFED FOCACCIA WITH TALEGGIO AND PANCETTA

MAKES 1 HALF-SHEET PAN
(18 BY 13 INCHES/
45 BY 33 CM)

Once you master focaccia, going to the store and buying sandwich bread will be a thing of the past. You can stuff focaccia with whatever you like, but I'm partial to the classic northern Italian pairing of Taleggio cheese and pancetta. Here, the filling is baked right into the dough.

515 grams (3¾ cups)
King Arthur bread flour

307 grams (1⅓ cups) water
at 55°F (13°C)

7 grams (2¼ teaspoons)
active dry yeast or 14 grams
(1½ tablespoons) fresh yeast

9 grams (1½ teaspoons)
fine sea salt

13 grams (1 tablespoon)
extra-virgin olive oil, plus
some for the bowl, pan,
and drizzling

8 ounces (227 g) Taleggio
cheese, shredded

4 ounces (113 g) pancetta,
very thinly sliced

Flake salt, such as Maldon

Freshly ground black pepper

TO MIX AND KNEAD: Put the flour and water in the bowl of a stand mixer, fitted with the dough hook. Add the yeast and mix on low speed for 2 to 3 minutes. Switch to medium speed, add the sea salt, and, stream in the oil. Mix until the dough is smooth and silky, about 10 minutes.

TO FERMENT: Transfer the dough to an oiled bowl, cover, and let rise in a warm place until doubled in size, about 1 hour.

Lightly oil a half-sheet pan (18 by 13 inches/45 by 33 cm) and then punch down the dough and turn it out onto the oiled pan. Fold the dough over itself in thirds, cover, and let rise in a warm spot for 30 minutes more. After 30 minutes, punch down the dough, fold it over itself in thirds again, cover, and let rise in a warm spot for another 30 minutes.

TO SHAPE, STUFF, AND FERMENT AGAIN: Cut the dough in half with a bench knife and press half of the dough into the baking sheet so it is about ¼ inch (0.6 cm) thick. Roll up that piece of pressed-out dough and set it aside on your work surface. Reoil the pan and press the other half of the dough into the pan so it is about ¼ inch (0.6 cm) thick. Arrange the Taleggio and pancetta over the dough in the pan, leaving a ¼-inch (0.6 cm) border around the edge. Unroll the other half of the dough over the Taleggio and pancetta and pinch the edges to seal. Dimple the surface all over with your fingertips, cover, and let rise in a warm spot for 30 minutes.

TO BAKE: Preheat the oven to 500°F (260°C). If you have convection, turn it on. Drizzle the top of the focaccia with oil and sprinkle on some flake salt and pepper. Bake until golden brown, 20 to 25 minutes (or 15 to 20 minutes with convection). Cool in the pan on a wire rack and then cut into 3-inch (7 cm) squares. Serve warm or at room temperature.

TURMERIC SOURDOUGH FOCACCIA

MAKES 1 HALF-SHEET PAN
(18 BY 13 INCHES/
45 BY 33 CM)

Claire Kopp McWilliams is our miller and baker at Vetri. She experiments with wheat varieties and creates amazing new breads for our guests. This focaccia is one of the most special things that she has come up with, and it opens the door to endless possibilities—just sub in other spices and fillings for the turmeric and onions. And if you can, use fresh-milled flour.

FILLING

2 tablespoons (30 ml) extra-virgin olive oil, plus some for the pan

1 large onion (at least 300 g), finely chopped

3 tablespoons (26 g) poppy seeds

1 tablespoon (6.5 g) ground turmeric

Generous pinch of fine sea salt

DOUGH

675 grams (5⅔ cups) high-extraction hard red wheat flour, preferably fresh milled, plus some for dusting

53 grams (⅓ cup) very active Whole Grain Sourdough Starter (page 84)

473 grams (2 cups) water at 80°F (27°C)

5 grams (1¾ teaspoons) ground turmeric

16 grams (2⅔ teaspoons) fine sea salt

Flake salt, such as Maldon

DAY 1: For the filling, heat the oil in a medium sauté pan over medium heat. When hot, add the onions and sauté until soft and translucent, about 5 minutes. Add the poppy seeds, turmeric, and salt and reduce the heat to medium-low. Continue cooking gently until the onions cook down and develop a little color, about 15 minutes. Remove from the heat and cool completely before using. This filling can be made a few days in advance and chilled. Return the filling to room temperature before mixing it into the dough. To be really precise, weigh the filling. You should have about 200 grams. If you have a lot more, use the excess for something else (like a curry dish).

TO MIX THE DOUGH: Combine the flour, starter, and water in the bowl of a stand mixer, fitted with the dough hook. Mix on low speed for 8 minutes. Cover with plastic wrap and let the dough rest for 15 minutes. Then add the filling, turmeric, and salt and mix on low speed for 4 minutes. Increase the speed to medium and mix for 6 minutes more. The dough should be shiny and strong enough to cling to the hook, but it will feel rather wet and sticky to the touch. The exact texture will depend on the flour you use. Cover the bowl with plastic wrap and let the dough rest for 15 minutes.

TO FOLD AND FERMENT: Stretch and fold the dough by digging a dough scraper (or a wet hand) between the dough and the bowl, grabbing about one-fourth of the dough, lifting it, stretching it, and folding it over the top of the dough. Turn the bowl a quarter turn and repeat the folding motion. Repeat this stretch-and-fold process about 4 times total, until all of the dough has been folded over itself. Cover and let rest for another 15 minutes.

Repeat the stretch-and-fold move a total of 3 more times with 15-minute rests between each move, covering the dough during the rests.

Cover tightly with plastic wrap or transfer the dough to a container with an airtight lid and refrigerate the dough overnight.

DAY 2: Pull the dough from the refrigerator about 2 hours before you plan to bake it. After 2 hours, the dough should have risen some and feel slightly full of air. If it does not, give it a little more resting time at room temperature (about 70°F/21°C).

TO BAKE: Place a pizza stone on the middle rack of your oven and preheat the oven to 500°F (260°C) for at least 45 minutes. At the same time, generously flour a work surface and turn the dough out onto the flour. Sprinkle the top of the dough with more flour. With a light hand, repeat the stretch-and-fold move, folding pieces of dough from the edges in toward the bulk of the dough. Gently roll the dough into a ball, cover, and let rest with the seam down.

When ready to bake, lightly oil a half-sheet pan (18 by 13 inches/45 by 33 cm) up the sides as well. Flour the work surface and dough again as necessary and, working with a light hand, stretch and press the dough ball into a rectangle that roughly matches the pan. Grab and stretch the center and edges as necessary to stretch the dough into an evenly thick rectangle. When the dough is just slightly smaller than the pan, transfer the dough to the pan by flipping it over one forearm and then lifting the remainder with the back of the other hand. This action will likely finish off the stretching process as the dough is lifted and set in the pan, but tug any edges into place if it needs further adjustment. Press the dough into the pan all the way to the edges in an even layer. Use your fingertips to dimple the dough with deep indentations all over the top.

Drizzle the top with oil, tipping the pan to make sure each dimple has a little oil in it. Sprinkle with flake salt and load the focaccia into the oven. If you have convection, turn it on, and bake until the top crust is mottled yellow and brown, 15 to 20 minutes, rotating the pan once for even browning. If you don't have convection, add 5 minutes to the baking time. Transfer to a wire rack to cool, at least until it is barely warm, about 15 minutes, which gives the interior time to set up.

10

—

DESSERT

I HAVE ALWAYS STRUGGLED WITH DESSERT PASTAS. They usually taste as if they were made for the surprise factor and not for the pasta itself. There have been one or two rare occasions when I came across something interesting that worked, but on the whole, dessert pasta has just never tasted right in my mouth. So when I thought about making dessert pizza, my initial thought was, "Don't mess with it."

Then came Nutella.

My first experience with dessert pizza was one of those earth-shattering, life-changing moments. It was 1997, and I was working at Bella Blu in New York City. We had a stuffed pizza on the menu made with robiola cheese and truffle oil (see page 148). One day, the chef, Matteo Pupillo, made the same pizza but stuffed it with Nutella. He put two dough balls together, stretched them out to the usual size, and docked the dough with a docker (see page 23). He baked it in the wood oven until it was a little underdone, and then he pulled it out, cut it horizontally through the side, and scraped out the uncooked dough on the inside. Then he spread on some Nutella, put it back together, and put it back in the oven to crisp up.

I was completely mesmerized but still skeptical. When he removed the pizza from the oven, you could smell the charred hazelnut. He cut the pizza, dusted the top with confectioners' sugar, and gestured with his hand for me to taste it. I can't describe the feeling when I put it in my mouth.

From there, my openness to dessert pizza just snowballed. Compared to pasta, pizza is a little closer to bread. And sweet bread has a long history, so it makes more sense to me. In fact, some of Italy's earliest yeast breads like schiacciata were flat breads topped with sweet toppings. Why not play around with pizza dough and have some fun? In this chapter, we revisit some of the pizza shapes from previous chapters that really work well, but this time they come with a sweet twist. The ice technique shows up on a Naples-style pie, but here it becomes crème brulee pizza, one of my favorite new discoveries. We also make a big pizza al metro and put fresh berries and mascarpone whipped cream on it. It's the perfect ending to a big pizza party. And then there's some fried dough tossed in fennel lemon sugar and a rotolo made like a sticky bun with caramel and pecans. The one new shape here is pizzette, which are small dough rounds pressed into little pans and filled with caramelized apples and a crumbly oat topping like mini–apple pies. As with the other recipes in this book, that one is a great template to work from. Fill your pizzette with whatever you want, from pudding to pie fillings. Make it how you like it. For that matter, experiment with all the dessert ideas here. The important thing is not to be creative for the sake of creativity but to be creative for the sake of deliciousness.

HOME OVEN NUTELLA-STUFFED PIZZA

MAKES ONE 12-INCH
(30 CM) ROUND
STUFFED PIZZA

A few marshmallows make this now-classic dessert even more gooey. I love it when some of the marshmallow melts through the crust and burns a little. It's like the best s'more ever!

2 dough balls, preferably Roman Dough at 67% Hydration (page 78), about 500 grams/17.6 ounces each

6 tablespoons (111 g) Nutella or other chocolate-hazelnut spread

8 large (or 1 cup mini) marshmallows, optional

Confectioners' sugar, for dusting

Flour, for dusting

Let the dough warm up at room temperature for at least 1 hour or up to 4 hours. As it warms up, the dough will relax and become easier to shape.

Place a baking steel or stone on the upper rack of the oven 4 to 6 inches (10 to 15 cm) beneath the broiler for an electric oven or 6 to 8 inches (15 to 20 cm) beneath the broiler for a gas oven. Preheat the oven to its highest setting (usually 500° to 550°F/260° to 288°C) for 45 minutes.

Have your fillings ready to go.

When the oven is preheated and you are ready to bake pizza, open the oven door for 10 seconds if you have an electric oven. This step lets some heat escape to make sure the electric broiler will actually turn on even though the oven has reached its maximum temperature. Reset the oven to broil and preheat the broiler for 5 to 10 minutes. The next steps of shaping and filling the pizza should take only 5 to 10 minutes if your fillings are ready to go.

TO SHAPE THE DOUGH: The goal is to combine the dough balls and stretch the dough to a 12-inch (30 cm) circle with an even thickness across the middle with no rim around the edge. There are lots of ways. For 67% hydration dough, you'll need a bit more flour and a gentler hand, since the dough is softer. It's best to shape it completely on your work surface. If you try to pick it up, it may tear a hole. Generously flour a work surface and a wooden pizza peel. Use a dough scraper to scrape the dough balls from the tray to the floured surface. Stack one dough ball on top of the other and press them together into one bigger disk of dough. Gently poke your fingers about ¼ inch (0.6 cm)

from the edge of the dough ball all around it. The center should look thicker like a hat. Press your fingers and palm gently into the center of the hat, moving your fingers and thumb outward to begin stretching the dough away from the center (see the photos on page 95). At this point, you should have a disk of dough 4 to 5 inches (10 to 12 cm) in diameter. Slip one hand under the disk and quickly flip it over. Repeat the poking and pressing process on the other side, poking your fingers around the edge first, and then placing your palm on the center and gently stretching your fingers and thumb outward to stretch the dough from the center outward. As you work, gradually rotate the dough on the flour to keep it round. The dough should be soft enough to continue this process until it is stretched to a 12-inch (30 cm) circle with an even thickness across the middle with almost no rim. It should be about ½ inch (1.3 cm) thick. If the dough tears a hole, patch it by pulling a little dough from one side of the hole and pressing it over the hole with your thumb.

Lay the stretched dough onto the floured peel. The easiest way is to simply drape it over the peel and then remove your hands from beneath the dough. Reshape the dough round as necessary. Dock the dough by poking holes all over it with a fork or a dough docker, which helps prevent it from puffing up too much in the oven. Give the peel a quick shake to make sure the dough can slide easily.

TO BAKE THE PIZZA: At this point, your oven should be on broil. Slide and shake the pizza from the peel onto the

CONTINUED

cooking surface. Cook until the dough is slightly puffed and very light brown on top, 3 to 4 minutes total. Check the dough during cooking and as it begins to puff up, use a long metal spatula or half-sheet pan to press down on the dough to keep any one bubble from puffing up and browning too much. Ideally, you want an evenly puffy and lightly browned disk of dough. Use your hands or a long spatula to rotate the dough as necessary for even cooking.

Remove the pizza from the oven to a wire rack to cool for a minute or so, just to keep the steam from making the crust soggy. Transfer the pizza to a cutting board and use a long serrated knife to cut the cooked dough in half through the side to make two thinner dough rounds (see the photos on page 149). Cut all the way around the outside edge first, gradually working the knife toward the middle until the dough is cleaved in two. Keep the knife perfectly flat at all times to avoid cutting a hole in the top or bottom crust.

Separate the two halves and open them like a book. Use a spoon or your fingers to scrape away any soft, undercooked dough from both halves. You want to scrape away and discard most of the undercooked dough. Smear the Nutella evenly across the bottom half of the dough, leaving about a ¼-inch (0.6 cm) border around the edges. Arrange the marshmallows, if using, over the Nutella. Put on the top half and return to the oven just until the Nutella and marshmallows start to melt, about 2 minutes (another minute if using marshmallows).

Remove the pizza to a cutting board and let cool slightly to firm up the filling. If you will be baking another pizza, reset the oven to its maximum temperature. Cut the stuffed pizza into 6 wedges and finish it with the confectioners' sugar.

HOME OVEN FRESH BERRY MASCARPONE PIZZA AL METRO

MAKES 1 LARGE
RECTANGULAR PIZZA,
ABOUT 21 INCHES LONG
BY 10 INCHES WIDE
(53 BY 25 CM)

Some dessert pizzas seem forced, but there's nothing forced about fresh seasonal berries and whipped cream! If you have a large baking stone or steel, this dessert is a crowd pleaser for a big dinner party. For a smaller pizza, just cut the recipe in half and roll a single dough ball into a smaller oval to fit your baking stone.

2 dough balls, preferably Roman Dough at 57% Hydration (page 76), about 460 grams/1 pound total

½ cup (116 g) cold mascarpone cheese

¼ cup (30 g) confectioners' sugar, plus some for dusting

¼ cup (50 ml) cold heavy cream

1 teaspoon (5 ml) vanilla extract

Flour, for dusting

3 cups (454 g) mixed fresh berries such as blueberries, blackberries, and halved strawberries

2 tablespoons (25 g) sugar

Finely grated zest of ½ orange, optional

12 fresh mint leaves

Let the dough warm up at room temperature for at least 1 hour or up to 4 hours. As it warms up, the dough will relax and become easier to shape.

Chill a medium metal bowl and the whip attachment for an electric mixer in the freezer for about 10 minutes. Combine the mascarpone, confectioners' sugar, cream, and vanilla in the cold bowl and beat with the whip attachment on medium speed until thickened and smooth, 2 to 4 minutes. Spoon the whipped mascarpone cream into a piping bag fitted with a star tip (or into a zipper-lock bag and cut off one corner of the bag so you can pipe the cream). Refrigerate until ready to use. This mixture can be made up to 4 hours ahead of time.

Place a large baking steel or stone (at least 22 inches long and 11 inches wide/56 by 28 cm) on the upper rack of the oven 4 to 6 inches (10 to 15 cm) beneath the broiler for an electric oven or 6 to 8 inches (15 to 20 cm) beneath the broiler for a gas oven. Preheat the oven to its highest setting (usually 500° to 550°F/260° to 288°C) for 45 minutes.

TO SHAPE THE DOUGH: The goal is to stretch the dough to a large rectangle, about 21 inches long by 10 inches wide (53 by 25 cm) with an even thickness across the middle

and a thicker rim around the edge. There are lots of ways. Here's how I usually do it for a pizza al metro. Lightly flour a large work surface and a large wooden pizza peel or cutting board (a board big enough to fit the stretched-out dough). Use a dough scraper to scrape the dough balls from the tray to the floured surface. Position the dough balls end to end and press the ends together, pinching them and reshaping the dough balls to make one larger piece of dough in a rough rectangular shape. Gently poke your fingers about ½ inch (1.3 cm) from the edge of the dough all around it to begin forming the rim. The center should look thicker at this point. Leave the rim alone and press your fingers and palms gently around the center portion to begin stretching the dough away from the center. At this point, you should have a rectangle of dough about 12 inches long by 4 inches wide (30 by 10 cm). Slip one hand under the rectangle and quickly flip it over. Repeat the poking and pressing process on the other side, poking your fingers around the edge first to make the rim, and then placing your palms on the center and gently stretching your fingers and thumb outward to stretch the dough from the center outward into a large rectangle about 21 inches long by

CONTINUED

10 inches wide (53 by 25 cm). Use both hands to stretch the dough and as you work, keep the rim thick. If the dough is difficult to stretch, let it relax for 5 minutes or so and then stretch it again. If the dough tears a hole, patch it by pulling a little dough from one side of the hole and pressing it over the hole with your thumb.

Lay the stretched dough onto the floured peel or cutting board. The easiest way is to slide it onto the peel or board, one end at a time, removing your hands from beneath the dough each time. Reshape the rectangle as necessary on the peel or board and then give the peel or board a quick shake to make sure the dough can slide easily.

Arrange the berries evenly over the pizza all the way to the rim. Sprinkle the sugar over the top. Give the peel or board another quick shake to make sure the dough slides easily.

TO BAKE THE PIZZA: At this point, your oven should be on broil. Slide and shake the pizza from the peel or board onto the cooking surface. Cook until the rim is puffed, the dough blisters and chars in spots, and the bottom is crisp, 6 to 8 minutes. Use your hands or a long spatula to rotate the dough as necessary for even cooking.

Remove the pizza from the oven to a large cutting board to cool for a minute or two before slicing. For this pizza, I like to cut the entire pizza in half lengthwise, then make 5 crosswise cuts to make rectangles. Slice and then pipe a dollop of whipped mascarpone cream on each slice. Sprinkle the orange zest, if using, over the top. Finish with the mint leaves and a dusting of confectioners' sugar.

WOOD OVEN CRÈME BRÛLÉE PIZZA

MAKES ONE 10-INCH
(25 CM) ROUND PIZZA

When I was playing around with the ice technique on pizza (see page 10), my mind started wandering. The pizza started looking less like a pizza and more like a tart shell. It could be filled with almost anything! But I like to keep it simple. A creamy custard of crème brûlée is all you need, plus a kitchen torch. You can make this dessert in a home oven, too (see "Option," page 243).

1 dough ball, preferably Naples Dough at 60% Hydration (page 72), about 250 grams/8.8 ounces

Flour, for dusting

½ cup (70 g) coarsely crushed ice

1 egg

3 egg yolks

1 cup (237 ml) heavy cream

½ cup (100 g) sugar, plus some for sprinkling

Fresh mint leaves, optional

Confectioners' sugar, optional

Light a wood fire on the oven floor directly where you will be cooking the pizza (for details on starting a fire, see page 15). Feed the fire until the ambient temperature in the oven is around 700°F (371°C), 1 to 2 hours. Quickly rake the fire to one side of the oven, containing it in a neat pile near the edge. Brush the cooking surface clean.

Let the dough warm up at room temperature for at least 1 hour or up to 4 hours. As it warms up, the dough will relax and become easier to shape.

TO SHAPE THE DOUGH: The goal is to stretch the dough to a 10-inch (25 cm) circle with an even thickness across the middle and a thick rim around the edge, at least ½ inch (1.3 cm) high. You want a thick rim for this pizza because it will have to contain the ice as it melts to water on the pizza shell. Here's how I usually do it. Lightly flour a work surface and a wooden pizza peel. Use a dough scraper to scrape the dough ball from the tray to the floured surface. Gently poke your fingers about ½ inch (1.3 cm) from the edge of the dough ball all around it to begin forming the rim. The center should look thicker like a hat. Leave the rim alone and press your fingers and palm gently into the center of the hat, moving your fingers and thumb outward to begin stretching the dough away from the center (see the photos on page 95). As you work, gradually rotate the dough and keep your thumb against the rim to make the rim thick and round. As the dough round stretches and gets wider, you

can begin to use both hands instead of just one. The dough should be soft enough to continue this process completely on your work surface until it is stretched to a 10-inch (25 cm) circle with an even thickness across the middle and a rim about ½ inch (1.3 cm) thick. If the dough tears a hole, patch it by pulling a little dough from one side of the hole and pressing it over the hole with your thumb.

Lay the stretched dough onto the floured peel. The easiest way is to simply drape it over the peel and then remove your hands from beneath the dough. Reshape the dough round as necessary, making sure the rim is nice and thick, at least ½ inch (1.3 cm) high. Give the peel a quick shake to make sure the dough can slide easily.

TO TOP AND BAKE: Spread the ice evenly across the dough.

Slide and shake the pizza from the peel onto the cooking surface. Cook until the rim is puffed and charred in spots and the bottom is crisp, 1 to 2 minutes. The ice will melt and almost completely evaporate. Pop any large bubbles that form in the center of the pizza. Essentially, you are creating a pizza shell or tart shell. Use a metal pizza peel to rotate the dough as necessary for even cooking. If the rim is done before all the water melts, use a pastry brush to brush excess water over the rim; this will shine it up a bit.

Remove the pizza from the oven to a wire rack to cool.

CONTINUED

Meanwhile, make the custard filling. Set up a large bowl of ice. Whisk the egg in a metal bowl that will fit over a saucepan of simmering water (to make a double boiler). Whisk the egg until the whites and yolks are fully blended and no streaks of white remain. Whisk in the yolks, cream, and sugar and then place the bowl over the saucepan of simmering water. Cook gently, whisking almost constantly, until the mixture thickens enough to thickly coat the back of a spoon, 10 to 15 minutes. You should see some trails in the custard as you whisk, and its temperature should be around 182°F (83°C). When thickened, set the bowl or saucepan of custard in the bowl of ice and whisk until the custard cools and thickens a bit more, 4 to 6 minutes. When cooled, you should see deeper trails in the custard as you whisk, and its temperature should be around 95°F (35°C).

Pour the cooled custard into the pizza shell. It should be thick enough to pour in a wide ribbon. Chill the pizza, uncovered, until firm, about 1 hour or up to 3 hours. When chilled, you can refrigerate the pizza for up to 24 hours before finishing it.

Before serving, sprinkle a thin layer of sugar over the top of the custard and quickly brûlée (broil) it by waving a kitchen torch back and forth over the sugar until it melts and caramelizes to a nice amber brown, 2 to 3 minutes. A few burnt spots on the custard are okay, but try to point the torch toward the center of the pizza to avoid scorching the crust. Return the brûléed pizza to the refrigerator just long enough to firm up the custard so it doesn't run when you cut the pizza. As the caramelized sugar cools off, it will harden into a top crust that is cracklingly crisp. Remove the pizza to a cutting board, and slice it into 6 pieces. Finish it with some fresh mint and powdered sugar, if you like.

OPTION

HOME OVEN CRÈME BRÛLÉE PIZZA: Place a baking steel or stone on the upper rack of the oven 4 to 6 inches (10 to 15 cm) beneath the broiler for an electric oven or 6 to 8 inches (15 to 20 cm) beneath the broiler for a gas oven. Preheat the oven to its highest setting (usually 500° to 550°F/260° to 288°C) for 45 minutes. When the oven is preheated and you are ready to bake the pizza, open the oven door for 10 seconds if you have an electric oven. This step lets some heat escape to make sure the electric broiler will actually turn on even though the oven has reached its maximum temperature. Reset the oven to broil and preheat the broiler for 5 to 10 minutes. Shape the dough as described in the recipe and top it with the ice. Bake the pizza on the hot steel or stone beneath the broiler until the rim is puffed and charred in spots, the bottom crust is crisp, and the ice melts and almost completely evaporates, 1 to 2 minutes. Remove the cooked pizza shell to a wire rack to cool and then proceed with the rest of the recipe.

FRIED DOUGH WITH FENNEL LEMON SUGAR

MAKES 9 PIECES

You can fry anything, and it will taste good. These little nuggets, coated in sugar with lemon zest and ground fennel, go right past good to great. The perfect ending on pizza night!

1 dough ball, preferably Roman Dough at 57% Hydration (page 76), about 230 grams/8.1 ounces

Finely grated zest of ½ lemon

½ cup (100 g) sugar

½ teaspoon (1 g) fennel seeds, finely ground

Vegetable oil, for frying

Flour, for dusting

Warm Nutella, for dipping

Let the dough sit out at room temperature for 1 hour to take the chill off.

Put the zest in a bowl and place the bowl in a warm spot to let the zest dry out. We do it on top of our wood ovens at the pizzeria. You could also put it on your stovetop while your oven heats up for pizza or on top of a warm radiator. About 90°F (32°C) is the temperature you're after. Within an hour or two, the zest should be nice and dry. Don't leave it too long, or it will get brittle.

Mix the dried zest, sugar, and fennel seeds together in a medium bowl. (By the way, you can grind the fennel seeds in a clean coffee grinder or a spice mill. A good mortar and pestle works, too.)

Heat the oil in a deep fryer to 400°F (204°C). At least 2 inches (5 cm) of oil is a good depth, and a large deep pan like a wok will let you fry a bunch of these at once without crowding them.

TO SHAPE AND CUT THE DOUGH: When you're ready to fry, lightly flour a work surface and use a dough scraper to scrape the dough ball from the tray to the floured surface. Lightly flour the top of the dough and then shape and pat the dough ball into a nice, thick 8-inch (20-cm) square. Use a bench knife to cut the square like a tic-tac-toe board into 9 square pieces.

TO FRY THE DOUGH: Fry the dough squares in batches. Don't crowd the fryer or the dough will get greasy. Adjust the heat to keep the oil at a constant temperature of 400°F (204°C). Fry until the pieces are golden brown, about 2 minutes, turning with tongs as necessary. Remove from the oil with tongs or a spider strainer, let drip dry, and immediately toss the pieces in the fennel lemon sugar, coating every nook and cranny. Serve hot with Nutella for dipping.

HOME OVEN DOLCI ROTOLO

MAKES TWELVE 3- TO
4-INCH (7 TO 10 CM)
ROTOLOS

A few years after Brad Spence, the chef at our Philadelphia trattoria Amis, came up with the Mortadella and Pistachio Rotolo (page 211), we revisited the whole idea of rotolo. That mortadella rotolo had been inspired by cinnamon buns, so we thought, why not make a sweet version? Even better, let's make it into sticky buns with pecans!

DOUGH AND FILLING

3 dough balls, preferably Naples Dough at 60% Hydration (page 61), about 750 grams/26.5 ounces total

14 ounces (400 g) ricotta impastata

6½ tablespoons (80 g) sugar

2¾ tablespoons (41 ml) heavy cream

1 teaspoon (2.6 g) ground cinnamon

Flour, for dusting

TOPPING

½ cup (112.5 g) packed light brown sugar

⅔ cup (158 ml) heavy cream

2¾ tablespoons (37.5 g) unsalted butter

¾ cup (82 g) pecans, toasted and chopped

FOR THE DOUGH AND FILLING: Let the dough warm up at room temperature for at least 1 hour or up to 4 hours. As it warms up, the dough will relax and become easier to shape.

Meanwhile, mix together the ricotta, sugar, cream, and cinnamon in a medium bowl. Cover and refrigerate until ready to use, up to 6 hours.

TO SHAPE THE DOUGH: The goal is to stretch the dough to a rectangle about 18 inches long by 13 inches wide (45 by 33 cm) with an even thickness across the middle and no rim at the edge. Flour a work surface and lay the dough balls end to end in a horizontal line in front of you. Gently flatten and pinch the ends of the dough together to make 1 bigger piece of dough. Dust the top with flour and then press the dough with your palms and fingers, stretching outward to shape the dough into a large rectangle that roughly matches the dimensions of a half-sheet pan (18 by 13 inches/45 by 33 cm). If the dough is stiff, you can also pick up the edges of the dough to stretch it outward, or use a rolling pin. As you work, loosen the dough from the work surface with a bench knife and reflour the work surface as necessary. You don't want the dough to stick. When the dough is an even thickness of about ½ inch (1.3 cm), square up the edges with your hands to make a nice rectangle.

Spread the ricotta filling in an even layer all the way to the edges of the dough. Fold the short sides of the dough rectangle over the filling, about ½ inch (1.3 cm). Then starting at the long side (nearest you), begin rolling the dough over the filling into a tight roll, enclosing the filling in a spiral. The sides will want to spread as you roll. Try to keep the roll tight. When fully rolled, compress gently around the roll with your palms to make it nice and compact. Cut the roll crosswise into 12 pieces, each 1½ to 2 inches (3 to 5 cm) wide.

Lightly oil a half-sheet pan (18 by 13 inches/45 by 33 cm). Place the rotolos, cut sides up, on the baking sheet, reshaping them as necessary so each is a nice, stable spiral. Cover and let stand at room temperature until puffy and almost doubled in size, about 1 hour.

Preheat the oven to 450°F (232°C) and place a baking stone or steel on the middle rack. Let the oven preheat for at least 45 minutes.

CONTINUED

TO BAKE THE ROTOLOS: Bake the rotolos until puffed and golden brown, 15 to 20 minutes, rotating the pan once or twice for even cooking. Remove the entire pan from the oven, let cool for a minute, and then use a metal spatula to transfer the rotolos to a platter or plates. These rotolos may spread a bit, which is fine. Each one will have its own unique character.

FOR THE TOPPING: While the rotolos bake, combine the brown sugar, cream, and butter in a small saucepan. Heat over low heat until everything is melted and smooth, stirring occasionally, 10 to 15 minutes. Spoon the sauce over the rotolos and top with the pecans.

OPTIONS

To make these ahead of time, proof the filled and cut rotolos in the fridge instead of at room temperature. Cover and let them ferment in the fridge for 2 to 6 hours.

If you don't have ricotta impastata, which is creamy and not grainy in texture, use regular ricotta and blend it in a blender along with the cream, sugar, and cinnamon until everything is creamy.

MINI-DOLCI ROTOLOS: After rolling out the dough, cut the rectangle of dough in half lengthwise to make 2 smaller rectangles. Top, roll, cut, proof, and bake as directed. Each rotolo will come out a little smaller.

HOME OVEN APPLE PIZZETTE

MAKES SIX 3-INCH (7 CM)
ROUND TARTLETS

These pizzette are like mini–apple pies made with pizza dough. In the fall, I make them with my kids, and they're usually all gone before they cool off. Don't forget the vanilla ice cream!

DOUGH AND FILLING

1 dough ball, preferably Roman Dough at 57% Hydration (page 76), about 230 grams/8.1 ounces

Spray oil, for pans

1 tablespoon (14 g) unsalted butter, melted

2⅓ cups (262 g) apples, peeled and sliced into half-moons ¼ inch (0.6 cm) thick

¼ cup (50 g) sugar

2 tablespoons (16 g) cornstarch

Heaping ¼ teaspoon (0.75 g) ground cinnamon or nutmeg or a combination of both

6 tablespoons (89 ml) apple cider

1⅛ teaspoons (6 ml) fresh lemon juice

TOPPING

1 cup plus 1 teaspoon (131 g) all-purpose flour, plus some for dusting

7 tablespoons (87 g) sugar

1 cup plus 1 tablespoon (55 g) old-fashioned rolled oats

6 tablespoons (85 g) cold unsalted butter, cut in small pieces

FOR THE DOUGH AND FILLING: Let the dough sit out at room temperature for 1 hour to take the chill off.

Heat the oven to 500°F (260°C). Coat six tartlet pans (3-inch/7-cm diameter by 3/4 inch/2 cm high) with spray oil. You can also bake these tartlets in a jumbo muffin tin or individual 3-inch (7 cm) diameter shallow carbon steel frying pans or other small frying pans.

Melt the butter in a medium saucepan over medium heat. Add the sliced apples and toss to coat. Whisk together the sugar, cornstarch, cinnamon, and nutmeg in a medium bowl. Then whisk the cider and lemon juice into the cornstarch mixture until evenly moistened. Pour the mixture over the apples in the saucepan and bring everything to a simmer, stirring until thickened, about 5 minutes. Remove from the heat and let cool slightly in the pan.

FOR THE TOPPING: Mix together the flour, sugar, and oats in a medium bowl. Use your fingers to rub the butter into the dry ingredients until crumbly, walnut-size pieces form in the bowl.

Lightly flour a work surface. Use a dough scraper to scrape the dough ball from the tray to the floured surface and then use the scraper or a bench knife to cut the dough into 6 pieces. Press a piece of dough into each prepared pan, filling the pan completely and evening the tops to make a tartlet shell about ¼ inch (0.6 cm) thick.

TO BAKE THE PIZZETTE: Divide the cooled filling evenly among the tartlet shells. Sprinkle the crumb topping evenly over the filling and bake until the pizzette are golden brown and bubbly, 10 to 12 minutes.

ACKNOWLEDGMENTS

From Marc Vetri

Every book I have worked on has been an evolution, and this one is no exception. Our last book *Mastering Pasta* took us deep into the scientific world of grain and agriculture. I read more papers, theses, and studies in the three years we spent writing it than I had probably read in my entire life. Looking back, I can say that the research for *Pasta* was simply a precursor to the adventure that was to become *Mastering Pizza*. The cast of characters that helped bring this book together—some aware, some unaware of her or his role—was simply the most inspiring group that I have ever had the pleasure of learning from.

DAVID JOACHIM: A big thanks to the best writing partner of all time. After four books, and looking for more, it's safe to say that he speaks my voice better than I do!

CLAIRE KOPP MCWILLIAMS: Always there to debunk the myths, state the obvious, or just create a new process, Claire has been an integral part of this book as well as the entire Vetri Cucina team.

KATIE PARLA: It's not too often you meet someone who can simultaneously organize a journey that will put you in a food coma and make an Italian taxi driver feel like a child as she scolds him for trying to cheat us out of a couple bucks.

ED ANDERSON: Ed is simply a master at making the most mundane picture seem extraordinary and jump off the page! Always a treat to work with him.

MARCO ROSSI: The best friend and travel partner one could ever ask for, and a true inspiration to so many of my projects.

STEPHEN JONES: He is the wheat whisperer and taught me that wheat, like people, should strive to be different. It's where the magic happens.

ITALY PIZZAIAOLOS: There is so much amazing pizza in Italy, and there are so many pizzaiolos to mention. Yet there are a few who take something so traditional and reinvent it in such an original way that it pushes far beyond the perceived limits of what pizza can be. Stefano Callegari, Franco Pepe, and Gabrielle Bonci are true innovators and inspired much of this book.

USA PIZZAIOLOS: Whether it's their books, their restaurants, or their friendship, these chefs had so much impact on the direction of the research and the outcome of this book. I can't even begin to express all my thanks to Chris Bianco, Jim Lahey, Ken Forkish, Anthony Mangieri, Nancy Silverton, Joe Beddia, Lachlan Mackinnon-Patterson, Mark Iacono, and Anthony Tassinello.

THE TEN SPEED TEAM: After four books with these guys, it's easy to see why the relationship has gone so well. Always fair, always supportive, and always working as a team, Aaron Wehner, Kelly Snowden, Betsy Stromberg, and Serena Sigona are quite simply as good as it gets in publishing.

MEGAN AND THE KIDS: For putting up with a house that looked like a movie set for a week!

From David Joachim

To write a cookbook on how to make something that brings so much joy to so many people, I feel truly lucky. Heartfelt thanks to those who schooled us and joined us in the exploration of this food that is so very much alive, especially:

MARC: For welcoming me into your dough-shaped world and showing me all the beautiful things you can make in it.

CLAIRE KOPP MCWILLIAMS: For making complex baking seem so simple.

SEAN COYNE: The Buddha of baking, for incomparable dough lessons.

PETER REINHART: For your continued pizza quest, the introduction to Wolfgang Mock, and an invite to the "International Symposium on Bread" at Johnson and Wales University.

FRANCISCO MIGOYA, co-author of *Modernist Baking*, for answering my nerdy science questions.

STEPHEN JONES: For being the kindest, most badass, disruptive scientist ever.

KATIE PARLA: For chewing out that Roman cab driver with aplomb.

MARCO ROSSI: For being smooth like Sunday morning.

PAUL LEBEAU: For turning us onto the Mock mill.

WILLIAM RUBEL: For the quote from David Rains Wallace.

JOHN SPENCER: At Inizio Pizza Napoletana for letting me geek out on wood ovens, doughs, and pizzas.

PAT CORPORA: For pizza testing in your mac daddy wood-fired oven.

BILL MELCHER, JORDAN CZAJKA, AND CHARLIE SOUTHGATE: For stealth recipe testing.

LISA EKUS: For introducing me to Marc four books and fourteen years ago. What a *viaggio* it's been!

SALLY EKUS: For continuing to introduce me to some of the raddest human beings in the food world.

CHRISTINE, MADDOX, AND AUGUST: For always lighting up with smiles when I said again and again that for dinner tonight we were having . . . pizza.

SELECTED BIBLIOGRAPHY

Books

Artusi, Pellegrino. *Science in the Kitchen and the Art of Eating Well*. New York: Marsilio Publishers, 1997.

Basey, Marleeta F. *Flour Power: A Guide to Home Milling*. Salem, OR: Jermar Press, 2004.

Beddia, Joe. *Pizza Camp: Recipes from Pizzeria Beddia*. New York: Abrams, 2017.

Bianco, Chris. *Bianco: Pizza, Pasta, and Other Food I Like*. New York: Ecco, 2017.

Bonci, Gabriele. *Pizza: Seasonal Recipes from Rome's Legendary Pizzarium*. New York: Rizzoli, 2013.

Corriher, Shirley. *BakeWise: The Hows and Whys of Successful Baking*. New York: Scribner, 2008.

_____. *CookWise: Secrets of Cooking Revealed*. New York: William Morrow and Company, 1997.

Davidson, Alan. *The Penguin Companion to Food*. London: Penguin UK, 2002.

Delcour, Jan A., and R. Carl Hoseney. *Principles of Cereal Science and Technology*. St. Paul, MN: American Association of Cereal Chemists, 2010.

Field, Carol. *The Italian Baker, First Revised Edition*. Berkeley, CA: Ten Speed Press, 2011.

Forkish, Ken. *The Elements of Pizza: Unlocking the Secrets to World-Class Pies at Home*. Berkeley, CA: Ten Speed Press, 2016.

_____. *Flour, Water, Salt, Yeast: The Fundamentals of Artisan Bread and Pizza*. Berkeley, CA: Ten Speed Press, 2012.

Gemignani, Tony. *The Pizza Bible*. Berkeley, CA: Ten Speed Press, 2014.

Helstosky, Carol. *Pizza: A Global History*. London: Reaktion Books Ltd, 2008.

Italian Academy of Cuisine. *La Cucina: The Regional Cooking of Italy*. New York: Rizzoli, 2009.

Joachim, David, and Andrew Schloss. *The Science of Good Food: The Ultimate Reference on How Cooking Works*. Toronto: Robert Rose, 2008.

Lahey, Jim. *My Pizza: The Easy No-Knead Way to Make Spectacular Pizza at Home*. New York: Clarkson Potter, 2012.

Levine, Ed. *Pizza: A Slice of Heaven*. New York: Universe, 2005.

López-Alt, J. Kenji. *The Food Lab: Better Home Cooking Through Science*. New York: W. W. Norton & Company, 2015.

May, Tony. *Italian Cuisine: Basic Cooking Techniques*. New York: Rizzoli, 1992.

McGee, Harold. *On Food and Cooking: The Science and Lore of the Kitchen*. New York: Scribner, 2004.

Miscovich, Richard. *From the Wood-Fired Oven: New and Traditional Techniques for Cooking and Baking with Fire*. White River Junction, VT: Chelsea Green Publishing, 2013.

Myhrvold, Nathan, Chris Young, and Maxime Bilet. *Modernist Cuisine: The Art and Science of Cooking*, 5 vols. Bellevue, WA: The Cooking Lab, 2011.

Myhrvold, Nathan, and Francisco Migoya. *Modernist Bread*. Bellevue, WA: The Cooking Lab, 2017.

Parla, Katie, and Kristina Gill. *Tasting Rome: Fresh Flavors and Forgotten Recipes from an Ancient City*. New York: Clarkson Potter, 2016.

Pomeranz, Y., ed., *Wheat: Chemistry and Technology*, 2 vols. St. Paul, MN: American Association of Cereal Chemists, 1988.

Reinhart, Peter. *American Pie: My Search for the Perfect Pizza*. Berkeley, CA: Ten Speed Press, 2003.

Steinkraus, Keith H., et al. *Applications of Biotechnology to Fermented Foods*. Washington, DC: National Academies Press, 1992.

Tassinello, Anthony. *The Essential Wood-Fired Pizza Cookbook: Recipes and Techniques from My Wood Fired Oven*. Berkeley, CA: Rockridge Press, 2016.

Vetri, Marc. *Il Viaggio di Vetri: A Culinary Journey*. Berkeley, CA: Ten Speed Press, 2008.

_____. *Mastering Pasta: The Art and Practice of Handmade Pasta, Gnocchi, and Risotto*. Berkeley, CA: Ten Speed Press, 2015.

_____. *Rustic Italian Food*. Berkeley, CA: Ten Speed Press, 2011.

Young, Daniel. *Where to Eat Pizza*. New York: Phaidon Press, 2016.

Zanini de Vita, Oretta. *Popes, Peasants, and Shepherds: Recipes and Lore from Rome and Lazio*. Oakland, CA: University of California Press, 2013.

Articles

Adler, Jerry. "Artisanal Wheat On the Rise." *Smithsonian Magazine*, December 2011.

Brouns, Fred J. P. H., Vincent J. van Buul, and Peter R. Shewry. "Does Wheat Make Us Fat and Sick?" *Journal of Cereal Science* 58, no. 2 (September 2013).

Chen, X., and J. D. Schofield. "Changes in the Glutathione Content and Breadmaking Performance of White Wheat Flour During Short-Term Storage." *Cereal Chemistry* 73, no. 1 (1996).

Czerny, Michael, and Peter Schieberle. "Important Aroma Compounds in Freshly Ground Wholemeal and White Wheat Flour—Identification and Quantitative Changes During Sourdough Fermentation." *Journal of Agricultural Food Chemistry* 50, no. 23 (October 2002).

Di Cagno, Raffaella, Maria De Angelis, Paola Lavermicocca, Massimo De Vincenzi, Claudio Giovannini, Michele Faccia, and Marco Gobbetti. "Proteolysis by Sourdough Lactic Acid Bacteria: Effects on Wheat Flour Protein Fractions and Gliadin Peptides Involved in Human Cereal Tolerance." *Applied and Environmental Microbiology* 68, no. 2 (February 2002).

Hartwig, Pam, and Mina R. McDaniel. "Flavor Characteristics of Lactic, Malic, Citric, and Acetic Acids at Various pH Levels." *Journal of Food Science* 60, no. 2 (March 1995).

Hrušková, Marie, and Dana Machová. "Changes of Wheat Flour Properties During Short Term Storage." *Czech Journal of Food Sciences* 20, no. 4 (2002).

Jones, Stephen. "Kicking the Commodity Habit." *Gastronomica: The Journal of Food and Culture* 12, no. 3 (Fall 2012).

McWilliams, Margaret, and Andrea C. Mackey. "Wheat Flavor Components." *Journal of Food Science* 34, no. 6 (November 1969).

Miś, A. "Influence of the Storage of Wheat Flour on the Physical Properties of Gluten." *International Agrophysics* 17 (2003).

Nishio, Zenta, Kanenori Takata, Miwako Ito, Tadashi Tabiki, Norio Iriki, Wakako Funatsuki, and Hiroaki Yamauchi. "Relationship Between Physical Dough Properties and the Improvement of Bread-Making Quality During Flour Aging." *Food Science and Technology Research* 10, no. 2 (2004).

Pico, Joana, José Bernal, and Manuel Gómez. "Wheat Bread Aroma Compounds in Crumb and Crust: A Review." *Food Research International* 75 (September 2015).

Robbins, Jim. "A Perennial Search for Perfect Wheat." *New York Times*. June 5, 2007.

Strom, Stephanie. "A Big Bet on Gluten-Free." *New York Times*. February 17, 2014.

Struyf, Nore, Eva Van der Maelen, Sami Hemdane, Joran Verspreet, Kevin J. Verstrepen, and Christophe M. Courtin. "Bread Dough and Baker's Yeast: An Uplifting Synergy." *Comprehensive Reviews in Food Science and Food Safety* 16, no. 5 (2017).

Wang, Linfen, and Rolando A. Flores. "The Effects of Storage on Flour Quality and Baking Performance." *Food Reviews International* 15, no. 2 (1999).

Wink, Debra. "Lactic Acid Fermentation in Sourdough." *Bread Lines, a Publication of The Bread Bakers Guild of America* 15, no. 4 (December 2007).

INDEX

Published in the United States by Ten Speed Press, an imprint of
the Crown Publishing Group, a division of Random House LLC,
New York, a Penguin Random House Company.
www.crownpublishing.com
www.tenspeed.com

Ten Speed Press and the Ten Speed Press colophon are
registered trademarks of Random House LLC.

Library of Congress Cataloging-in-Publication Data
Names: Vetri, Marc, author. | Joachim, David, author. | Anderson,
    Ed (Edward Charles), photographer.
Title: Mastering pizza : the art and practice of handmade pizza,
    focaccia and calzone / Marc Vetri and David Joachim ;
    photography by Ed Anderson.
Description: California : Ten Speed Press, [2018] | Includes
    bibliographical references and index. |
Identifiers: LCCN 2017049095 (print) | LCCN 2017050438 (ebook)
Subjects: LCSH: Pizza. | Cooking, Italian. | LCGFT: Cookbooks.
Classification: LCC TX770.P58 (ebook) | LCC TX770.P58 .V48
    2018 (print) | DDC 641.82/48—dc23
LC record available at https://lccn.loc.gov/2017049095

Hardcover ISBN: 978-0-399-57922-6
eBook ISBN: 978-0-399-57923-3

Printed in China

Cover design by Betsy Stromberg

Interior design by Rita Sowins / Sowins Design based on a design
by Betsy Stromberg

10 9 8 7 6 5 4 3 2 1

First Edition